Political Women

Political Women

Fifteen Campaigns that Shaped Twenty-First-Century Britain

Maggie Andrews

First published in Great Britain in 2024 by
Pen & Sword History
An imprint of Pen & Sword Books Limited
Yorkshire – Philadelphia

Copyright © Maggie Andrews 2024

ISBN 978 1 39901 234 8

The right of Martyn Beardsley to be identified as
Author of this Work has been asserted by him in accordance
with the Copyright, Designs and Patents Act 1988.

A CIP catalogue record for this book is
available from the British Library

All rights reserved. No part of this book may be reproduced or
transmitted in any form or by any means, electronic or mechanical
including photocopying, recording or by any information storage and
retrieval system, without permission from the Publisher in writing.

Typeset by Mac Style
Printed in the UK by CPI Group (UK) Ltd, Croydon, CR0 4YY.

Pen & Sword Books Limited incorporates the imprints of After
the Battle, Atlas, Archaeology, Aviation, Discovery, Family History,
Fiction, History, Maritime, Military, Military Classics, Politics,
Select, Transport, True Crime, Air World, Frontline Publishing, Leo
Cooper, Remember When, Seaforth Publishing, The Praetorian Press,
Wharncliffe Local History, Wharncliffe Transport, Wharncliffe True
Crime and White Owl.

For a complete list of Pen & Sword titles please contact

PEN & SWORD BOOKS LIMITED
47 Church Street, Barnsley, South Yorkshire, S70 2AS, England
E-mail: enquiries@pen-and-sword.co.uk
Website: www.pen-and-sword.co.uk
or
PEN AND SWORD BOOKS
1950 Lawrence Rd, Havertown, PA 19083, USA
E-mail: uspen-and-sword@casematepublishers.com
Website: www.penandswordbooks.com

Contents

Abbreviations vi
Acknowledgements viii
Twentieth-Century Timeline ix
Introduction xiii

Chapter 1 Glasgow Rent Strike (1915) 1

Chapter 2 *Voters Awake* (1920s) 12

Chapter 3 The Suppression of *The Well of Loneliness* (1928) 22

Chapter 4 'Every mother should be entitled to anaesthetic' (1930) 33

Chapter 5 Equal Pay in the Aeronautical Industry (1943) 44

Chapter 6 Gowns and Mortarboards (1940s and 1950s) 55

Chapter 7 'We got a little hall and took our children there with their toys' (1961) 67

Chapter 8 Avoiding Unwanted Pregnancy for the Young (1964) 77

Chapter 9 The Miss World Protest (1970) 90

Chapter 10 'We appreciate the cards and flowers but they are not enough' (1972) 102

Chapter 11 Airport Protest against Virginity Tests (1979) 115

Chapter 12 Prostitutes Sit-in at Holy Cross Church (1982) 127

Chapter 13 'How dare the government presume the right to kill others in our name?' (1982) 138

Chapter 14 Equal Pay for Equal Value (1988) 149

Chapter 15 Tell me what you want, what you really, really want' – Girl Power (1996) 158

Notes 167

Abbreviations

ACAS	Advisory, Conciliation and Arbitration Service
AEF	Amalgamated Union of Engineering and Foundry Workers
BBC	British Broadcasting Corporation
BFBPW	British Federation of Business and Professional Women
CADP	Campaign Against Depo-Provera
CBI	Confederation of British Industry
CND	Campaign for Nuclear Disarmament
CWCS	Council of Women Civil Servants
ECC	Equal Compensation Committee
ECP	English Collection of Prostitutes
FPA	Family Planning Association
GWHA	Glasgow Women's Housing Association
IRA	Irish Republican Army
JCWCS	Joint Committee on Women in the Civil Service
LNSWS	London and National Society for Women's Service
NAWCS	National Association of Women Civil Servants
NBCC	National Birth Control Council
NFWI	National Federation of Women's Institutes
NFWT	National Federation of Women Teachers
NSEC	National Union of Societies for Equal Citizenship
NUPE	National Union of Public Employees
NUT	National Union of Teachers
NUVB	National Union of Vehicle Builders
NUWSS	National Union of Women's Suffrage Societies
NUWT	National Union of Women Teachers
NUWW	National Union of Women Workers of Great Britain and Ireland
OWAAD	Organisation of Women of Asian and African Descent
PLA	Pre-school Learning Alliance
PPA	Pre-School Playgroups Association
SWCG	Scottish Women's Co-operative Guild
TGWU	Transport and General Workers Union
TUC	Trade Union Congress

WAPC	Women Against Pit Closure Group
WAR	Women against Rape
WILPF	Women's International League for Peace and Freedom
WSPU	Women's Social and Political Union
WTRL	The Women's Tax Resistance League

Acknowledgements

This book would not have been written without the help and support of many people.

Thanks must go to all with whom I have discussed the campaigning women featured in this publication: in particular, Paula Bartley, Janis Lomas, and Alyzn Johnson. A special thank you also goes to the students and friends who have joined me in regular online writing retreats, without whom I don't think I would have been able to keep writing through the challenges that the last three years of Covid-19 have thrown at us all: Hayley Carter; Lisa Davies; Janis Lomas; Lyndsey Jenkins; Anna Muggeridge; Kristin O'Donnell; Linda Pike; Lesley Spiers and Diana Russell. Likewise, my furry writing companions, Alfie and Poppy, have shared my study with me while I have written, and have walked with me when I was unable to write. My gratitude also goes to Janis Lomas and Oliver Morgan, for kindly reading drafts of the chapters, and to all at Pen and Sword for being patient about my tardiness in completing the manuscript.

Finally, this book would never have been completed without the forbearance and support of my husband Neil; children, Lynton, Oli, Dom and Annie, and my grandchildren, Lucia, Erin, Edu, Florence, Stanley and Remi – who all put up with more discussion of politics and women than they see the need for. This book is dedicated to you all.

Twentieth-Century Timeline

1883   Women's Co-operative Guild formed.
1894   The Local Government Act is passed, enabling some married and single women to vote in elections for county and borough councils.
1897   Twenty suffrage societies amalgamate to form the National Union of Women's Suffrage Societies (NUWSS).
1902   Women textile workers from the North of England present a petition with 37,000 signatures to Parliament asking for votes for women. Midwifery Act to regulate midwifery profession.
1907   Qualification of Women Act allows women to be elected onto borough and county councils and to become a mayor.
1904   Equal pay league formed.
1906   National Federation of Women Teachers formed becomes National Union of Women teachers 14 years later.
1909   Tax Resistance League formed: no taxation without representation.
1914   Glasgow Women's Housing Association formed; Catherine Macmillan and other suffrage supporters draft an International Manifesto of women seeking to prevent the outbreak of war.
1915   Rent Strikes take place in Glasgow and other urban areas.
Women's Right to Work March takes place. The first Women's Institutes are set up.
1917   House of Commons passed the Representation of the People Act entitling women aged 30 or above with the necessary property qualifications to vote.
1918   The enfranchisement of some women finally becomes law on sixth of February, and they vote for the first time in December. Of the 17 women parliamentary candidates, only Constance Markievicz wins her seat, but as a member of Sinn Fein, she never sits in the House of Commons. National Federation of Women's Institutes is formed.
1919   NUWSS renamed National Union of Societies for Equal Citizenship (NUSEC).
Nancy Astor becomes the first woman to take a seat as an MP. Housing and Town Planning and Sex Disqualification (Removal) Acts are passed.

1920	University of Oxford first awards degrees to women.
1921	Maggie Wintringham, the first English born women MP, enters parliament. The Walworth Women's Welfare Centre which included birth control provided by a doctor is opened.
1923	Welsh Women's Peace petition gathers 390,296 signatures.
1924	Eleanor Rathbone published The Disinherited Family promoting family endowment.
1928	Women are at last entitled to vote on the same terms as men. Radcliffe Hall's *The Well of Loneliness* is published, and following a court case, is suppressed by the Government. National Birthday Trust, to campaign for improved maternity services and analgesics in childbirth, is formed.
1929	The first general election, where women can vote on the same terms as men, produces 14 women MPs. Margaret Bondfield becomes first Cabinet Minister. The Anaesthetics Appeal Fund is set up to promote the availability of analgesics in childbirth.
1930	National Birth Control Council (NBCC) set up, renamed the Family Planning Association (FPA) in 1939.
1933	Women's Co-operative Guild introduced White Poppy, as an alternative to be worn on Remembrance Day as a sign of a commitment to end peace.
1934	Over 30 women's groups organise a mass public rally in support of equal pay.
1936	Midwifery Act passed, and local authorities become responsible for domiciliary midwifery service.
1940	Women's Power committee set up by women MP.
1941	Women conscripted into war work in December.
1943	Equal Pay strike at Rolls Royce factory, Hillington, Glasgow. Equal compensation for war injuries finally introduced after campaigning by women's groups.
1945	Family Allowance Act passed, giving family allowances for second and later children.
1948	National Health Service (NHS) set up. Women are finally awarded degrees and admitted to be full members of Cambridge University.
1949	Radcliffe Hall dies and *The Well of Loneliness* is published unopposed in Britain.
1955	Equal Pay in the Civil Service introduced.
1959	Women were instrumental in organizing the First Notting Hill Carnival followed by others, for example in Leeds.

1961	Belle Tutaev's letter to the *Guardian* sparks the formation of the Pre-school Playgroups Association (PPA). The contraceptive pill for women first becomes available on the NHS.
1964	Dorothy Hodgkin wins the Nobel prize in Chemistry. First Brook Advisory Centres to provide birth control to young unmarried women opened.
1967	Abortion Act legalises abortion, when two doctors propose that the continuation of pregnancy might be a risk to the mental or physical health of women.
1970	Equal Pay Act passed. First Women's Liberation Conference held in Oxford. Feminists protest at the Miss World Competition. Women in Media Group formed to combat gender bias in media industries.
1972	First edition of *Spare Rib* published. Wages for Housework Campaign set up. First Women's Refuge opens.
1973	Virago Press, to publish women's writing, is set up.
1974	Child Benefit Bill to amalgamate child tax allowances and family allowances, and replace with child benefit to be paid for all children.
1975	Sex Discrimination Act passed. Gertrude Maretta Paul becomes first black headmistress to be appointed in Leeds. The English Collection of Prostitutes is formed.
1976	Industrial dispute at Grunwick Factory Strike begins. The Domestic Violence and Matrimonial Proceedings Act is passed. The first Rape Crisis centre is opened.
1977	Reclaim the Night marches, to challenge violence against women, first take place in Leeds, Manchester and other places.
1978	Organisation of Women of Asian and African Descent (OWAAD) formed. The Campaign Against Depo-Provera (CADP), a contraceptive injection, was established.
1979	Protests against virginity testing of Asian women held at Heathrow airport. Margaret Thatcher is the first woman prime minister to be elected. First OWAAD held. Southall Black Sisters formed.
1981	Greenham Common Peace Camp set up.
1982	More than 30,000 women take part in surrounding the base at Greenham Common. London prostitutes occupy the Holy Cross Church objecting to their treatment by the police.
1983	Open University begins running *The Changing Experience of Women* course.
1984	Black Women and Media Conference held in London.
1986	Claire Short seeks to introduce bill to make Page 3-type pin-ups of (semi-)nude women in newspapers illegal.

1989 R versus R case begins, which will establish that rape can occur between a married couple.
1990 Off the Shelf campaign launched, seeking to remove the sale of pornography from high street newsagents.
1996 Nursery education voucher scheme introduced. The Spice Girls' Wannabe song released.

Introduction

When my grandmother, Catherine Barriball, was born in 1900, women could not vote or sit on juries; they had limited educational or career opportunities, and if married, were likely to experience multiple pregnancies and had little time for leisure. The lives of my granddaughters, born over 100 years later, would have been unimaginable to my grandmother. They inhabit a world where domestic technologies such as washing machines are commonplace; there is health care, access to reliable birth control, preschool education for all, and housing with indoor water and sanitation; a twenty-first century world changed by political women. Catherine Barriball had the good fortune to come from a middle-class, respectable Cornish family, and so escaped much of the grinding domestic labour and struggle with economic uncertainty experienced by many working-class women. My grandmother had only one child, apparently thanks to sexual abstinence, rather than access to birth control or safe abortions. Many of the women who feature on the pages of this book had no contraception or possibility of refusing their husbands advances, and suffered the consequences.

Catherine Barriball was, nevertheless, very much a twentieth-century woman, her experiences intimately tied to the changes in the era in which she lived. She voted for the first time in the 1920s, drove a car in the 1930s, was divorced in the 1940s, and worked in a family business from the 1950s onwards. In the years before she died in the 60s, she remained a nattily dressed lady who smoked black Russian cigarettes, and left a small legacy to her younger gentleman friend, John. Even so, Catherine would never have entertained nor comprehended the lifestyle, options, expectations, behaviour, dress and demeanour of the confident young women who joined the 2.5 million revellers sharing a night out in London on New Year's Eve in 1999. The things twenty-first-century women may perhaps take for granted: equal pay, participation in the political system, the right to go to university, and to go out on their own at night, would all have been beyond Catherine's wildest imagination when she was in her youth.

These changes to women's lives since 1900, have not just been brought about by technological and economic advances, or by society gently shifting to become more liberal and enlightened. Rather, they are the result of a multiplicity of small and large, local, national and international political campaigns. This book is about the political efforts of hundreds and thousands of women who participated in such campaigns. A few like Maggie Wintringham and Nancy Astor were MPs. Others, like Mary Barbour, became local councillors. However, women's access to traditional areas of political power has been limited: even when Britain had its first woman prime minister in 1979, she was one of only 19 women in a parliament of 635 MPs. Consequently, women sought other spheres of activity in which to fight for change, using all the resources and imagination at their disposal to challenge injustice and abuse. Women have employed deeds and words, petitions and protests, legal and illegal devices, peaceful and violent strategies, to further their political aims.

The activities of the Edwardian suffrage campaigns are the most well-known examples of these fights for equality and justice. Supporters of women's suffrage marched, held demonstrations and conferences, and refused to pay their taxes or complete census returns. They distributed leaflets from air balloons, lobbied MPs, signed petitions, and held sit-ins. They burnt down buildings and disrupted meetings, wrote novels, songs, poems and plays, and argued their case in court. They were imprisoned, suffered ill health, poverty and abuse, for the causes they believed in. Suffrage campaigners set a precedent, which was followed by a multitude of campaigning groups and organisations seeking to improve women's lives in concrete, pragmatic ways in the years that followed. The majority of the women featured in this book were engaged in less well-known political struggles, which they fought with equal tenacity, sacrifice, inventiveness, and many other similar tactics. These women influenced decision makers and cultural values, and exercised and challenged power throughout their lives, sometimes through organisations such as the Scottish Women's Co-operative Guild, the Women's Institute Movement, the Pre-School Playgroups Association, the English Collection of Prostitutes, Women of Asian and African Descent, or Women against Rape.

Many women in the earlier part of the twentieth century were involved with the suffrage campaigns in the years prior to 1928, when all women were finally able to vote in parliamentary elections on the same terms as men. Several women featured in this book, who took part in campaigns and activities in the 1970s and 1980s, participated in what was nicknamed women's lib: the Women's Liberation Movement, sometimes referred to as second wave feminism. These two well-known waves of feminist activity are not really the core focus of this book; these were moments of intense campaigning through a multiplicity of protests and political channels. There are, after all, already many fascinating histories of the suffrage campaigns, and also of 1970s and

1980s feminism, providing some interesting overviews of women's activism in the twentieth century.[1] This book does not aim to compete with them, rather instead, it seeks to challenge perceptions of women's politics in both the twentieth and twenty-first centuries.

The chapters that follow consider a selection of 15 campaigns and thematic clusters of activities, which made up an overall attempt to bring about social change. They explore the histories which led up to each particular event, and the issues and people who shaped these campaigns and activities. In so doing, this book aims to encourage women's political activity to be recognised as shaped, and often experienced, in very different ways from that of men. The 15 campaigns I have chosen could have been replaced by 15 or 50 other campaigns; anyone could have chosen a different 15. I am seeking to showcase different strategies of campaigning from court cases to peace camps; a range of motivations from housewives defending their homes to confident, sassy young girls celebrating their sexuality, and girl power. I apologise to those who feel I have omitted many important campaigns and admit my own priorities influenced my choice of these campaigns which all brought about change in ordinary women's lives.

With limited financial resources and hefty domestic responsibilities, women have often chosen to pick their political battles very carefully. Some fought for workers' rights or the right to education, some prioritised stopping male-violence on the streets, in the home or between nations. Others like Radcliffe Hall campaigned so that women could define their own sexuality. Women organised self-help childcare, rape crisis centres and peace camps. They set up birth control clinics and women's refuges. Ordinary women took on exploitive landlords, immigration officers, international companies, local councils, the media and successive governments. This book explores how women did this, and the tactics that they used. It records some of the sacrifices women made to be involved in these political battles and their motivations. It discusses the thousands of unsung heroines who picked their battles, fought them and managed to make a difference.

Women's political activities were often shaped by their own, sometimes very personal experiences, where they lived, their homes, friends or communities. Lucy Baldwin's concern for maternal welfare and analgesics in childbirth stemmed from her own tragic loss of the first of her six children. The Glasgow rent strikers' tactics and solidarity were in some respects products of the physical environment of the tenement blocks in which they lived. Many women campaigned for things dear to them – such as Family Endowment or Wages for Housework, only to see their campaigning undermined or critiqued by not only men, but by other women. There was no consistent philosophy across, or even within, some of the campaigns. Many women did not necessarily choose to call themselves feminist because 'they regarded feminists as women who denied the needs of working-class mothers and workers by demanding equality for professional women.'[2] These women, whatever the label they chose for themselves or were given, whose political activities were sometimes small-scale or local, short lived or seemingly unsuccessful, despite all the setbacks, together helped to transform women's lives. We should thank these women for having shaped the twentieth century - first century in which we now live.

Chapter 1

Glasgow Rent Strike (1915)

Working-class housewives who lived in overcrowded and cramped tenements in the Clydeside area of Glasgow during the First World War, took direct action to oppose rent rises in 1915. Theirs was a heavily industrial area of the city, running along the banks of the River Clyde, with shipyards, factories and workers housing. The women initiated rent strikes, which spread to many other urban areas. The housewives thwarted attempts by the landlords' representatives to evict families for non – payment of rent. Their campaign was inspired by tactics used to fight for women's suffrage, but like many of the campaigns which followed, it was also rooted in women's experience of domestic life. Like many women's political campaigns in the twentieth century, the rent strikes did not challenge the assumption that women were homemakers, carers, mothers, wives, and primarily responsible for the domestic sphere. Instead, housewives articulated what historian Annmarie Hughes has described as, 'the politics of the kitchen' whereby the conditions and availability of housing, the costs of renting or running a home, have repeatedly been the focus of women's political campaigning.[1]

Well before the outbreak of the First World War, Clydeside was already experiencing a housing crisis and overcrowding; as 'an industrial powerhouse, the second city of the Empire'.[2] A high proportion of its accommodation was in three or four-storey buildings known as tenements, which were entered via a close providing access to shared stairs and the back court. These multi-storied buildings rarely had internal sanitation or water supplies; instead, a shared privy and hand pump for water were located in the court. Glasgow's population increased by 70,000 between 1912 and 1915, but less than 2,000 tenements were built to house migrants to the city.[3] Landlords' profits grew in line with the increase in overcrowding in these often-unsanitary tenements. Organisations such as the Glasgow Women's Housing Association (GWHA), established in 1914, fought for better housing conditions and campaigned to make landlords maintain properties adequately.[4] In wartime, thousands more people poured into the city, to work in the shipyards and munitions factories, exacerbating the already existing housing shortage.[5] Unscrupulous landlords took advantage of the situation and put up rents by as much as 25%, creating difficulties for housewives already facing increasing food prices.

In the years before the war, Britain was far from self-sufficient in food. Its reliance on imports at that time, included the majority of the sugar consumed which came from the Austro-Hungarian Empire. The supply of nearly 80% of the country's grain from the USA was likewise interrupted by the war.[6] Wheat, an essential ingredient in bread, as with other staple foods in the working-class diet, faced price increases, due to panic buying, shortages and profiteering. For example, in the first week of the conflict, a housewife in Bermondsey, London, was dismayed to discover a grocer attempting to charge eight and half pence for a packet of Quaker oats, which had retailed for five and half pence only a couple of weeks before, as well as four pence for sugar, previously sold for two pence. The housewife refused to take the goods, asked for her money back and left, speedily returning with twenty others who threw produce around and threatened to wreck the shop before the police were called to take charge of the situation.[7] Housewives' finances faced further pressure when separation allowances, paid to the wives of husbands in the forces, took weeks to come through. Newspapers were full of stories of those who, with already precarious finances prior to hostilities, found such delays disastrous. The Prince of Wales Fund's appeal sheets, issued in Glasgow in September 1914, argued efforts should be made to: 'guarantee to soldiers and sailors serving with the colours, that the wives, families and dependents will be looked after and that their homes will remain intact'.[8] But in many parts of the country, this did not happen, and soldiers' wives were evicted from their homes.[9]

Housewives whose husbands were in local employment fared no better: the Munitions of War Act of 1915 enabled the Ministry to declare factories 'controlled establishments' and restrict the freedom of workers to leave or go on strike.[10] Hence, landlords who increased rents were referred to in the language used for the enemy, were labelled unpatriotic, described as Prussians, likened to spies, and called 'huns at home'.[11] Committees were formed in working class districts to resist rent increases and housewives initiated rent strikes.[12] There were calls for a city-wide strike with early support in Clydeside in the Govan and Patrick districts, which lay on opposite sides of the River Clyde, in April 1915. This was, as Annmarie Hughes and Valerie Wright argue, 'a protest organized by women for women with community being the most important motivation'.[13]

Local groups linked together through the Glasgow Women's Housing Association (GWHA), which organised open-air meetings on street corners and had gained approximately 3,000 members by the end of 1915. The GWHA, which had former suffragette, Helen Crawfurd (1877–1954) as its secretary, benefitted from the 'practical framework' that suffrage militancy gave them.[14] Helen was one of six children in a religious family, headed by a master baker. She originally lived in the Gorbals on the South side of the Clyde, but spent a number of years in Ipswich, returning to Glasgow at the age of 17, where she married the much older Rev. Alexander Crawfurd in 1898.[15] A fervent suffrage supporter, Helen was initially a member of the Women's Social and Political Union (WSPU) led by Mrs Pankhurst. However, she rejected the Pankhurst's cessation of suffrage activities at the outbreak of war, and instead formed a branch of the United Suffragists in Glasgow in 1915, and became an active peace campaigner.[16]

A number of women in local tenants' groups also co-ordinated activities, including Mary Barbour (1875 -1958), who became the most famous leader of the rent strikers. Mary had left school at fourteen; she was the third of seven children of a carpet weaver in Kilbarchan, Scotland. She also worked in carpet factories, before marrying David Barbour in 1896. By 1915, Mary Barbour was living in the Govan district of Glasgow, the mother of two young boys, her first child having died of meningitis at only 10 months old. She became a member of Scottish Women's Co-operative Guild (SWCG), formed at the end of the nineteenth century to provide women with education, companionship and the chance to exchange and formulate their views on political and social issues. Arguably, the SWCG provided Barbour with the training in organising and speaking in public that she would later draw on when involved in the rent strikes.[17] Mary who was the leader of the Tenants Defence Association, set up the South Govan branch of the GWHA, and was described by the socialist, William Gallagher, as 'a typical working-class housewife' who 'became the leader of a movement such as had never been seen before.'[18] Mary used drums, bells, trumpets, and notoriously, a noisy football rattle to summon women to meetings held in the streets or back-courts of tenements. Her skills in inspirational public speeches drummed up support for the rent strikes and opposition to evictions, and led to fellow activists being nicknamed 'Mrs Barbour's army'.

Bailiffs who sought to remove those who had not paid rent from their properties, were greeted by hundreds of women who jostled them, preventing them from entering the tenements, pelted the landlord's representatives with flour and peasemeal, seized notes, and occasionally lifted up and dumped bailiffs in the midden. Empty houses were picketed and new tenants were not allowed to take possession of any such homes. Women worked collectively to bring about change, justifying their illegal actions by appeals to natural justice and 'women's instinct to protect her family and home'.[19] Consequently, when landlords sought to evict tenants behind with their rent, including the wife of a soldier on active service in Clydeside, they found themselves confronted by hundreds of angry residents.

Posters produced by the Glasgow Labour Party Housing Association, and printed cards which carried the words *Rent Strike: We are not Removing* appeared in thousands of properties windows in the city. Attempts to evict the strikers were met with resistance and made more successful by the style of housing. Pam Currie has pointed out the 'forced proximity of the tenements reinforced opportunities for collective action, facilitating contact between women and overcoming the isolation of the housewife'.[20] Helen Crawfurd later recalled:

> One woman with a bell would sit in the close, or passage, watching while the other women living in the tenement went on with their household duties. Whenever the Bailiff's Officer appeared to evict a tenant, the woman in the passage immediately rang the bell, and the women came from all parts of the building. Some with flour, if baking, wet clothes, if washing, and other missiles. Usually the Bailiff made off for his life, chased by a mob of angry women.[21]

By September 1915, over 20,000 households were taking part in the Glasgow rent strike. The following month, the local newspaper, *The Courier*, reported that Sheriff Thompson had dealt with applications to evict 'nine of the 130 tenants who had refused to pay increased rents' in the Partrick area of Glasgow.[22] Court actions were met with large demonstrations involving thousands of women, who, like many suffrage campaigners, emphasised their respectability. This was remarked upon by a number of newspapers, including *The Times*. Placards were carried inscribed with the familiar refrain, *We are not Removing*, but also demanding the root causes of the housing crisis; profiteering, private landlords and the need for government funded housebuilding were addressed. One poster read: 'Our Husbands Sons and Brothers are Fighting the Prussians of Germany. We are fighting the Prussians of Partrick. Only Alternative: Municipal Housing'.[23]

As the social unrest grew, the government became concerned the strikes would spread to other parts of the country, and that such actions would impact on the morale of fighting men and productivity in factories and appointed shipyards on Clydeside. The Secretary of State for Scotland set up a departmental committee to look into the matter, which planned to begin work within a week. One impatient landlord sought to serve summons on 18 tenants before the committee met. A local newspaper reported the problems the landlord faced in his initial attempt to put ejection warrants into force against Glasgow tenants in Maryland Street, Govan.[24] Mrs Barbour addressed a demonstration gathered to resist the entry of Sherriff's officers who sought to evict one tenant; officers were attacked with peasemeal, flour and whiting leading to one woman being arrested. After discussion between the protester's leader, Mrs Barbour, and the Sherriff's officers, it was decided not to proceed with the warrant, as the occupant, a widow, was ill.[25]

As tensions mounted further, strikers were served with court citations on the 17 November. Six of these tenants were from households where men worked in shipyards. When the tenants were summoned to appear in the small debt court, women marched again, accompanied by a band of improvised instruments such as drums, whistles or hooters. This time, men from the shipyards and munitions factories threatened industrial strikes in support of the rent strikes. The court decided that as the whole issue of rents was under consideration by government, it was in the public interest to take no action on this occasion. Yet three warrants for eviction were soon granted, albeit with a special dispensation which ensured the evictions, which usually occurred within 48 hours, would not take place for 4 days.

By this time, other housewives in areas such Aberdeen, Gretna and Annan, were following Clydeside's example and undertaking rent strikes. In Dundee, militancy was strongest in the Jute-producing districts of the city where one third of households 'were female headed, by widows, women separated from partners and young single working women' often sharing households with friends and sibling.[26] An attempt to evict a soldier's wife with three children, who was two weeks behind with her rent, fuelled anger against greedy landlords. In Birkenhead, on Merseyside in Cheshire, two thousand women marched to the town hall with banners bearing the slogan, *Father is fighting in Flanders, We are fighting the landlords here.* In the Lozells district of Birmingham, a large number of tenants refused to pay the rent increases demanded by their landlords, despite threats to double rents if they failed to comply.[27] At the end of November 1915, an increasingly anxious government froze all rents at pre-war levels, and the Rent and Mortgage Interest Restriction Bill was speedily passed by Parliament, gaining Royal Assent before 1915 drew to a close. These legal changes, had been brought about by women's direct action seeking to prevent other women being evicted; women's informal unorganized, spontaneous protests were responsible for stopping landlord's war time profiteering.[28]

For much of the twentieth century, women have been housewives, responsible for the lion's share of work within the home and the household budgets. Wartime created particular cost of living challenges, rent rises, increased food prices and food shortages. Local newspapers carried letters from women struggling to survive on separation allowances. (These were the financial allowances paid by the Government to wives whose husbands were in the armed forces.)

The suffragette, Sylvia Pankhurst, documented wives' and families' struggles and reliance on charity.[29] When submarine warfare intensified in 1916, food became increasingly expensive and scarce, women waited hours in queues to obtain necessities, such as margarine, while shopkeepers and farmers made profits. One well-connected middle-class woman with brutal honesty, recalled: 'my grandfather was a farmer, and farmers have never hated war'.[30] Housewives used their power as consumers in imaginative ways, to express their displeasure at inflated prices and profiteering. In the Rugby Muddling Strikes, housewives bought their usual amount of milk on some days, but on others, bought none. Retailers lost money when they found themselves unable to sell the milk.[31]

Food riots were common in wartime Germany, but rarer in Britain. Nevertheless, in 1917, when potatoes became prohibitively expensive, a lorry carrying potatoes destined for prosperous areas of Glasgow was attacked. The protest was sparked by an elderly woman saying: 'they've got money because you haven't, because you're not in the same class as them.'[32] Housewives looted the potatoes and lifted up their skirts to make impromptu bags to carry them. When the police and another driver tried to intervene, they were attacked. There were also potato riots in Maryport, Cumbria, England, and in Wrexham, north-east Wales, a riot broke out as women fought over a cartload of potatoes.[33] Whilst in Nottingham, England, housewives invaded a chip shop and demanded that their stock of potatoes was sold to them. Once more, government intervention was needed. Food Control Committees were set up in towns, National Kitchens, government-subsidised cafes providing cheap meals for the poor, were opened and rationing was introduced on some foods to alleviate housewives' grievances.[34]

The Rent Strikes had led to rent control and helped to shift responsibility for working-class housing onto the government, even in peacetime.[35] Lloyd George's decisive victory in the first parliamentary election in which women could vote, rested in part on his promise to build *Homes Fit for Heroes*. Homes were to be a physical and ideological embodiment of the better future the country had fought for. Housing had become a political hot topic, spurred on by Glasgow Rent Strikes, and also by the Spanish Flu pandemic responsible for approximately a quarter of a million deaths in Britain between 1918 and 1919. The flu spread quickly in overcrowded inner-city urban areas and many put the blame for this firmly at the door of poor housing. The 1919 Housing and Town Planning Act embodied the idea that the state was now responsible for housing a significant proportion of the working class. Municipal housing, for which Mrs Barbour's army had advocated, was introduced in the years after the war and continued to be built until the 1980s. A principal, supported by all political parties which significantly increased the housing stock.[36]

This new housing policy gave local authorities the power to build houses, but was open to widely varying interpretation. Women's counsellors and women's groups had a key role in ensuring the implementation of the 1919 Housing and Town Planning Act. The newly formed National Federation of Women's Institutes (NFWI) which we will explore further in later chapters, campaigned determinedly to improve housing in rural areas.[37] The NFWI joined forces with other campaigning organisations, such as the Rural Housing and Sanitation Association (RHSA). Simultaneously, the Women's Labour League and Women's Co-op Guild, for whom the home and housing were key areas of political struggle, also sought to influence local and national government to take action to build and improve housing.[38] Notwithstanding the determination of these women's campaigners, their resolutions and petitions, their letter writing and meetings, the housing problem was large, and progress was limited and slow. In Glasgow, it was estimated that 50,000 to 60,000 homes were needed in the city, but in the first years after the war, plans were only passed to build a few hundred.[39] Building costs increased and rents charged by private landlords began to climb again. Furthermore, even when councils built houses, the government insisted that economic rents were charged, putting them beyond the budgets of many working-class families.

By 1919, Socialist groups on Clydeside were calling for direct action to be taken on housing while the *Govan Pioneer*, a local newspaper, concluded: 'The standard must be higher; better housing, and everything that makes life what it should be, in the future must come first; the paying for it is the secondary consideration.'[40] Political agitation and direct action began again: on 23 August, 1920, 60,000 people attended a demonstration in the city organised by the Housing Committee and 'certain leaders of public opinion' in Glasgow. Legal challenges, rent strikes and demonstration continued to be supported by the Scottish Labour Party Housing Association, but local newspapers indicate that the response to calls for a 'no-rent strike' in Glasgow and in Edinburgh struggled to win the support they had received in 1915. In December 1922, *The Times* reported that 20,000 householders in Glasgow, and tens of thousands in West Scotland, deliberately withheld rent in protest against new rent rises.[41] Tensions rumbled on, Clydeside tenants were threatened with eviction for non-payment of rent and took actions to resist. Vigils were kept every night and hand bells were rung to warn tenants of the potential arrival of the Sherriff's officers. By 1924 however, their actions were beginning to run out of steam.[42]

Women fared no better in rural areas, where the absence of amenities, such as water and drainage, and the poor condition of many houses, were political issues for women. The 1919 act set minimum suggested standards for council house building and the approximate floor area of the properties, but as the economic crisis deepened in the 1920s, successive governments weighed down by the debt from the First World War sought to reduce these standards.[43] Proposals to cut the number and size of rooms met with criticism from housewives and the first English-born woman MP Maggie Wintringham. In 1923, she expressed housewives' concerns when the new Housing Bill did not include provision for houses to be built in rural areas. She also critiqued austerity measures, which reduced the size of three-bedroom houses to 850 square feet, with one of the children's bedrooms being only 6ft by 6ft 10 inches. Maggie made her point eloquently, explaining to the almost totally male House of Commons:

> I visualize that room in my mind, and I compared it with the Table in front of the Treasury bench, and afterwards I was interested to go down and measure the Table. I found that the smallest bedroom would be half-a-foot less in length than the Table. I ask the Minister, how would it be possible to use such a room as a bedroom for the accommodation of two girls or two boys?[44]

Rural women with no domestic water supplies found that their exasperation was compounded in the Second World War. Villages which had campaigned unsuccessfully for rural water supplies for years, discovered that when the army was stationed nearby, their camp had water and drainage in no time at all. Why, one woman wanted to know, 'couldn't such action be taken for ordinary people in peacetime?'[45] In 1943, it was agreed at the AGM of the National Federation of Women's Institutes: '…the three main services – water, sewage and electricity – should be a national responsibility, and it should be possible to compel Local Authorities to take necessary action to ensure to adequate provision in the countryside as well as towns.'[46] Their campaigning made slow progress: even in the 1950s, half the rural housing stock had no indoor water supply.

Wartime bombing destroyed a large number of properties in urban areas throughout the county. In London, 160,000 houses needed repairs before they could be lived in, whilst a further 780,000 were habitable despite the damage they had suffered during the war – but repairs took time.[47] Although repairs to the housing stock were carried out in the 1940s and thousands of council houses were built in the 1950s and 1960s, housing continued to be an issue for many women. In the early 1950s approximately one in six London households were living in buildings converted for multiple ooccupancy. Families lived in one room and shared a sink tap and lavatory with other families. One in five households shared a home with either strangers or their in-laws.

The practicalities of people's lives were not always considered in the design of new homes. New estates were often built on the edges of conurbations where women sometimes felt isolated. Tower blocks also presented problems for women with small children in pushchairs, or with shopping to carry, particularly when the lifts were not working. Other women struggled to get adequate housing because of racism, or prejudice against single mothers. Once again, women were compelled to take direct action: Beverley Bryan, Stella Dadzie, and Suzanne Scafe have argued in their book, *Heart of the Race:* 'Black women organised both individually and collectively against the housing policies of racist councils.'[48] They organised rent strikes and demonstrations. On one occasion, exasperated at the council's slow progress in addressing issues around electricity and heating in a London estate, which was supposed to provide short-term housing, women occupied the town hall and let their children run loose in the building. This action speedily brought council officials to the negotiating table.[49]

Squatters had moved into disused army camps across the country in the 1940s, and women's groups followed their example in the 1970s.[50] In Greater London, nearly a third of the housing stock was built before 1875, and two thirds between 1875 and 1919.[51] There were 23,100 empty dwellings awaiting demolition in London alone, which were reclaimed and repaired by women squatters.[52] Lynne Harne lost her job at the social security office when she became pregnant and struggled to find housing as private renters often did not want children. She recalled how she 'was living basically in one room, with a tiny kitchenette and a separate toilet and bath' and so decided squatting was a better option.[53] Hers was not a singular experience: other mothers of young children also took direct action, when stuck on the council waiting lists for housing for years, unable to find suitable accommodation. Thus, 'by the late 1970s an estimated fifty women-only households were scattered throughout the streets behind Broadway Market, including one continuous terrace of seven women's squats on Lansdowne Drive' in London.[54] Local residents, keen to avoid living next to a boarded-up house, often tipped off squatters' groups when a house became empty. Women acquired the necessary skills to reinstate the water and electricity; some took courses in plumbing and helped repair the houses; others grew vegetables and kept chickens in the gardens at the back of the property.

As historian Christine Wall has argued, the squats, 'enabled radical experiments in collective living', including shared childcare in an 'extensive network of women-only housing' which provided new 'social spaces'.[55] Women's centres were created in squats; one in London's Caledonian Road offered free pregnancy tests. Olive Morris, feminist activist and founder member of the Organisation of Women of Asian and African Descent (OWAAD), squatted in 121 Railton Road, Brixton, London from where she facilitated a number of community groups in the area. The initial disapproval of the authorities towards squatting, however, had its consequences: women and children faced evictions, and prejudice meant that mothers sometimes lost custody of their children if they lived in a lesbian squat. In time, a more organised system of co-operation with local councils evolved and short-life licences were granted to squatters so they could live in empty properties awaiting demolition or redevelopment.

For many women, political campaigns around housing led to their involvement in other campaigns, and some of these campaigns are discussed in the next chapters. Mary Barbour continued to fight to improve working class women's lives in the post-war world when she became a magistrate and local counsellor. She worked for the introduction of washhouses; laundries; public baths; free milk for school children; child welfare centres; play areas; pensions for mothers; home helps, and municipal banks. She was also Chairman of the Glasgow Women's Welfare and Advisory Clinic, Glasgow's first family planning centre providing birth control for married women.[56] In 2018, a sculpture portraying Mary Barbour leading rent strikers was unveiled on International Women's Day in Govan, Glasgow. The fundraising to erect the statue was led by the Remember Mary Barbour Association, whilst an award in her name was launched by Parkhead Housing Association, in recognition of women's roles in campaigning and working in the voluntary sector in Glasgow. Its first winner in 2016 was Anna Stuart, a mother of six who founded the Castlemilk East Housing Co-operative, which has provided low-cost housing in Glasgow since 1984.[57]

Mary Barbour's army; Maggie Wintringham and the campaigning members of the Women's Institute; the London squatters and the black women activists who occupied the local town hall with their children in the 1970s; and Anna Stuart, were all important political campaigners. They opened up for housewives the possibility of change when battling with the cost of living crisis and poor housing conditions in which they had to live and work. These campaigners, and women's growing power in the ballot box, had achieved improvements in housing by the 1990s. The supply of housing, and the cost and standards of some housing, still left much to be desired, but tenants had gained new rights and landlords had new responsibilities. An inside water supply, drainage and electricity were provided in almost all British homes by the end of the twentieth century. The importance of this cannot be overlooked, as one housewife from Longdon in Staffordshire explained in the 1930s:

I have lived in this cottage for over six years and for the first four and half years we had not water supply on the premises and had to fetch it from a draw well 40 feet deep from a cottage 70 yards away We had to make three journeys a day which would take about half an hour..... My supply is now from a sink in the back kitchen ... You will understand what a blessing it is to us.[58]

Chapter 2

Voters Awake (1920s)

On Saturday 14 December 1918, for the very first time, women were able to vote in parliamentary elections. The polls opened early, and despite Spanish Flu raging across Britain, a poll clerk in Leeds described this historic day as one of the 'jolliest of all elections.'[1] The local newspaper report also went on to explain: "it had been a day of smiles." Nine out of ten of the women voters had a smile for the policeman .... and he, gallant man, returned the glad look unfailingly.'[2]

Women's enfranchisement came after years of struggle by thousands of women from all walks of life, in all parts of the country. Their long, slow and overall painstakingly polite and peaceful political campaigning for the vote had lasted for more than seventy years, gathering pace in the Edwardian era (1901–1912). A multitude of organisations and groups, including Mrs Pankhurst's Women's Social and Political Union (1903) and The Tax Resistance League (1909), attended a lot of meetings, went on many marches, smashed the occasional window, set light to a few post-boxes and buildings, and refused to pay any taxes, even dog licences. In 1914, less than 60% of men could vote in parliamentary elections; the vote was restricted to men over 21 who rented or owned their own homes. Both the Liberal and Conservative parties were concerned any changes to the franchise should be focused on groups likely to vote for them. Certain Conservative politicians felt inclined to give the vote to wealthy women, who were thought most likely to vote for their party. Liberals were worried enfranchising women, on the same limited terms as men, might favour the Conservatives. The Labour party was all in favour of adult suffrage, but it had too few MPs to have any significant influence.

Popular myth suggests that suffrage campaigns came to a halt at the outbreak of First World War, and that women were enfranchised as a reward for their contribution to the war effort. It certainly required a wartime coalition government to extend the franchise, giving the vote to all men and to some women in 1918. Excluding women under thirty and many more who could not meet complex property qualifications, ensured that almost all the munitionettes, land girls, and many other women war workers, continued to be denied entry to the ballot box and citizenship for many years. Campaigning for all women to have the vote on the same terms as men was a priority for women's groups which continued to protest at the unfairness of the electoral system. For, as suffrage campaigner, Anna Munro, pointed out at a meeting of the National Council of Women at Church House, Westminster, London in 1926, 'a girl came of age morally at sixteen, industrially at eighteen, and legally at twenty-one.'[3]

Getting the vote was, however, only one part of the battle to ensure that women exerted political influence: a long and concerted campaign was required to persuade ordinary women to use it. Since the 1870s, women had been able to vote in elections for their parish and district councillors, but many had not bothered to do so; in the city of Worcester, for example, less than 10% of women reportedly voted in local elections. Some apparently avoided politics, as they did not want to 'engender arguments with their neighbours'.[4] So, despite the historical significance of the December 1918 election, many of those who had campaigned for women's suffrage were anxious about how many women would actually turn out to vote. Would women, people wondered, find the time or the inclination to vote, given the multiple other tasks and responsibilities they had to contend with – particularly as the post-war election was condemned by many as staged, sinister, chicanery and innately moderate. Austin Chamberlain, writing to his sister, claimed he had never hated an election so much, as 'the voters are apathetic; the dividing lines of parties obscure and uncertain, the issues ill defined, cranks and numerous worse elements very much in evidence'.[5]

On election day, the 14, December 1914, newspaper reports were mixed. *The Birmingham Mail* suggested: 'some women refused to vote at all unless they were accompanied by their husbands. They had literally to be pushed into the polling stations.'[6] Going on to say polling was low in the morning 'In some working-class districts – of which Aston, in Birmingham may be quoted as an example – the number of women voters in the early hours of polling was negligible .... In a thickly populated ward at Nechelles, too, only six votes were recorded in the first two hours.'[7] It was insinuated that poor weather might have had a detrimental impact on the turnout at the election. In the St Pancras district in London, apparently it did, especially in the poorer districts, where 'women go thinly shod. Yet even in such a quarter one would find workers at the polling booths declaring that the proportion of men to women voters was six or eight to one.'[8] Nevertheless, evening newspapers included images of women who had turned up with children accompanying them, or with babies in prams. In Stourbridge, West Midlands, where the Trades Unionist, Mary Macarthur was standing, it was reported that one woman looked after sixty babies, presumably not all at once, while their mothers went to vote for Macarthur.[9]

Many reports were upbeat about the election, claiming 'From all parts of the country there have come in reports that the women voted in larger proportions than the men, although they made no fuss about it.'[10] But the national turnout was generally low: it transpired that only 57% of the total electorate had voted. Although pamphlets and leaflets had been distributed giving guidance on which women could vote, as historian Anna Muggeridge has argued, uncertainty and confusion may have contributed a low turnout of women voters.[11] Furthermore, while some women it seemed had greeted their new status as citizens with elation and excitement, others were more anxious or indifferent about it. Consequently, in the years that followed throughout the 1920s and 1930s, women's magazines; suffrage campaigners; the great and the good of the chattering classes and women's organisations, including the National Women Citizens Association, the National Council of Women, the National Council of Equal Citizenship (NSEC), and the National Federation of Women's Institutes (NFWI), all sought to persuade the newly enfranchised women to become active citizens and campaigners; they all encouraged women to try and exert influence in local and national politics.

A mixture of optimism and anxiety was expressed about the potential effects of women voters on the parliamentary system. Mrs Abbethnot from Warwick and Leamington National Union of Suffrage Societies suggested: 'the old political parties will remain, but although women are docile and perhaps easily led, I do not believe that they will readily fall in with the party cries and ambition of recent years. We owe our actual enfranchisement to no one party'.[12] The Conservative party's principal agent in 1921 suggested women would make politics 'more parochial', being more concerned with the cost of living, and that women would vote on 'purely home questions.'[13] Such an approach may explain Conservative Stanley Baldwin's comment, when explaining his unwillingness to reduce the price of sugar, describing the housewife as 'Chancellor of the Exchequer in her own right.... I am, as Chancellor of the Exchequer, the housewife of the nation.'[14] Political parties have, of course, their own agendas to persuade women to vote for them. They all created magazines targeting the women voter: *Labour Women* (1913–71), the Conservative Party's *Home and Politics* (1921) and the Liberal Party's *Women's News* (1925). In each publication there was more than a whiff of condescension adopted towards women readers from the male politicians who were trying to persuade women to support them.[15]

Having women as prospective candidates for parliament was perhaps one way to encourage women to vote, but they were few to be found. There were over 700 parliamentary constituencies in 1918, but a mere seventeen women stood in the December election. They were, however, greeted with some enthusiasm. In the Birmingham constituency of Ladywood, where Margery Corbett Ashby was standing, one woman said she wanted to get her 'vote in for the lady before the housework', another 'old lady of 68 told the lady clerk that she felt it a privilege that on her first opportunity of voting she could choose a woman to represent her'.[16] Only one woman, was elected to the House of Commons in the 1918; Constance Markievicz, became MP for the Irish constituency of Dublin St Patrick's. As a member of Sinn Fein, she did not take up her seat at Westminster but continued to take an active role in Irish politics, campaigning for independence. In the years that followed, progress towards women taking an active role in parliamentary politics was slow, as Jon Lawrence had argued 'the gender dynamics of electoral politics changed little between the wars...men's grip over electoral politics was barely loosened.'[17] Helena Norman noted *in Good Housekeeping*, 'Men do want women in politics. Yes, so far as rough work is concerned, canvassing for instance, and in short as the charwoman of the political world. Scrubbers – yes, Cabinet Ministers, Premiers and Presidents – no.'[18]

A very small number of women became MPs in the 1920s, included Margaret Bondfield, who was elected as the Labour MP for Northampton in 1923 and went on to become the first woman cabinet minister, when she served in Ramsey McDonald's Labour Government from 1929–31. Nancy Astor was the first woman to take up a seat in the House of Commons, as Conservative MP for Plymouth Sutton in 1919, when her husband the serving constituency MP, was elevated to the House of Lords. Likewise, Maggie Wintringham inherited her husband's seat, Louth in Lincolnshire. She was adopted as the Liberal candidate after her husband died in the Palace of Westminster, aged only 53. As she was still in mourning, it was agreed that she would not make public speeches during the campaign, although she attended meetings where others, including her two sisters, spoke on her behalf. This led to her being nicknamed 'the silent candidate'. *The Pall Mall Gazette* noted, 'Mrs Wintringham the Liberal candidate is the widow of the late member, sentiment in the circumstances is naturally on her side, and women's societies irrespective of party have gone to her aid. Old-fashioned farmers, on the other hand, are said to be averse to being represented by a woman.'[19] Maggie won the election, with 8,386 votes, being 42.2% of the vote, and was re-elected in 1922 and 1923, but only served as an MP for a brief three years. Observing the difficulty of getting women into parliament, feminist, Rose Macaulay, ironically suggested it was not considered good form to vote for a woman as a candidate, unless:

she is the wife of your former member, who has disqualified himself from standing by means of death, peerage or his conduct in elections. A little thought will show you that all lady members of Parliament obtain their seats in one of these ways. It is not thought very nice for a woman to get into parliament though merely on her own account; there is something a little unwomanly about it. There is only one path to this position; they must marry a member and then put him somehow out of action, by whatever method seems most suitable.[20]

Once elected, these women MPs worked together across party lines to campaign on women's issues, including the need for women police, widow's benefits, and for women to have equal guardianship of children with men.

In celebrating the enfranchisement of women in 1918, Mrs Fawcett, as leader of the largest suffrage organisation – the National Union of Women's Suffrage Societies (NUWSS) – had discussed the 'exhilaration of feeling the power of the vote behind them' when addressing the organisation's annual conference. The NUWSS went on to demand that the franchise should be extended to all women on the same terms as men; that women were to be introduced as magistrates; and that women should be allowed to sit on juries and a variety of legislation to protect women. For example, the NUWSS wanted the machinery for obtaining and enforcing maintenance orders against neglectful, cruel or dissolute husbands to be simplified and made more effective; for married women to have more control over their money; and for women police with full powers of arrest to be introduced. The NUWSS and other women's organisations were gratified to see the passing of the 1919 Sex Disqualification Removal Act, which enabled women to take on a range of civic roles, including jury service and serving as magistrates.[21] Catriona Beaumont has argued that a diverse range of women's organisations, including The Townswomen's Guild, Mothers' Union, the National Council of Women and the Catholic Women's League, sought to encourage women to take an increasing role in public life as both citizens and housewives.[22]

Yet not all women were convinced that voting was really their bag, so to speak, or were even a tiny bit excited by politics, and a tone of desperation seeped into the articles written by suffrage campaigners in women's magazines during the period. Rose Macaulay's article 'Problems for the Citizen' in *Good Housekeeping* in 1923, adopted a tongue-in-cheek and justifiably sceptical approach to explaining the political process to readers: 'The Government seems to go on along its own way without much reference to public opinion. But every now and then there is a parliamentary election and then every voter has to decide which of the various candidates who offer themselves as representative of his constituency he least dislikes. Be sure that they will all be quite foolish, quite useless and quite unable to show any reason why they should represent you.'[23] Even when the extension of the franchise to all women over 21 on equal terms with men in 1928 resulted in women outnumbering male voters, many ordinary women did not seem to have warmed to the idea of, or even used, the term citizenship.

Women's relationship with politics was ambivalent and often unconfident. The feminist, Storm Jameson's article in *Women's Journal*, entitled 'Voting Need not be Difficult', drew upon the old suffragette adage of the symbolic significance of the vote stating: 'The second fact that you and I and Mary Smith must get securely into our heads is that the vote is our symbol of personality. It is a badge we wear, inscribed "I am a real person". It is a sign of power. It means that ultimately, we are in this terrific business of government.'[24] Storm Jameson went on to explain it was 'a privilege and a duty to vote', and that government actions interfered with everything that mattered to women: 'from your silk stockings to your men's lives'. But convincing women of this was not easy, as the Women's Institute Movement soon discovered. *Home and Country*, the monthly magazine of the National Federation of Women's Institutes (NFWI) introduced a series of short monthly pieces entitled 'Voters Awake', which explained any business before parliament affecting women – for example, legislation on housing, maternity provision or women police. But the very title of the series, 'Voters Awake' linguistically suggests that women were somewhat less than alert when it came to parliamentary politics.

Formed in 1915 as part of the national war effort to stimulate the production, preparation and preservation of food to help alleviate wartime shortages, the Women's Institute movement developed to see the political education of rural women as one of its core functions. It was run by many women who had been actively involved in the suffrage campaigns, such as Lady Denman, Grace Hadow, Mrs Auerbach, Edith Rigby, Lady Isabelle Margesson, and Elizabeth Robins, who all saw the organisation as an extension of their suffrage activities.[25] By the mid 1920s, the NFWI had become the largest women's organisation in Britain, with in excess of 250,000 members and an institute in nearly one out of every five villages. The movement's Annual General Meeting was held at the Albert Hall in London, nicknamed the Countrywomen's parliament; it was broadcast on the radio, discussed in newspapers, and listened to by governments. The NFWI argued that women's points of view were needed in the political decision-making process. In 1921, an AGM resolution advised: 'That it be the recognised duty of individual institutes to educate their members in the powers of the Parish Councils, Rural District Councils and County Councils with a view to getting local women on all these bodies'.[26]

The NFWI was led and guided and chaired by Lady Denman, who also was very active in the Women's Liberal Federation and the Birth Control Movement, and her deputy Grace Hadow, a suffrage campaigner, Oxford Don and Conservative Party supporter. Eve Colpus has argued that Hadow placed emphasis 'upon facilitating women's active role in community politics... [as] part of a distinctive vision for adult education'.[27] These movements' leaders campaigned on national, county, and village issues they believed would improve the quality of rural women's lives. They liaised with a multitude of other feminist, women's and social welfare organisations, including the League for Health, the Maternity Child Welfare League, and the National Council for Unmarried Mothers.

In attempting to bring together rural women across religious, class, and party lines, there was potential for conflict. Lady Denman and Grace Hadow strongly advocated the prevention of controversy, asking that nothing which might cause friction or lead to serious differences should be discussed, and institutes must be non-sectarian and non-party-political. *Home and Country* sought to educate and encourage its readers to partake in the electoral process as voters, council and parliamentary representatives, and with whichever party they went on to choose to support. The organisation's non-party-political stance was frequently misunderstood, with the general secretary of the National Union of Agricultural Workers insisting in the *Daily Herald* in 1922, that the Women's Institute Movement was working 'insidiously against the Labour Party and the trade unions and in favour of 'leaving things as they are'.[28] *Home and Country* just as determinedly sought to increase the voters, by including articles by politicians of all political persuasions, such as the Liberal MP, Megan Lloyd George, and Nye Bevan, from the Labour Party.

Politically educating rural women and teaching them to think for themselves, required not only informing and lecturing them, but also giving them the opportunity to participate in political processes within the safe spaces that women's organisations like the NFWI could provide. Learning to speak in public, to chair meetings, and to exercise their democratic right, gave women the chance to practice politics. Local WIs were run by a committee elected by secret ballot; an alien approach in many of the villages of rural Britain, where parish councillors were still selected by a show of hands. The institute's democratic principle (of one member, one vote), which caused a shift in rural power relationships, was not always well received. One horrified lady of the manor, on discovering that she would not be elected president, automatically declared: 'she had no intention of allowing such a radical movement in their village'.[29] Helen McCarthy has pointed out how in 1920, an article in the Conservative Agents' Journal reflected fearfully upon the growth of new organisations for women: 'Operating under all sorts of disguises, in name non-party, but in very truth, manipulated by socialistically inclined women'. The editorial declared these bodies to be 'to the disadvantage of our own party organisations, in money, membership, in energy and in influence'.[30]

While outsiders from all sides of the political spectrum were concerned that the Women's Institute Movement was too political, ordinary members were often dismissive of the NFWI's political campaigns. In the 1980s, when I interviewed women who were members in the inter-war years, what they cared about were local issues and village-centred concerns. Chidham Women's Institute in West Sussex was proud of having prevented the local bus company raising the fare to the local market town, for instance. Others talked of having exerted pressure to ensure the local doctor's surgery remained open in their village. In 1931, the Anglesey Federation reported the local activities in which they were engaged:

> Many Institutes take an active interest in the children of the village. One has, in co-operation with the school managers, formulated a scheme for helping necessitous children by providing clothing, boots, etc., in the winter. Christmas parties have been given in several villages for the school children. Clinics have been run in co-operation with the district nursing associations. Model outfits for infants have been made, under the direction of the Superintendent of nursing for North Wales. Local hospitals and village halls have been generously helped.[31]

Likewise, in Worcestershire, institutes collected farm eggs for local hospitals, ran infant welfare clinics, or helped fund the local district nurse. Such activities could be seen as community service – a continuation of the First World War traditions of volunteerism. But they were also ways of organising health provision prior to the introduction of the National Health Service (NHS) in 1948, which ran alongside the organisation's demands for social welfare legislation. A 1926 AGM resolution demonstrated this when the meeting urged 'all Women's Institutes to study the different methods of National Health and other Insurance, in the interests of members and the families of members.'[32]

Health, welfare and public amenities, like housing, were political issues that women cared about in the inter-war years. One of the direct results of women's new power as voters and citizens was politicians slowly recognized the significance of these areas, which became central to interwar political discourse and the formation of the 1945 welfare state.[33] But it was a slow recognition, and in the meantime, perhaps one of the reasons women felt alienated from the political process was because whatever they were told, they remained unconvinced that their actions and their vote would really change the things that mattered to them in their everyday lives.

Education, maternal and child welfare, like housing, were regionally varied and organised under the auspices of local government, and this is where many women chose to focus their efforts to politicise women. Nevertheless, Mrs Perkins of Boulder WI, in Lancashire admitted: 'one of the difficulties in the past has been the indifference of the public to parochial affairs and the people themselves are to blame, not the Councils.'[34] *Forward*, a Scottish newspaper, with a strong commitment to left-wing politics, noted:

> The growing political power of women and their intense desire for better home conditions will be a great aid in effecting the peaceful revolution in the municipal administration. Women are practical and more concerned about securing a fuller life for their children. We are on the threshold of tremendous developments; politics are rapidly being domesticated.[35]

Local councils were seen as a core area for women's political activities. Indeed, when *Woman's Magazine* ran a series on 'The Citizenship of Women', they included a detailed explanation of the working of the local county councils. For, if women struggled to acquire interest or influence in national politics, they were beginning to make headway in local politics in the inter-war years.[36] In Edinburgh, for example, a Women's Citizenship Association was formed in 1919, which supported women candidates (many of whom were Conservatives) in local elections and campaigned for improvements in maternity care and improvements in housing.[37]

Across the country, women played an active role in local politics. Ada Croft Baker, a staunch liberal and Temperance supporter became the first woman in Lincolnshire to gain a council seat in 1919. She joined the Maternity and Child Welfare Committee, and took over the role of chair within three years. She was also one of the first women magistrates, and after many years of service on Lincolnshire county council, became Alderman in Cleethorpes.[38] In Wolverhampton, suffragette Emma Sproson, who had been imprisoned for refusing to pay for a dog license on the basis of no taxation without representation, also sought to become a Labour counsellor. After two failed attempts, she was elected to represent the Dunstall Ward in 1921, when she waved a red flag on the Town Hall balcony, she gained the nickname of 'Red Emma'. Her council committee work focussed on helping the blind, distressed and the mentally ill. She was appalled by the malpractice she discovered, and wrote a pamphlet, *Fever Hospital Facts and Fairy Tales*, claiming goods were stolen and staff underpaid.[39]

Often the women who became counsellors were only too aware of the struggles to feed and care for families during the economic recession and high unemployment of the interwar years. Hannah Mitchell, as well as becoming a magistrate, served on Manchester City Council from 1924 to 1935, and she was on a number of committees including the Poor Relief Committee. Hannah recalled: 'I knew just how much food could be bought out of the allowance, knew the cost of children's clothes and footwear; could tell at a glance if the applicant was in ill health.'[40] Likewise, in Stepney, London, Annie Barnes was elected to the local council in 1934; she lost her council seat in 1937, but returned to serve between 1941 and 1949. She later recalled, 'I was on lots of different committees at different times, sometimes as many as five at a time. I always tried to be on Housing or Public Health every year, but I was also at various times on the committees for markets, General Purposes, Libraries and Museums and Sick and Accident Pay. I was vice-chairman of the Public Health Committee three times.'[41] These women brought their experience as chancellors of exchequers of their own households into managing local council budgets, but it is interesting to note that nearly 100 years later, Britain has never had a woman appointed to the role of chancellor of exchequer in a national government.

Between 1918 to 2023, there have only been 561 women elected to take a seat in the House of Commons. Progress was slow until 1997, when 120 women were elected, 101 of whom were Labour MPs. In the run up to the election, pollsters identified someone they called 'Worcester woman' as the median voter who could swing the election for Labour. She was perceived to be a working-class woman in her thirties, with two children, concerned about the quality of life and with little interest in politics.[42] Politicians, as well as women's organisations, were still trying to wake up ambivalent women voters – a project that momentarily at least seemed successful. A report, published by the Electoral Commission in April 2004, found no gender gap in voter turnout at national, regional or local elections. Women, however, continued to be more likely to get involved in cause-orientated activities, such as signing a petition or boycotting products for ethical reasons.[43] More than 100 years after women excitedly voted in their first parliamentary election, some women fulfill the expectations of their suffrage predecessors and enthusiastically participate in parliamentary politics. Others, it seems, still see other forms of political activities as more likely to bring change and social justice.

Chapter 3

The Suppression of *The Well of Loneliness* (1928)

The publication of Radclyffe Hall's novel *The Well of Loneliness* (1928) is best understood as one woman's campaign to elicit recognition and compassion for lesbian women. According to Diana Souhami, Radclyffe Hall wanted to end public silence about homosexuality, to bring about 'a more tolerant understanding', and to 'spur all classes of inverts to make good through hard work...and sober and useful living'.[1] Radclyffe Hall borrowed the term 'invert' for a lesbian, from the writing of contemporary sexologists such as Havelock Ellis. It is a term which seems uncomfortable to many modern readers, but should be seen as indicative the complex attitudes and prejudices which surrounded same-sex relationships at the beginning of the twentieth century. These prejudices lay behind a crusade to suppress the novel, led by the editor of *The Sunday Express*, and resulted in the book becoming the subject of a widely publicised obscenity trial. This not only provided huge exposure for *The Well of Loneliness*, but also ensured that there was extensive public discussion of lesbianism. In the years that followed, art, literature, culture, and the courts, continued to provide arenas for ideas about women's sexuality to be explored and challenged.

Marguerite Antonia Radclyffe Hall, who was born in Bournemouth in 1880, was already an established writer, with five novels and a number of volumes of poetry to her name, when *The Well of Loneliness* was published. Her novel, *Adam's Breed* (1926), had been a best seller, winning the Prix Femina and James Tait Black prizes. She had achieved literary success, despite apparently being dyslexic, and having been slow to learn to read as a child. Throughout her life, Marguerite's spelling was appalling, and she often asked her companions to read for her. This did not, however, deter her from becoming a writer. As a consequence of significant wealth inherited from her father, Radclyffe Hall was financially independent. She was free of many of society's constraints and, most importantly, any pressure to marry or earn a living in an era when women's career prospects were limited. She was able to be open about her sexuality, to dress in masculine clothes, and to live with her life partner, the sculptor, Una Troubridge, for many years.

In many respects Radclyffe Hall was an unlikely radical. Her wealth and lifestyle placed her firmly within the establishment. As a couple, she and Troubridge attended the opening nights of theatrical performances in London, bred and raised dogs, and were photographed with their dachshunds at Crufts. As well as a residence in London, they purchased a cottage near Rye in Sussex. Their political sympathies lay with Stanley Baldwin, the leader of the Conservative Party. Given their settled lifestyle, and aware of the potential furore the book might cause, Radclyffe Hall ensured that she had her partner's support before she embarked upon writing *The Well of Loneliness*. Others shared Radclyffe Hall's awareness of the novel's potentially contentious subject matter. The book was rejected by three publishers before Johnathan Cape agreed to publish it. Radclyffe Hall explained to her editor that the text must not be altered, for she had put her 'pen at the service of some of the most persecuted and misunderstood people in the world'.[2]

The Well of Loneliness charts the childhood, coming out, and early relationships of Stephen, a girl born to well-off parents of the late Victorian era. Stephen's parents, who lived in rural Worcestershire, had expected to have a son, and had already selected their infant's name prior to her birth. Although they had a daughter, they did not change their chosen name, which throughout the novel is a signifier of the heroine's non-conformity to the gender roles of the era. As Stephen grows up, her own sense of difference grows. Her inner emotional turmoil is signified when she expresses her hatred of dresses and demands to have her hair cut, aged only seven. When Stephen reaches adulthood, her father dies and she begins to dress in masculine clothes. After falling in love with the wife of a neighbour, the heroine goes to London, publishes two novels, and is encouraged to travel to Paris, where she encounters gay subcultures. Serving as an ambulance driver on the front in the First World War, Stephen falls in love with Mary, a fellow driver. However, this is no fairytale romance, although Mary and Stephen do live together in Paris for a while after the war. The narrative ends when Stephen, believing that she will never be able to make Mary really happy, pretends to have an affair, driving Mary into a relationship with a man. The novel's last words, uttered by Stephen, are a plea to God: 'Give us also the right to our existence!'.

The novel has no explicit sexual content, something that a number of readers found rather disappointing. It was controversial because the main protagonist, despite having been born a woman, in dress, behaviour, and sexual preference, adopted roles society assigned to men. It is often seen as semi-autobiographical. Radcyffe Hall herself was known to her friends as John or Jack. It is, as Heather Love points out, an indication of the values of the time which led Radclyffe Hall to describe her own sexuality as innate but also different, and what she described as 'inverted'. In her letters to Evguenia Souline, one of her many lovers, Radclyffe Hall explained: 'I have never felt an impulse toward a man in all my life, this is because I am a congenital invert. For me to sleep with a man would be an outrage against nature'.[3] Thus, Radclyffe Hall's writing, in both her private letters and in *The Well of Loneliness*, articulates her struggle to live a lesbian life within a prevailingly hostile culture.[4] The book was for Radclyffe Hall, both a personal and political publication: one woman's campaign against society's prejudices.[5]

Ideas about homosexuality were both shifting and contested in the inter-war years. Once seen in terms of religious morality and deemed to be a sin, same-sex relationships and intimacy were increasingly being understood as a sickness, something requiring medical intervention. *The Well of Loneliness* campaigns against both of these perceptions of lesbianism. Instead, the novel portrays lesbianism as an inherent characteristic, not a sign of immaturity or mental instability, perversity, aberrance, or immorality, and it argues for acceptance based upon this different type of understanding. That the heroine is innately lesbian is marked out as physical difference. Thus, at birth Stephen is described as 'narrow-hipped wide shouldered little tadpole of a baby'.[6] Radclyffe Hall had herself converted to Roman Catholicism in 1912 and the novel is also a deeply moral and religious text which 'has been repeatedly described as the "bible" of lesbian literature'.[7] Nevertheless, as Ed Madden, argues 'by writing the life of a lesbian as a kind of gospel of inversion, Hall turns a language of condemnation into a language of validation'.[8] It was this very validation of lesbianism and its portrayal of the main character Stephen as a 'lesbian messiah' that seemed to cause such consternation to the moral critics of *The Well of Loneliness*.[9] Most significantly, it portrayed lesbian relationships without suggesting they were 'in any way blameworthy'.[10] This was an incredibly radical idea at a time, when, for some, the very mention of lesbianism was offensive.

Male homosexuality had been illegal since the Tudor period, punishable by death until 1828, and by imprisonment with hard labour after that. In Britain, however, it has never been illegal for two adult women to have sexual relations with each other. In part, this was consistent with the assumptions of some Victorians that women, or at least middle-class women, had limited sexual desire. Dr William Acton, an eminent medic in the era sought to reassure young men 'the majority of women (happily for society) were not much troubled by sexual feeling of any kind'.[11] Some people in the early twentieth century seemed to assume that without the active presence of a certain male appendage, sex could not possibly take place. Thus, lesbianism found itself placed firmly in the closet, not by punitive and cruel laws, but by deafening silence. Nevertheless, waves of anxiety, precipitated by women's apparent independence during the First World War, the surplus-women problem after the conflict, the enfranchisement of some women in 1918, and the advent of the supposedly 'new women', all seem to have increased anxiety about lesbianism. Support grew, particularly in some religious groups, to amend the 1885 Criminal Law Act, and to ensure that 'any act of gross indecency between female persons shall be a misdemeanor, punishable in the same manner as any such act committed by male person.'[12]

When this attempt to criminalise lesbian acts reached the House of Lords on 15 August, 1921, the Earl of Malmesbury explained that he was 'extremely sorry to raise a discussion' of what he felt must be for all his fellow peers 'a most disgusting and polluting subject'. He expressed his concern that any change in the law would lay women open to blackmail. Furthermore, there would difficulties in obtaining evidence for convictions. Finally, he reiterated his view, this 'vice has been increasingly partly owing to the nervous conditions following on the war'.[13] The amendment, and consequently any change to the law, were finally rejected on the grounds that it was best not to mention such topics, as it might give women ideas. The Earl of Desart, opposing the legislation, described lesbianism as sinful, and linked it to neurosis, asking:

> How many people does one suppose really are so vile, so unbalanced, so neurotic, so decadent as to do this? You may say there are a number of them, but it would be, at most, an extremely small minority, and you are going to tell the whole world that there is such an offence, to bring it to the notice of women who have never heard of it, never thought of it, never dreamed of it.[14]

The Lord Chancellor was equally convinced 'except [in] a sophisticated society in a sophisticated city', that 999 out of thousand women had 'never even heard a whisper of these practices'.[15] Arguably, much of *The Well of Loneliness*'s expected readership would probably have been members of this supposedly 'sophisticated society', but, seven years after the House of Lords debate, attempts to suppress the novel ended the silence around lesbianism, bringing the subject to public's notice.

The train of events which brought debates about lesbianism into numerous ordinary homes across Britain was not the publication of 1,500 copies of *The Well of Loneliness* on the 27 July, 1928. It had a black cover with a plain jacket and was cautiously placed on sale for 15 shillings (75 pence in modern money). The novel was discussed and considered in literary circles, praised and critiqued in equal measure (some felt the novel structurally left a great deal to be desired). It would probably have been read by only a few, had it not been for articles published by James Douglas in the *Daily Express*. Douglas was not shy about launching moralistic and self-righteous campaigns about all manner of topics, including the horrors of extending women's suffrage to all over the age of 21 in 1928. His front-page headline, 'A book that Must be Suppressed' appeared on Sunday 19 August, 1928; extra publicity had been drummed up by billboard teasers carrying this headline the day before.

Douglas's article described lesbian relationships in bigoted and prejudicial terms as 'sexual inversion and perversion' and 'horrors' that 'flaunted themselves in public places with increasing effrontery and more insolently provocative bravado'. He went on to talk of 'decadent apostles of the most hideous and most loathsome vices' which were no longer 'concealing their degeneracy and degradation'.[16] Finally, in a flourish of absurdity, he suggested he 'would rather give a healthy boy or a healthy girl a phial of prussic acid' than *The Well of Loneliness*, and called upon the publishers and the Home Secretary to take action to ban the book. In the days and weeks which followed, other newspapers and magazines waded into the debate. *The People* and the *Sunday Chronicle* gave the *Sunday Express* their support. Others, such as *The Daily Herald*, *Country Life*, and *The Lady's Pictorial*, were supportive of both the book's literary qualities, and intentions. Some pointed out that it was not a book anyone intended to be given to a child.

Nevertheless, Johnathan Cape panicked and sent a copy of the book to the Home Secretary, William Johnson-Hicks, and offered to withdraw the novel if it were considered to be in the public interest to do so. The Home Secretary had already made a name for himself by cracking down on nightclubs, gambling, and alcohol, and predictably was not of a mindset to take a permissive approach in matters of sexuality. Furthermore, the Director of Public Prosecutions, in a report to the Home Office, drew attention to the campaigning nature of the novel:

> The book has been widely and favourably reviewed in the Press (see the numerous reviews forwarded to the Home Office by the publishers). It is described (see "Times" Literary Supplement) as sincere, courageous, high-minded, and beautifully expressed. The fact however remains that it is in effect, as described in another review, a plea not only for toleration but for the recognition of sexual perversion amongst women. With regard to the contention which might be made on behalf of the authoress that she did not intend to corrupt her readers, intent is immaterial....
>
> In my view the book would tend to corrupt the minds of young persons if it fell into their hands and its sale is undesirable.... My view however,

is that there would be reasonable prospect of a conviction in this case. Incidentally it would appear to be clear that the authoress is herself what I believe is known as homo-sexualist, or as she prefers to describe it as an invert.[17]

The Home Secretary informed the publishers that if the book was not withdrawn a prosecution would take place.[18] Jonathan Cape stated they had withdrawn the text at the request of the Home Office, but quietly sold the rights to Pegasus Press, an English language publisher in France. Appalled and outraged, Radcyffe Hall wrote a defence of her work, which was published in part or full by a number of papers, including, for example, *The Scotsman*. She pointed out that:

> far from encouraging depravity my book is calculated to encourage a mutual understanding between normal persons and the inverted, which can only be beneficial to both and to society at large. I am proud to have taken up my pen in defence of the persecuted. As a pioneer I have been attacked, but then pioneers must always expect that fate; and the attacks in my case whatever their material consequences to my book have not come from those whose approval would have conferred any honour. Finally, I most emphatically claim that my book is eminently Christian.[19]

Jonathan Cape's partner, Wren Howard, popped across the English Channel and delivered the papier-mâché moulds for the type-setting to the Pegasus Press in Paris, from where the book continued to sell well for many years to come. By the end of September, 1928, the London bookseller Leopold Hill had become the distributor for *The Well of Loneliness* for Pegasus in Britain. All these shenanigans and controversy increased interest in the novel and demand for the book rose exponentially. When a shipment of 250 copies being imported through Dover was stopped, the Chairman of the Board of Customs, who had read the book himself and admired its literary merits, overruled the decision. The Home Secretary responded by issuing a warrant for the books to be seized. The Metropolitan Police searched Leopold Hill's premises on 19 October, and both Jonathan Cape and Leopold Hill were summoned to appear at Bow Street Magistrates Court, prosecuted under the Obscene Publications Act. The stage was set for a high-profile and widely publicised court case.

The case appeared to provide an opportunity for the publisher, the distributor, and many others, to defend the book and prevent copies of the novel being destroyed. The book was prosecuted under the Obscene Publications Act and the case was scheduled for Friday November 9, 1928 at Bow Street Police

Court, London. At a time when very few women worked in the legal profession, it is unsurprising that the prosecution was led by an all-male legal team with Conservative views – Eustace Fulton and Vincent Evans – whilst the defence was made up of Harold Rubenstein and Norman Birkett. Radclyffe Hall was not on trial herself and the defence barristers decided not to ask her to give evidence. She was reduced to watching from the visitors' gallery whilst *The Evening Telegraph* reported that: 'Half an hour before the Magistrate took his seat, a number of fashionably-dressed women appeared in Court. Among them Miss Radclyffe Hall, with her neatly cropped hair and dressed in a black suit and hat to match. She was accompanied by a lady friend.'[20]

The corridors of the magistrates' court were thronged with the public, press, and many willing to testify in support of the novel. As Marc Vargo points out, there were 'forty eminent men and women gathered in the courtroom to speak on the merits of *The Well of Loneliness* amongst them physicians, educators, journalists, ministers, social workers, biologists, and booksellers'.[21] However, the magistrates it seemed were not interested in any views that might be expressed about the potential literary or moral qualities of the book. The Chief Magistrate, Sir Chartres Biron, was determined to make the decision alone. He was not interested in the novel's literary qualities, and he announced that he did not 'think people are entitled to express an opinion upon a matter which is the decision of the court', and refused to hear from them. Instead he withdrew for a week's deliberations.

The Bow Street Magistrates Court was again crowded when the magistrates returned on the 16 November to give their verdict. Sir Chartres Biron found the book obscene and ordered it to be destroyed. The defendants were ordered to pay costs. As he detailed his reasons for regarding the book as obscene, he argued that 'The unnatural offences which are the subject of the book involve acts which between men would be criminal and involve the most horrible, unnatural, and disgusting obscenity'. His prejudicial and intolerant rant continued, but, when he claimed 'there was a suggestion in the book that a number of women at the front, during the First World War in the ambulance work were addicted to what he referred to as 'these practices', Radclyffe Hall could remain silent no longer. She jumped to her feet and, addressing the magistrate directly, shouted: 'I protest, I emphatically protest. I am the author of this book and I cannot let that remark pass.' She was threatened with removal from the court if she could not remain silent.

At the end of the proceedings, as she left the court, Radclyffe Hall was heard to say to friends 'Believe me, the end is only the beginning'.[22] The following week newspapers across the country, including the *Dundee Evening Telegraph*, announced first that the order to destroy the books would not be put into effect immediately as an appeal was being considered, and then that an appeal had been lodged against the magistrates' decision. However, the appeal was also unsuccessful with another stinging judgement, this time delivered by Sir Robert Wallace. On 15 December, it was announced: 'the view of this Court is that this is a disgusting book when properly read. It is an obscene book prejudicial to the morals of the community. In our view, the order made by the magistrate is perfectly correct, and the appeal must be dismissed with costs.'[23] Radclyffe Hall appeared on the steps of the court after the appeal and accepted that there was no possibility of continuing the fight to get the book published. Two days later, news appeared that the copies of the books which had been seized in police raids and had been held under lock and key would soon be burned in large furnaces. Despite this announcement, the campaign to change social attitudes to women's same sex relationships in which Radclyffe Hall had played such an important part, was not lost.

The coverage of *The Well of Loneliness* obscenity trials was not restricted to the national newspapers but also appeared in local newspapers. Across the country, interest in, and sympathy for, the campaign, the book, and its publication, grew. Well-known feminists expressed their support. These included the writer and lecturer, Vera Brittain, who became the author of *The Testament of Youth* in 1933, and the suffragette composer, Ethel Smyth, who had written the *March of Women* (1911) as an anthem for the suffragettes. Smyth was also rumoured to have been suffragette leader Emmeline Pankhurst's lover. George Bernard Shaw's campaign against the suppression of *The Well of Loneliness* garnered support from the National Union of Railwayman and the South Wales Miner's Federation. A Doncaster coalminer, who was married, wrote to Radclyffe Hall to say he 'marvelled at the bigoted outlook of so-called "thinking men", who are ashamed to let broader minded folk than themselves delve into the great sex problems', going on to add, 'Some day we will wake up, and demand to know ourselves as we profess to know about everything else'.[24] Radclyffe Hall's private papers, and archives which have come to light since her death in 1943, also indicate that she received thousands of letters of support from ordinary women and men, many offering to send money to help her fight the book's suppression.

Sleeveless Errand, a novel by Norah James was also suppressed the following year; the promiscuous behaviour of its lesbian protagonist and her friends was similarly condemned. On February 21, 1929, newspapers carried the headline: 'Women's Novel Seized'. *Sleeveless Errand* had been seized from booksellers and was to be destroyed.[25] The author, who had read *The Well of Loneliness* and thought it 'a fine and sincere piece of work', discovered her 'experience neatly replicated that of Radclyffe Hall'. Other books, such as Compton Mackenzie's novel *Extraordinary Women* (1928), managed to avoid the controversy and ban that Radcliffe Hall's and James's books had suffered. Intriguingly, Mackenzie's novel caricatured some well-known lesbian women of the era, including Radclyffe Hall herself. Likewise, Virginia Woolf's novel, *Orlando* (1928), which describes a poet who changes from a man into a woman as she travels in time, escaped the attention of the censors. The novel was inspired by the aristocratic family of Virginia Woolf's lover, Vita Sackville-West, and was critically and financially successful. Both Woolf and Sackville-West had been amongst the throngs of experts ready to testify at *The Well of Loneliness* trial. What all of these authors did in their books, using different styles and plots, was to lift the veil of secrecy surrounding lesbianism.

Renewed interest and media coverage were sparked once again when *The Well of Loneliness* was published in the USA, and an unsuccessful legal attempt to suppress the novel followed. As Leslie Taylor has argued, 'from December 1928 to April 1929, New York City attorneys, courts and the public pondered "sex matters" … The scandal forced publishing houses, vice societies, attorneys, and the courts to articulate the manner in which a lesbian novel could and could not corrupt.'[26] These deliberations resulted in *The Well of Loneliness* being given 'a clean bill of health' by the Commissioner of the United States Customs, who announced he had read the book and agreed it was 'not offensive to clean minded persons'.[27] The results of the legal proceedings were followed closely in many British papers, and the public was reminded, although the book was still banned in Britain and Canada, that it was now on sale elsewhere. Thus, lesbianism remained firmly in the public eye, and was widely discussed beyond the limited literary readership that the original publication might have hoped to reach. Radclyffe Hall became something of a celebrity. She and her partner, Lady Una Troubridge, continued to be photographed together and frequently graced the pages of the society magazine *The Tatler* in the inter-war years. In 1930, Radclyffe Hall received the Gold Medal of the Eichelbergher Humane Award. In 1931, the *Leeds Mercury* covered a debate between Radclyffe Hall and Yves Ranaud over a private performance Renaud was putting on entitled *The Well of Loneliness*.[28] Indeed, as Diana Souhami has suggested, launching the book 'into public consciousness' through widely publicised trials on both sides of the Atlantic, resulted in *The Well of Loneliness* gaining 'a notoriety that may have exceeded its literary merits.'[29]

The notoriety and significance of the novel lasted for years afterwards. It has never been out of print. Published in France, it sold well and copies of the book continued to find their way into Britain, where they were shared and read – no doubt enjoyed all the more because of the prohibition on their purchase in British bookshops. Six years after Radclyffe Hall's death, a new edition was published in Britain (in 1949), and this time there was no challenge to it. Its position as the most widely read lesbian novel written in the English language was established. As Blanche Cook has pointed out, '[M]ost of us lesbians in the 1950s grew up knowing nothing about lesbianism except Stephen Gordon's swagger [and] Stephen Gordon's breeches'.[30] *The Well of Loneliness* featured in many coming-out stories, and until the 1970s, it was 'the go-to book for women... questioning their sexuality'.[31] It was a predecessor of the lesbian pulp fiction of later eras, and, even in 1999, was placed at number seven on a list of the top 100 lesbian and gay novels compiled by The Publishing Triangle.[32]

In 1996, Radclyffe Hall was voted number 16 in the Pink Paper's top 500 lesbian and gay heroes, her book and the controversy around it having played a pivotal role in changing attitudes to sexuality. In 1967, homosexuality – between consenting men over the age of twenty-one in private – was decriminalised, facilitating the rise of the gay-pride movement which, alongside second-wave feminism, enabled Radclyffe Hall's campaign for acceptance to gain wide support. However, to 70s' feminists *The Well of Loneliness*' 'butch-femme romance, and tragic ending' was not always regarded so positively.[33] Whilst 'few would argue with Hall's intention to champion the female invert's right to exist, many are still troubled by the means she employed to this end, and have rejected *The Well* as excessively dark.'[34] Rumour has it that one reader was so horrified by the tortuous portrayal of lesbianism that she wrote a note in a library copy of the book, to tell other readers that loving another woman can also be beautiful.[35]

Sociologist, feminist, political activist, and campaigner for lesbian and gay rights, Mary MacIntosh later recalled that 'During the 1970s, as women met, talked and worked together in women's centres on campaigns, they began to debate every aspect of their sexuality, linking gay politics with feminist politics'.[36] Like Radclyffe Hall, many wanted greater sexual freedom – the right to decide when, where, and with whom, they enjoyed sexual intimacy. The 1974 National Women's Liberation Movement conference in Edinburgh adopted 'The right to a self-defined sexuality – an end to discrimination against lesbians' as a fundamental tenet of feminism.[37] Some women went further than this, putting forward the argument that 'all feminists can and should be lesbians', and defining 'a political lesbian' as 'a woman-identified woman who does not fuck men'. Rather than 'compulsory sexual activity with women' in a pamphlet entitled *The Debate Between Heterosexual Feminism And Political Lesbian*, the Leeds Revolutionary Feminist Group encouraged women to get rid of men 'from your beds and your heads'.[38]

Such suggestions, while hotly debated within the women's movement, met with a mixed response and did not address the widespread discrimination many lesbian women still experienced. In 1978, Mary Winter, a Burnley Bus Company driver in Lancashire, wore her 'Lesbian Liberation' badge to work, as she claimed it helped to stop unwanted sexual advances from men. When she refused to comply with the bus company's order to stop wearing it, she was sacked. Although her trade union gave her little support, her campaign received backing from women's groups. Vanessa Redgrave, a famous actress and a member of the Workers' Revolutionary Party, called for Mary's reinstatement and held a demonstration outside the Bus Company's office. As there were no employment rights for LGBT (lesbian, gay, bisexual, and transgender) people in Britain at the time, the campaign was unsuccessful. Despite such disappointments, by the end of the century, in books, films, and broadcasting, the idea that women had the right to choose their own sexual identity was gaining traction. Vita Sackville-West's colourful personal life was portrayed in the BBC television series *Portrait of a Marriage* (1990), and a dramatisation of Jeanette Winterson's semi-autobiographical coming-out novel, *Oranges Are Not the Only Fruit* (1985), was shown the same year. Either production would have driven apoplectic, all those who fought so hard to suppress *The Well of Loneliness*. As the century came to a close, lesbianism was finally out of the closet.

Chapter 4

'Every mother should be entitled to anaesthetic' (1930)

Before the National Health Service was established in 1948, the antenatal and perinatal care of mothers and the attention they received when giving birth was varied and ad hoc. It depended on local and national insurance schemes, poorly funded ex-workhouse public hospitals, and large prestigious hospitals – such as University College Hospital and Queen Charlotte's (both in London) – which relied on charitable donations and fundraising. The vast majority of babies were born at home where the wealthy, who funded their own care, could afford to pay skilled midwives and doctors to look after them, while those on limited means had to keep the expenses of childbirth to a minimum, and often relied upon the support of untrained midwives, friends, and family only. Campaigns led by the National Birthday Trust to both improve the safety of childbirth, and give all women the right to analgesics, were part of wider political struggles to develop maternal welfare and decrease maternal mortality in the first half of the twentieth century. These included the opening and running of mother and baby clinics, funding district nurses and midwives, and petitioning politicians to improve the regulation and provision of midwives, which culminated in the 1936 Midwifery Act. The campaigns and actions led to the alarmingly high maternal mortality rate finally beginning to decline in the late 1930s.[1]

One of the most significant early campaigning organisations was the Women's Co-operative Guild, founded in 1883 as part of the Co-operative Society. Margaret Llewelyn Davies became its Honorary Secretary in 1889, holding the post until 1921, when she became President. Under her influence the organisation grew. It had 32,000 members by 1910, and it became one of the very few organisations to give a voice to working-class housewives. The Guild campaigned to get maternity benefits included in the 1911 National Insurance Act, and for maternity benefits to be paid to (and to be the property of) mothers when the act was amended two years later. As a key player in early campaigns to improve maternal care, they gathered more than 400 letters from guild members about their experiences of pregnancy, childbirth, and motherhood. A selection of these letters was published as *Maternity:*

Letters from Working Women in 1915. The harsh reality of many working-class women's lives, coping with multiple pregnancies and domestic labour in homes with few amenities, was brought into sharp relief by the letters. It was perhaps the first real social investigation of an area of women's lives which had been hidden behind closed doors, as it was not considered a suitable topic for public discussion. Carolyn Tilghman argues, writing the letters 'gave working-class women the opportunity to document their suffering as victims of obscurity and dependence in which they continually gave birth to children in ignorant, unhealthy, and economically strained conditions'.[2] They shed light on the horrible toll of multiple pregnancies. As one woman wrote: 'My grandmother had twenty children, only eight lived to about fourteen years of age, only two to a good old age. A cousin (a beautiful girl) had seven in about seven years; the first five died in birth, the sixth lived, and the seventh died and the mother also'.[3]

The 1902 Midwives Act sought to regulate the midwifery profession, requiring certification for practicing midwives and making it illegal for anyone who was not a certified midwife or medical practitioner to assist a woman in labour. The Central Midwives' Board was established to regulate the training and examination of licensed midwives, to whom it would also issue certificates. At the time, not everyone called out a midwife to assist during childbirth, as a member of the Women's Co-operative recalled:

> I had a severe labour lasting two nights and two days. (This was twenty-three years ago.) No effort was made to obtain help for me, although at that time my mother was starting to practice as a midwife, and had all a mother's fears for her daughter in her first labour. At that time, it was much more usual to trust to providence, and if a woman died it only proved her weakness and unfitness for motherhood. My baby lived only seven months. In spite of all this trouble, I was very glad when I found a year later, I was to become a mother again.[4]

Many certified midwives had had little training and many women chose to seek assistance from a neighbour or the local handywoman, who was often also prepared to help with housework and care of the family, which mothers could not otherwise manage immediately after giving birth. With little space in the family budget to fund maternity care prior to 'the First World War and, in some areas, until the mid-1930s, the majority of working-class women in Britain were attended in childbirth not by a professional but by a local woman'.[5]

The physical and emotional trauma women experienced during childbirth was regarded as natural and inevitable, often because of religious beliefs. This was informed by the Biblical story of Adam and Eve in the Garden of Eden, which described in Genesis Chapter 3, how Eve, having eaten a forbidden apple was told: 'In sorrow thou shalt bring forth children'. Women's pain and suffering when giving birth was apparently punishment for Eve's sins, and many women's distress was met with an attitude of 'it'll get worse before it gets better'. As Joanna Bourke has pointed out, moral justifications for women's suffering were linked to religious ones. 'Sex was sin; childbirth pangs, the punishment. The author of an 1806 textbook for midwives even contended that women who suffered the most in childbirth were those who possessed strong passions, who have been used to have all their desires gratified.'[6] One woman explained in her letter to the Women's Co-operative Guild prior to the First World War: 'I must say that although it is a time that women suffer terribly, yet it is a time they get very little pity, as it is looked upon as quite a natural state of things... So if anything could be done to limit the suffering of the next generations I for one would be in favour of it'.[7] Despite her hopes, it was to be another thirty to forty years before women were treated differently, and even then, unmarried mothers could be told that their suffering would serve as a lesson to them. Whatever women may say at the time, the pain of childbirth has not proved to be a deterrent to further pregnancies.

There had been attempts in the nineteenth century, to alleviate the pain of childbirth using drugs, potions, massage, or even distraction. Physicians and chemists trialled the use of nitrous oxide for pain relief in surgical amputations and dentistry, practices which were then transferred to childbirth. Queen Victoria's use of chloroform for the birth of her eighth child in the 1850s did much to make painkillers more socially acceptable, particularly when there was a dire medical emergency. Some Women's Co-operative Guild members described how, in labour with life-threatening complications, they had indeed been given chloroform. One mother recounted, 'My next baby was born about eighteen months after, and when she was five I had the misfortune to go to bed again; I had a very bad time, although it was my tenth child. I was given chloroform, and the baby lived half an hour'.[8] For this mother, a dangerous labour meant the added expense of calling a doctor, the administration of analgesics, and an infant death.

Doctors' willingness to experiment with a potentially toxic mixture of morphine and scopolamine, administered to ensure that women were not even aware that they had given birth, seems rather alarming now. Such powerful drugs were not without danger. Women could become psychotic, screaming and hurting themselves, and having to be restrained. The drugs could also have a detrimental, sometimes lethal, effect on the baby's breathing. However, mothers did positively describe having experienced a 'twilight sleep', and feminists in the USA formed *The National Twilight Sleep Association*, in response to a very favourable account of the practice by two American women journalists in *McClure's Magazine* in 1914. Women in the USA campaigned, with some success, for every women's right to a pain-free labour. Few working-class British women had this luxury. In Britain, analgesics in childbirth were only allowed to be administered by doctors. The high cost of the drugs, and concerns over their side-effects, meant that in the first half of the twentieth century the vast majority of women gave birth without any form of pain relief. With huge demands on their limited funds, cash-strapped hospitals did not consider relieving a mother's distress during labour to be a high priority. Beds in hospitals were also scarce, and, as giving birth was regarded as a natural rather than a medical matter, it predominantly took place at home (although specialist private nursing homes began to emerge to cater for women of the wealthier classes). Those who had sufficient funds could pay for both a trained midwife and a doctor able to administer pain relief to attend women in labour.

The First World War brought infant and maternal care into sharp relief in the public consciousness. Both the number of potential recruits who were physically unfit to serve, and the death of so many young men on the battlefields during the conflict, led to a new focus on motherhood and the health of babies and young children. Infant mortality figures were certainly a cause for concern. The Bishop of London pointed out that while nine soldiers died ever hour in 1915, twelve babies also died every hour, so that it was more dangerous to be a baby living in the slums than a soldier on the Western Front.[9] An exponential growth in the provision of infant welfare clinics occurred, which Gerald DeGroot has suggested were run by 'middle class women who dispensed advice formulated by middle class men to working class mothers.'[10] This is perhaps a tad harsh, but it is certainly true that few of those involved in the infant welfare movement had much understanding of the realities of the lives of the working-class women who penned letters to the Women's Co-operative Guild. Some do-gooders also had little understanding of the work of midwives who cared for these mothers. In Stoke-on-Trent, trained midwives requested the visits of these 'zealous often autocratic meddlesome ladies, might be postponed until the tenth day after birth', and decried 'the habit of these ladies to descend on the hapless mother when her baby is a day old, armed to the tongue with lectures, pamphlets and even scales.'[11]

Infant and maternal welfare services during the First World War and in its aftermath were rather ad hoc, being provided by some charities, ex-workhouse hospitals, and insurance schemes. There were consequently huge variations in the provision, and in both infant and maternal mortality – with the latter rising during the inter-war years, even though infant mortality reduced.

Official statistics indicate the annual maternal mortality rate increased from 2,690 to 2,920 in 1928. This was the highest rate since these statistics were first compiled in 1911 and became a cause of public disquiet.[12] The National Birthday Trust Fund was established in 1928 by Ina Lady George Chomondeley in response to a speech by Queen Mary expressing her concern about the high maternal mortality rate. Its charitable objectives included: 'To assist towards the cost of establishing or maintaining voluntary maternal hospitals and training centres or classes for midwives or maternity nurses and generally improving the professional ability and standing and emoluments of such persons.'[13] It also had a wider, catch-all remit enabling it to include 'Any other purpose connected with maternity and the welfare of maternity patients and newly born children'.[14]

The organisation's slightly quaint name, the National Birthday Trust, which there were many attempts to change, stemmed from the notion that, if everyone in the country donated one shilling (5 pence in modern money) to the trust on their birthday, they would raise 42 million shillings which could be spent on improving maternal welfare (nearly £150 million in modern money equivalent).[15] The organisation supported improvements in midwifery training and the building of voluntary maternity hospitals, where ordinary working-class women could give birth in clean and sterile surroundings, cared for by professionals with the possibility of a few days rest to recover afterwards. The Royal Family, as well as shops, theatres, and newspapers, were all approached for birthday collections. High profile donations in honour of mothers and in celebration of births and birthdays came in. For example, a personal ad in the *Western Mail and South Wales News* announced that Lady Neville Pearson had sent a donation to the National Birthday Trust (for the extension of maternity services) as 'a thanksgiving for the safe arrival of her daughter and her own and the baby's well-being'.[16]

This was an organisation of the great and the good. Members were mainly influential wealthy women, almost all involved with, and members of, the Conservative Party. It included many well-known society hostesses, such as the Marchioness of Londonderry and from Worcestershire the Countess of Plymouth, and Lady Hindlip. It was an example of what Helen Jones has described as a 'group of women not personally affected by misfortune' but 'who understood the gendered impact of poverty" and took 'action to get women's issues on the political agenda.'[17] The organisation also gave the Conservative Party a softer, more caring image that was appreciated by the party grandees in a time of austerity, unemployment and cuts to welfare. While the Women's Co-operative Guild continued to campaign for maternal welfare, the Maternal Mortality Committee was set up in 1927 with supporters from across the political spectrum, including trade unionist Gertrude Tuckwell, and Lady Iveagh, the latter the chair of the Conservative Party.[18] Like the National Birthday Trust, they carried out research and were committed to explaining the high maternal mortality rates. At a conference they organised on 15 November 1932, it was reported that approximately 3,000 mothers a year were being lost as a consequence of childbirth. On the basis of a report into 6,000 maternal deaths, it was argued that the responsibility for the preventable deaths could be allocated as follows: 15% to the absence of antenatal care; 19% to an error of judgement on behalf of the doctor or midwife; 8% to the negligence of the mother; and 4% to the lack of available facilities at the time of birth. Many more 'young women were invalided at childbirth'.[19]

It was, however, Lucy Baldwin, then wife of the Conservative Prime Minister, who alongside Lady George Cholmondeley, spearheaded the launch of the Anaesthetics Appeal Fund in January 1929. Established by the National Birthday Trust, the fund aimed to improve women's very different experiences of labour, and to make it less traumatic and painful. Lucy Baldwin, neé Ridsdale, who was a keen cricketer, had married Stanley Baldwin in Rottingdean, on the Sussex Coast, on 12 September, 1892. Two years later, she suffered the trauma of giving birth to her first son, who was stillborn – an experience that shaped her political priorities for the rest of her life. She went on to produce a further six healthy children in the next twelve years. Meanwhile, her husband, a Worcestershire industrialist, and MP for Bewdley, progressed to become leader of the Conservative Party, and then to serve three terms as Prime Minister of Britain (1923–24, 1924–29, and 1935–37). As the wife of the Prime Minister and a vice-chairman of the National Birthday Trust Fund, in 1928 Lucy became an ardent campaigner for improvements to maternity services to reduce maternal mortality rates. During the First World War, she had taken a role in the care of wounded soldiers, as Commandant of the Wilden Auxiliary Hospital, and like many others, she had seen at first hand the injuries and deaths of men in the conflict. Indeed, Lucy evoked national memories of the horrors of wartime carnage when she likened the uncertainty that mothers faced when going into labour to men 'going into battle', arguing that 'Our women daily, hourly, are 'going over the top' risking 'death from childbirth as men did in the trenches.'[20]

So strong was Lucy Baldwin's commitment to maternal care, that her close friend and fellow cricket enthusiast, the wealthy philanthropist, Julien Cahn, funded the building of what became known as the Lucy Baldwin Maternity Hospital in Stourport-on-Severn, Worcestershire, near the Baldwins' family home, Astley Hall. Lucy's husband, then Prime Minister, was responsible for opening the hospital on 16 April, 1929. Over the main entrance, a bronze dedication plaque carried the words, *'What she wanted most in the world. Presented to her by Julien Cahn Esq.'* Cahn's funds and organisational skills were brought on board by the National Birthday Trust, when he was appointed to the chairmanship of the trust in May 1930 with the approval of Lucy Baldwin, who considered 'the fund will make vast and rapid advances under such able guidance.'[21] Cahn's main role was to organise fundraising activities, including the high-profile annual charity balls with quirky themes. These were big society events, attended by debutantes whose photographs appeared on the pages of society magazines. In 1931, for example, there was a Lace Ball held on 21 April, and a British Porcelain Ball held on 24 November. The latter, held at the Claridge's Ballroom, began at 10 pm with supper an hour and half later, followed by a 'Porcelain Buffet' with attendees continuing to party until 3 am. It was Julien Cahn who had persuaded leading pottery firms such as Wedgwood, Crown Derby, Doulton, and Minton, to become involved. This ensured not only that the tables were decorated with china, but that guests had china items as souvenirs to take home.

Lucy Baldwin was chairman of the China Ball and hosted a table with a party of guests, but by then her attention, alongside that of Lady George Cholmondeley, was particularly focussed on the Anaesthetics Appeal Fund. The two women used their political and social connections and networks to publicise their cause and to raise money, although the National Birthday Trust continued to rely heavily on donations from wealthy benefactors like Julien Cahn. The Anaesthetics Appeal Fund worked with hospitals, lobbying them to prioritise alleviating all women's pain during labour, giving them equipment, resources, and grants to go towards the cost of anaesthesia or employing an anaesthetist. In time, they also funded mobile anaesthetic equipment to be used by midwives. Their campaign was instrumental in the appointment of an anaesthetist at Queen Charlotte's Hospital in London, resulting in 60% of mothers receiving pain killers. University College Hospital, London, then followed their example. Other hospitals were also pressurised to commit to an 'analgesics for all women' approach. The organisers of the Anaesthetics Appeal Fund were so committed to this principle that they withheld giving the East End Hospital a grant as it only administered anaesthetics for difficult and abnormal labours.

Financing such actions and campaigns was costly and Lucy Baldwin's two broadcast appeals, the first in 1929, the second in 1935, shocked some by discussing what many perceived to be an unseemly topic on a public forum like the radio. Those who donated were contacted by the National Birthday Trust committee, and were asked to take part in a snowball chain-letter scheme, entitled Forge a Link. Those wealthy enough to have telephones were targeted as potential donors. The campaign employed booklets, donation slips, flags, stamps, and other sundry items to promote the cause. Lucy Baldwin also hosted entertainments from 10 Downing Street, and a number of theatre and cinema gala performances (sometimes attended by members of the Royal Family) also helped raise money. An air pageant, organised at Hanworth Flying Club (on the outskirts of London), was one of the more unusual fundraising events, and particularly evocative of the era. Flying clubs from outside of Britain sent teams, and the day included an air race around London. All the efforts of wives of local MPs drumming up publicity could not compensate for the disappointing weather, which consequently led to disappointing attendance figures and revenue. Nevertheless, donations and various fundraising activities resulted in the capital fund and the Anaesthetics Appeal Fund reaching £16,500 by November 1932 (equivalent to £1,227,187.05 in modern money), enabling them to support a number of experimental projects which would bring analgesics to more women.[22]

Backed by a number of distinguished campaigners, including Ethel Dawson of Penn, Margaret Ebbisham, Juliet Williams – the Honorary Treasurer of Queen Charlotte's Hospital Anaesthetics Fund – and E. G Dare – the Matron of Queen Charlotte's Hospital – Lucy Baldwin wrote a letter to the *British Medical Journal*. This appeared on 1 February, 1930, titled 'A Fund for Anaesthetics in Midwifery.' It sought to persuade doctors to support the campaign for anaesthetics to be given to mothers who wanted them during childbirth. It pointed to the rising maternal mortality rates, and linked mothers' suffering in childbirth to maternal mortality. If women had not suffered so unnecessarily in childbirth, it was argued, their nervous system would be able to cope with potentially life-threatening after-effects of childbirth, such as infections. The discovery and mass production of antibiotics, which would be prescribed for such infections today, had not yet taken place. Thus, the letter asked, 'Is it not time that the use of Anaesthetics was extended? The mother who can afford to, pays her fee for an anaesthetist, the mother who cannot has, as a rule to pay a further penalty for her suffering'.[23] Lucy Baldwin was the first name at the bottom of the letter, placed there by virtue of both alphabetical ordering, and her status as the wife of a British Conservative politician. Yet she was presenting an argument which might have been expected to come from those with more left-wing political allegiances, pointing to the social divisions around childbirth and the 'penalty of suffering'. The letter explained that they 'want it known far and wide that it is unfair that mothers should still be allowed to suffer as they do because of lack of money' and implored readers of the British Medical Journal to protest 'that every mother should be entitled to anaesthetic if she wishes it.'[24]

The vast majority of babies were not, however, born in hospitals, or with doctors in attendance. There was therefore a need for methods to be found for trained and skilled midwives to administer painkillers, something that the British Medical Council resisted. Even as late as 1939, they were refusing to sanction the administration by midwives of analgesics to women in childbirth, despite the plea of gynaecologist, Dame Louise McIlroy, who begged the conference, 'If you throw out this recommendation you will make these women go on suffering as they have in the past.'[25] Trials of chloroform capsules were carried out at Queen Charlotte's Hospital, London, with positive results, and reported on by Louis Carnac Rivett addressing the Royal Society of Medicine. In June 1932, the National Birthday Trust Fund offered to finance the wider distribution of this analgesic to hospitals and GPs, so that further investigations could be carried out. The development of portable machines to provide gas and air was also taking place. Once again, the National Birthday Trust sought to support this, being associated with the early trials of the Minnitt machine, and financing a survey by the British College of Obstetricians and Gynaecologists into analgesics suitable for use by midwives, which, in 1936, reported in favour of gas and air machines.[26] The fund sent these machines to hospitals and distributed them to nursing associations for a nominal fee of £5. Local organisations, such as Women's Institutes, raised this money while the New Zealand philanthropist, Robert McDougall, having heard Lacy Baldwin's 1935 Radio Broadcast, established a fund to distribute gas and air machines in memory of his mother.

The National Birthday Trust continued to campaign to improve maternal welfare, working with the Joint Council on Midwifery, to explore, for example, the benefits of antenatal care, abortion practice, and nutrition during pregnancy. From 1935 to 1939, the trust funded the distribution of supplementary food – mostly Marmite and dried milk – to pregnant women in areas with high unemployment, such as the Rhondda Valley in South Wales. This both alleviated suffering, and helped to prove that there was a link between poverty and maternal and infant mortality.[27] The trust was one of many groups whose campaigning led to the 1936 Midwives Act, which sought to ensure better training of midwives, greater regulation of their practice, and their employment. It sought to restrict the role of caring for mothers in labour to qualified midwives, although many women continued to find them too expensive. Regulating and continuing to improve the professional standing of midwives was a vital step in gaining support for midwives to be able to administer pain-killers to women in childbirth. Perhaps most importantly, local authorities had an obligation placed upon them to provide a secure, salaried, domiciliary midwifery service.[28] They now had a duty to work with local hospitals and charities, to harmonise provision, and to improve infant and maternal welfare in their area.

Support for the campaign for pain relief for women giving birth began to snowball in the 1940s. Individual women and women's organisations wrote to their MPs and to newspapers. The *Gloucestershire Echo* published a letter in 1942 signed by Six Expectant Mothers, who complained that 'any Cheltonian, rich enough to pay for [pain relief] can have it', but the 'poorer class' were 'damned'. They pointed out that, 'If a man wants a tooth out he has to have gas or cocaine. A soldier on the battlefield, when in great pain, has morphia administered to him' and asked what did a 'poor woman in the throes of childbirth' get? This campaign ran alongside increasing calls for the establishment of a National Health Service (NHS) which had grown during the Second World War.[29] When the NHS was formed in 1948, women were significant beneficiaries. Finally, they had access to free health care. Midwives and doctors were provided as needed when they were in labour.

In the 1940s, 68% of women in Britain had no form of analgesic during labour. The figure had halved within a decade, but not without a struggle. In 1949, Conservative Member of Parliament, Peter Thorneycroft, introduced a private member's bill 'calling for accessible pain relief for women giving birth', and Labour MP, Leah Manning, argued, 'if male MPs gave birth, they would ensure that there was something more than a towel…to pull on'.[30] The bill was sponsored by the National Birthday Trust Fund, arguably (like many women's organisations in the era) struggling to maintain their area of expertise in the face of a growing range of predominantly male medical experts employed by the health service. The bill, though it garnered wide support, was defeated. The NHS was financially struggling to cope as hundreds of thousands of patients, who had been unable to afford health care for decades, clamoured for its services. The pain women suffered in labour was once again not considered a priority.

Lucy Baldwin had died of a heart attack in 1945, at her family home in Worcestershire. Newspapers reported: 'Thousands of Mothers owe a debt of gratitude to her for the wider use of analgesics in childbirth.'[31] The National Birthday Trust, which had funded the development of an inhaler using tricholorethylene, also supported a nitrous oxide and oxygen machine manufactured by the British Oxygen Company in London. It provided a mixture of oxygen and nitrous oxide through a face mask to alleviate women's pain during childbirth. What was known as the 'Lucy Baldwin apparatus for obstetric analgesia' came into use in the late 1950s. The device was rather heavy. Although it had wheels to move it around within hospitals, for district midwives attending home births it was cumbersome. The apparatus's name was chosen as a tribute to the woman who had worked to improve women's experience of childbirth in the inter-war years: Lucy Baldwin.

The introduction of the NHS also heralded the transfer of giving birth into the medical environment of the hospital, the increasing involvement of doctors, and a more interventionist approach to childbirth. In 1956, the Cranbook Report recommended that 70% of births should take place in hospital. Only 14 years later, the Peel Report suggested that this figure should be 100%. Increasing numbers of women gave birth in hospital in the years after the Second World War. In many ways this was a safer place, and a positive response to the campaigns of Lucy Baldwin and the National Birthday Trust. However, women soon began to question whether the pendulum had swung too far in the direction of a medicalised approach to giving birth. Forceps began to be used routinely, as 'a quick delivery fix, rather than something to be used with great caution in the most difficult of situations.'[32] By the end of the 1960s, medical interventions such as induction, episiotomies, and electronic and foetal heart rate monitoring, were becoming increasingly common.[33] As Gill Thorn has argued, science and technology had become more valued than intuition and patience.[34]

Once again, women campaigned to improve their experience of childbirth. A small advert placed by a young mother, Prunella Briance, in the personal column of the *Times* on 4 May, 1956, invited women to join a new organisation: The Natural Childbirth Association. Like Lucy Baldwin, she was influenced by personal loss and what she describes as a horribly 'mismanaged birth and the loss of my precious baby girl.'[35] Briance was inspired by Grantly Dick-Read, a British obstetrician, who was a proponent of natural childbirth. The following year she set up the organisation now known as the National Childbirth Trust (NCT). Its aims are to 'help all parents enjoy an experience of pregnancy, birth and early parenthood which enriches their lives and gives them confidence in being a parent.'[36]

Some feminists in the 1970s argued that childbirth should be seen as a natural process, and that pain relief could stifle women's experience and the mother-child bonding process. However, more recently, women have reacted against the pressure to have a natural childbirth, arguing they should feel able to exercise choice over their own use of pain relief. Across the world, many women, like the working-class women Lucy Baldwin campaigned for, still do not have access to the facilities and the drugs which would enable them to exercise such a choice.

Chapter 5

Equal Pay in the Aeronautical Industry (1943)

In both the First and Second World Wars, women were called upon to replace men who had joined the forces and to work in war industries such as munitions. This was voluntary until the conscription of women into war work was introduced in 1941. By 1943, 7.25 million women were employed in industry, the armed services and civil defence. However, women's wages were consistently lower than men's. For example, in the Rolls Royce factory at Hillington near Glasgow, women workers received only 43 shillings (£2.15) per week, while men received 73 shillings (£3.65). A strike in 1943 led to changes ensuring wages were based upon the job being done, rather than the gender of who was doing the job. This is just one example in a long line of industrial conflicts and women's political campaigning in the first half of the twentieth century, as women sought equal pay for equal work. The campaigns, inside and beyond parliament, involved a multitude of different women's groups, women workers, trade unionists such as those at the Rolls Royce Factory, and women MPs who co-operated across party lines to advance the cause of equal pay.[1]

At the outbreak of the First World War, women's wages were typically about half that of men's; the pressing need for women's labour on the home front during the conflict offered the possibility of change. Women had worked in factories, on farms, shops and of course domestic service in the nineteenth century, but the First World War made their work more visible. As men joined the forces, and industry was required to produce the materials to fight a large-scale mechanised war, women's work became nationally important. In March 1915, the suffragette leader, Mrs Pankhurst, organised what became known as the Women's Right to Serve March. 20,000 women and 90 different bands marched through London waving flags and banners carrying messages such as 'Women believe in duty as well as rights' and 'We demand the right to serve.'[2] Not only was the march funded by the Minister for Munitions, Lloyd George, but there was significant support from the press. The *Labour Gazette* announced:

> We are satisfied that, in the production of shells and fuses, there are numerous operations of a nature that can be, and are already in some

shops, suitably performed by female labor. We therefore recommend that, in order to increase the output, there should be an extension of the practice of employing female labour on this work, under suitable and proper conditions.[3]

Many employers remained resistant to employing women, preferring to take on older men or boys below conscription age as workers, as they regarded women as poor timekeepers, sickly and not as productive. Where factories and small workshops were employed on Government contracts, producing 'everything from mercury thermometers and bronzed field glasses to soldiers' boots and horses' nosebags' they were pressurised to use women workers.[4] By 1916, there were just over 3,000 such establishments employing approximately 1.25 million people, of whom about one fifth were women. When they undertook unusual or extra-ordinary work, women were praised by politicians, heralded in newspapers and on film, photographed and painted. The new opportunities created in wartime led some young girls to leave their jobs in domestic service, choosing to work in factories, transport, workshops and shops, as chimney sweeps or land girls. Nevertheless, domestic service remained the industry employing more women than any other during the conflict. In 1918 out of total of 6.2 million women in paid work, 1 ¼ million were in domestic service.[5]

As women began to enter the workforce, an agreement was drawn up between the treasury and the unions, that if a woman replaced a man at work, they would receive the same wages he had done. However, women rarely directly replaced men. Instead, they were trained to undertake specific elements of men's jobs and received lower rates of pay. Despite evidence to the contrary, it was popularly believed at the time and since, that women, particularly if they worked in munitions, earned high wages and apparently became rather too independently minded. Government regulations, under various Defence of the Realm Acts, known as DORA, banned strikes, yet industrial disputes over wages and conditions of work continued throughout the war. In Plymouth, for example, in 1916, 'the co-operative society refused to increase the pay of its female workforce.'[6] In September 1917, '400 women at Dumfries munition factory went on strike for an adjustment in hours of work, improvements in the arrangements for night working and dismissal of the middle-class female supervisor'.[7] Trade Union membership amongst women increased significantly during the conflict, and some suffrage organisations such as the Women's Freedom League, called for women to be paid the same wages as men. The Labour economist and social welfare campaigner, Sidney Webb, writing in the *Daily News and Leader* in 1918, argued that demands for the principle of equal pay for equal work were on the increase following the passing of the Representation of the People Act in February 1918, which gave some women the right to vote in parliamentary elections.[8]

On August 17, 1918, women working on the London buses and trams went on strike 'in defence of the principle of equal pay for equal work.'[9] For, as the historian Cathy Hunt has explained, 'Despite promises that where men and women did the same jobs, pay would be the same, the Committee of Production had, earlier in the year, awarded an increase of five shillings per week to men only.'[10] The extra payment was to help workers deal with the spiraling cost of living. However, articulating arguments, which re-appeared again and again over the next fifty years, it was suggested only men needed this money, for they had to support wives and children. The injustice and inaccuracy of such reasoning led to the strike. The women tram and bus workers were supported by trade unions, other workers and many Londoners, despite the long queues and delays travellers had to endure during the strike. The transport companies argued women had higher rates of absenteeism than men, and were therefore more expensive to employ, and so should not receive the extra 5/- (25 pence in modern money). After a week of industrial action, the employers capitulated, and agreed women should be paid the same bonus as men.

Both the bus and tram workers' victory and the high employment of women in the First World War, were temporary blips on the long, slow journey towards equal pay for equal work in the twentieth century. With war factories closed and the economic recession of the 1920s, many women struggled to remain employed, despite the Sex Disqualification (Removal) Act being enshrined in law in 1919. Unfortunately, as Harold Smith has argued, 'the Act contained language that enabled employers to continue discriminating on gender and marital grounds.'[11] Historian, Gerry Holloway's assessment of women's work outside the home 'indicates women's participation was 35.3% in 1911; 33.1 % in 1921 and 34.2 % in 1931.'[12] Some even argued equal wages for equal work would ensure the continued preferential employment of men over women. The increasing implementation of marriage bars in many industries, such as teaching and nursing, whereby women were obliged to leave their jobs if they got married, also contributed to women's falling employment level.

The gendered division of labour and the notion that a skilled status was a facet of men's work, were used in many workplaces to ensure women's wages continued to remain low. It was, after all, the aim of most employers, to obtain the labour from their workers as cheaply as possible. Nevertheless, the genie of equal pay was out of the bottle, and it became a key demand made by women's groups, trade unions and women MPs in the inter-war years. Historian Harold Smith has argued feminist groups, including the London and National Society for Women's Service (LNSWS), viewed sex-differentiated pay both as a symbol of female subordination, and as a means by which women were kept dependent upon men. Gendered pay conveyed a powerful message of female inferiority, and it was part of a larger system of gender relationships, which feminists wished to reform.[13] Women politicians, although small in number, were themselves paid the same wages as their male colleagues and were also instrumental in keeping equal pay on the political agenda.

Much of the campaigning focussed on the teaching profession and the civil service – areas of employment which were under government control, and where women and men clearly did the same work. Women teachers had kept the education system going during the First World War, when many male teachers were conscripted into the armed forces. Likewise, the number of women in the civil service increased from 33,000 in 1911 to 102,000 by 1921.[14] A number of women teachers had themselves been arguing for equal pay since the beginning of the twentieth century and had formed the Equal Pay League in 1904. Initially, its members were drawn from the National Union of Teachers (NUT), and their group sought greater representation of women in the NUT and equal pay. In 1906, the National Federation of Women Teachers (NFWT) was formed, and as Hilda Kean and Alison Oram have argued, 'Exhausted and embittered by the relative lack of progress made inside the male dominated union, it broke away completely in 1920 to form a separate women's union, the National Union of Women Teachers' (NUWT).[15] Women teachers were exasperated that whatever their qualifications or experience, they were all paid less than their male colleagues. Furthermore, the significant number of women teachers who supported elderly parents was highlighted by the feminist writer and campaigner Rebecca West (1892–1983). She noted, 'It seems to me curious to defend a system which pays exactly the same salary to the bachelor, the childless widower, the father of one and the father of seven and then cuts it sharply when it come to the spinster who is keeping her father and mother and the widow who is keeping seven children.'[16]

In some local areas, where the NUWT were well organised, they did manage to persuade local authorities to agree to equal pay. However, there was consternation when Burnham Committee, set up in 1919, introduced a new system for settling teachers' pay; it led to salary scales which increased the gap between men and women's pay and abolished local authorities' autonomy to make their own equal pay agreements with teachers. In autumn of 1919, the NUWT declared itself as an autonomous union. By then 'feminists had already organised a mass meeting on equal pay at the Albert Hall, supported by 19 other organisations; collected ten thousand signatures in London for a petition at a few days' notice and organised militant lobbying of the LCC and demonstrations.'[17] This independent and feminist teaching union continued to campaign for equal pay and for the removal of the marriage bar in teaching throughout the inter-war years, working with other groups including the Labour Party.

Many supporters of equal pay were encouraged when the House of Commons passed a resolution in favour of equal pay in the Civil Service in 1920. This was shortly followed by dismay, when Stanley Baldwin, the Financial Secretary to the Treasury, explained, due to the pressure of work, the government was unable to reach a decision on equal pay in the civil service. Similar responses to further questions asked in the House of Commons, in 1925 and 1928, were no more positive.[18] The London and National Society for Women's Service (LNSWS) set up a Committee on Women in the Civil Service (JCWCS) to work with the National Association of Women Civil Servants (NAWCS) and the Council of Women Civil Servants (CWCS). As well as providing information about their arguments to the general public, in magazines, newspapers and at conferences, they also presented evidence to the Royal Commission on the Civil Service, which reported in 1931.

Another vociferous campaigning group supporting equal pay in this era was the Six Point Group, founded by Lady Rhondda (1883–1958) in 1921. She had been an active supporter of women's suffrage. Having inhereted her father's significant industrial interests, by the 1920s she was a wealthy woman who financed the feminist magazine *Time and Tide*. The Six Points Group campaigned for strict equality between men and women seeking changes in six areas of the law, including equal pay for men and women teachers, and equal opportunities for men and women in the civil service. The Six Points Group found the differentiation in teachers' pay both derogatory and offensive. One of its spokeswomen, Rebecca West, writing in *Time and Tide*, argued that the pay differential was based on sex-antagonism, male insecurity and a desire to keep women in a state of subjugation. This was possibly the case, although in 1920, the Minister for Education gave the impression that he 'favoured the principle of equal pay but was hamstrung by the cost'.[19] The Six Points Group soon discovered the difference between 'general sympathy' and 'practical help'. For although the government appeared to be 'in general sympathy with the demand for equal pay', it was 'strongly opposed in practice to granting it.[20] The government's reticence was initially blamed on financial pressures caused by economic crisis, but even when this began to ease in the 1930s, equal pay was not granted.

By this time, the campaign for equal pay had the support of a small but increasing number of women in the House of Commons. They made up 2% of the total number of members of Parliament, and they worked together on many women's issues. In March 1934, the LNSWS and the NAWCS, with the support of 29 other women's groups, organised a mass public rally in London to stir up public support for equal pay.[21] The meeting was chaired by Maggie Wintringham (1879–1955), who had become the first English-born woman MP in 1921. A suffragist, and a leading light in the Women's Liberal Association and the Women's Institute Movement, she campaigned on issues including housing, widows' pensions and equal guardianship of infants. The following December, 1935, Ray Stratchey (1897 – 1940), chair of the Joint Committee on Women in the Civil Service (JCWCS) and LNSWS president, addressed a House of Commons meeting attended by approximately eighty MPs. Ray Strachey is best known as the author of an early history of the women's suffrage movement and was a regular broadcaster on BBC radio. In 1931, she was appointed parliamentary secretary to the first woman to sit in the House of Commons, Nancy Astor, and in 1935, she became head of the Women's Employment Federation.

In seeking to gain support from predominantly male MPs across all political parties, Ray Stratchey adopted an unusual strategy. She argued, as male trade unions had done for decades, that equal pay would protect men's jobs and prevent women being employed in preference to men, merely because they were cheaper.[22] It was, according to Harold Smith, 'a deliberate political strategy designed to win support from those who had the power to change the policy of sex-differentiated pay.'[23] Lady Astor argued in favour of equal pay in a parliamentary debate 'as a means of maintaining traditional sex roles: "We want women to be women, and men to be manly."'[24] Such strategies were not, however, successful: despite discussions, debates and even votes in the House of Commons, there was no progress. When, on Tuesday 9 July 1935, the Conservative and Feminist MP, Thelma Cazalet-Keir (1899–1989), asked the Financial Secretary to the Treasury in the House of Commons whether he was prepared to apply the principles of equal pay to Civil Service staff, she received yet another negative response.[25] Campaigners sought a commitment to equal pay from prospective candidates during the 1935 general election, and the following year, Mavis Tate (1893–1947), another Conservative MP and campaigner on women's rights, explained in the House of Commons, 'The question really is one of principle. I believe that work should be done by the man or woman best qualified to do it, and that the pay should be commensurate with what the work is worth.'[26]

Women MPs of all parties supported the equal pay campaign. When a mass meeting involving more than 25 women's organisations was held at the Caxton Hall in London in March 1936, both the Conservative Lady Astor and the Labour MP Ellen Wilkinson (1891–1947) spoke in favour of equal pay. Ellen Wilkinson had worked for women's suffrage organisations and the trade union movement, and had been a member of both the Communist Party and the Six Points Group before she became Labour MP for Middlesbrough East in 1924. Described by the *Woman's Leader* as a 'vigorous, uncompromising feminist and an exceedingly tenacious, forcible and hard-headed politician', it was Ellen Wilkinson, by then the MP for Jarrow, who sought to introduce a private member's motion on equal pay in the House of Commons in April 1936.[27] Its wording required the Government to 'forthwith place women in the common classes of the Civil Service on the same scales of pay as apply to men in those classes.'[28] To the Government's shock, 156 MPs voted for equal pay and 148 against it. The initial excitement of this success was short-lived, as the result was vetoed by another vote, which Stanley Baldwin's government made a vote of confidence to ensure that they won. The lobbying, meetings, debates and agitation seemed to have produced no change; the campaign seemed to falter and many of those involved were disheartened. However, as Helen Glew has argued, the campaigns had laid much of the groundwork, created alliances between women's groups, and gained the support of many MPs, which would lead to change in the future.[29]

The Second World War, and the need for women in the workforce again, brought the issue of equal pay to the forefront of many people's minds. The government initially assumed that women would automatically move into essential work, covering for men who had been conscripted into the forces, or taking up jobs in the war industries, as they had done in the First World War. However, the first nine months of the conflict saw an increase in women's unemployment, and by February 1940, women backbenchers met with the financial secretary to lobby for greater use of women war workers. The following month, the Woman Power Committee (WPC) was formed to bring together women MPs to investigate possibilities for, and problems of, women's war work. Members included Conservative MPs Lady Astor and Mavis Tate, and Liberal Megan Lloyd George (1902–1966). Labour MPs Edith Summerskill (1901–1980) and Agnes Hardie (1874–1951) also joined, but Ellen Wilkinson did not, perceiving the group to be too upper-class and Conservative in outlook. The committee was initially under the chairmanship of the Conservative MP, Irene Ward (1895–1980), until Mavis Tate took over in 1941.

The WPC pressed for the appointment of 'a woman to a position in the Ministry of Labour who would be responsible for making and administering policies affecting women work', and sought ways of obtaining equal remuneration for women, in terms of both pay and equal compensation for war injuries.[30] The Personal Injuries (Civilians) Scheme, introduced in 1939, decreed women would receive 7 shillings less than the 21 shillings a week that men received if they were injured. One of those who objected to this plan was the Labour MP, Janet Laurel Adamson (1882–1962). She was then MP for Dartford in Kent. She and her husband, the Labour MP William Adamson, were the only husband and wife serving in the House of Commons at the time. She argued:

> In my judgment the Minister should for this purpose have regarded unpaid household duties as gainful employment. After all, the wife does work, though it is not paid work, and her work is perhaps more important to the nation than that of the breadwinner, but the Minister has determined – and the responsibility is entirely his – that if the woman in the pursuit of her domestic duties is disabled, if the woman with a basket is bombed when out shopping, nothing whatever is to be paid on her account.[31]

Discussion and debate about whether women should receive equal compensation for war injuries led to discussion about the value society placed on the domestic labour women undertook. The British Federation of Business and Professional Women (BFBPW), the London and National Society for Women's Service (LNSWS), the Open Door Council and the National Federation of Women's Institutes, were amongst the many organisations who voiced their objection to the discrimination enshrined in the Personal Injuries (Civilians) Scheme. Ministers were lobbied, letters were written to the national newspapers, and public meetings were held.

The WPC became increasingly critical of the unequal compensation for war injuries as the conflict progressed. Women were at risk from bombing when deployed in civil defence schemes, working as fire watchers in factories, ambulance drivers, air raid wardens or as members of first aid parties. The Government considered eliminating the differentiation between men and women's compensation for war injuries would lead to further discussion about equal pay. Something which 'was viewed by members of the government as being like a tinderbox which could easily explode into a raging fire of industrial unrest with serious consequences for the nation's war effort.'[32] In January 1941, members of over forty women's organisations met and selected a deputation to present their views on unequal compensation for war injuries to the Minister of Pensions, Lord Womersley. Frustrated at his and the government's responses in October, women formed the Equal Compensation Committee (ECC) with Mavis Tate MP as chairman.[33] Their lobbying began to be successful: by December 1942, more than 200 MPs had expressed their support, although equal compensation for war injuries was not introduced until 1943, by which time equal pay was once again a hotly debated topic.[34]

According to the Extended Employment Agreement signed in 1940, women with 32 weeks' experience were to receive the same wages as men. 'The actual rates of pay for most women industrial workers during the war ranged from 50 to 70 percent of the men's rates.'[35] The Transport and General Workers Union (TGWU) obtained equal pay for bus and tram conductors after their case was referred to an industrial court, but this was a rare success. Many employers found ways of suggesting women were not doing precisely the same work as men and should therefore receive lower wages. Furthermore, women employed in 'work commonly performed by women in the industry' retained the customary lower women's wages, leading to impassioned debates about which jobs should be regarded as 'women's work'.

As labour shortages became more acute, and it was acknowledged 'the voluntary principle' was not working, the government began to consider taking the unprecedented step of compelling women to undertake war work. Whilst the WPC saw this as an important step for the war effort, it wanted any introduction of compulsion linked to equal pay. In March 1941, a debate on woman power took place in the House of Commons. The government claimed that the principle of equal pay for women replacing men was already established, but members of the WPC described this as a myth. They also drew attention to differential rates of pay for men and women attending training centres for war industries. Public concerns about the conscription of women were allayed, when in December 1941, married women were initially excluded when the National Service (Number 2) Act was passed. Initially, conscription applied only to single women, aged 20 to 30. All these women were required to register at their local Employment Exchange from where they were directed into industry, the Armed Forces or Civil Defence. As the conflict progressed the number and range of women who could be directed into war jobs, at a distance or locally, depending on their 'Household Responsibilities', was steadily increased.[36] Thus, in October 1942, women aged between 18 and 45 and a half years were registered for employment.

The Six Point Group and other women's organisations demanded equal pay for conscripted workers, and 'members of these groups passed out leaflets bearing this message to women entering labour exchanges' – an activity some members of the police force considered to be subversive.[37] Far greater alarm was caused when a claim for equal pay led to industrial action and stopped the production of Rolls Royce Merlin V-12 aero engines, used in both Hawkers Hurricanes and Spitfire planes. The Rolls-Royce, Hillington Plant near Glasgow was by 1943 producing 400 engines each week, and employing 20,000 people, 39% of which were women. Hillington was a new satellite factory, set up to improve war production and reliant on new semi-skilled employees so the company did not feel compelled to grant women equal pay. As tensions escalated, a court of inquiry under Lord Wark examined the practices at the factory. It recommended a new grading system, which would give women higher wages, but still only 80% of those earned by men working on the same machines. The inquiry's findings were accepted by both the Amalgamated Engineering Union and the Transport and General Workers Union. However, in October 1943, sixteen thousand workers, mostly women, but with support from many male factory workers, went on strike.[38]

One of the striker's leaders was Agnes McLean, a crane driver at the factory. She had been brought up in Glasgow, in the shadow of Red Clydeside, where she attended a socialist Sunday school. By 1943, Agnes was an active trade union leader and a member of the Communist party, who, two years earlier, had instigated a strike at the factory to gain workers the right to join a trade union. Feelings were strong in 1943: union leaders who tried to persuade the workers to return to work were jeered, and it was thought the strike might spread to other factories. The employers eventually agreed a schedule by which each of the machines in the factory was placed in one of the four pay grades irrespective of who worked on them. Some historians, such as Angus Calder, have regarded this as a victory for the principle of a rate for the job, regardless of the sex of the worker.[39] However, the grades were still sex-related, with all the work in the bottom grade paid at the 'women's rate', while the other grades were related to the men's rate.

Equal pay was by this time gaining wider backing. In May 1943, the social investigators' Mass Observation recorded 'widespread support for equal pay for equal work.... Male respondents were in favour 82 to 11, with 24 "don't knows".'[40] With the issue of compensation for war injuries settled, the WPC and other women's groups launched a new equal pay campaign.[41] Mavis Tate took a key role in pulling together representatives of over 100 women's organisations, with 4 million members between them, for a meeting in London in January 1944. Once again, teaching and the civil service were high on their priority list. Trade unions representing those working in public services, including the National Union of Women Teachers, began to make deputations to parliament in favour of equal pay.

Hopes ran high when the 1944 Education Bill was being debated in parliament, particularly after the MP Thelma Cazelet-Kier proposed an amendment to introduce equal pay for teachers. This was opposed by the government and led to 'the only defeat suffered by Churchill's coalition government during the war'.[42] However, at Churchill's insistence, the vote was put to the House of Commons again. This time it was made a vote of confidence and was defeated, as all government members and supporters, including Ellen Wilkinson, had to vote against it. In an attempt to side-line the issue, a Royal Commission to consider the effects of equal pay on women's employment was appointed. Both the WPC and trade union's activities were stalled as everyone waited two years for the Commission's report. When completed, it tentatively suggested teachers and some civil servants might benefit from equal pay, but warned equal pay for equal work might 'prove disastrous in the long run even to young and strong women by heavily overtaxing their nervous and muscular energy.'[43]

Once again, those women who campaigned for equal pay sought ways to win support both inside and outside parliament. In July 1949, the Equal Pay Campaign Committee asked its members to fund a film to promote their cause. This was the stimulus for the radical feminist documentary filmmaker, Jill Craigie (1911 – 1999), to produce *To Be a Woman* (1951). This short film surveyed women's work, in industry, the professions, homes, local government, Parliament, managerial and executive posts. It drew attention to how undervalued women's work was, the problem of equal pay, and how this was part of a 'much wider problem'.[44] Demonstrations and petitions also continued in the 1950s. and finally, in January 1954, the Labour Party announced it would implement equal pay when next in power. Concerned about losing support from women voters, the Conservative government began a phased introduction of equal pay in the civil service in 1955.[45]

The Equal Pay Campaign Committee wound up in 1956, considering its work to have been done. By the early 1960s, both teachers and civil servants doing exactly the same job as men had indeed obtained equal pay. This was of no benefit to the multitude of typists, cleaners and secretaries employed in 'women's jobs' in the civil service and education, or to women working in the private sector. It would take further industrial action by trade unions at the end of the 1960s, and the appointment of Barbara Castle, as the first woman Secretary of State for Employment, to bring about wider change. The Equal Pay Act was passed in 1970, but as will be shown in Chapter 14, its scope was limited, and it did not solve the problem of the low status of women's work and gendered definitions of skill, which women at the Rolls Royce factory at Hillington, near Glasgow experienced. Further campaigns led by political women were required to address these issues later in the century.

Chapter 6

Gowns and Mortarboards (1940s and 1950s)

In 1948, after many years of campaigning, women at the University of Cambridge were awarded degrees and admitted as full members of the University, on equal terms as men. However, the number of women who studied at the elite and influential universities of Oxford and Cambridge, the training grounds for political, industrial and administrative leaders, remained limited until the 1970s and 1980s. Campaigns to give women equal access to higher education lasted over 100 years, dating back to the nineteenth century. When in 1928, the feminist politician, Ray Strachey (1887–1940), came to write one of the first histories of the struggle for women suffrage, titled: *The Cause, A Short History of the Women's Movement in Great Britain*, she included campaigns by women to undertake degrees and medical training.[1] Strachey recognised that women's access to higher education and women's struggles for political rights were intimately connected.

Gaining access for all women to higher education, perhaps more than any other political campaign, relied upon the activities of a multitude of individual women who battled with both public institutions and their families. The women who took on such fights became trailblazers and role models; they ploughed a path which others followed. Consequently, 133,316 women were awarded university undergraduate degrees in the year 2000, compared to only 109,930 men. The number of women gaining higher degrees was also fast catching up with that of men.[2] The list of often-forgotten women pioneers in higher education includes the scientist Dorothy Hodgkin, (1910–1994), who was a chemist, studied at Cambridge, became a Professor and a fellow at Wolfson College, Oxford, and was also a wife and mother. Yet when she received a Nobel prize in 1964, there were still only three men's colleges at the University of Oxford which would allow her, or any other woman, to visit as dinner guests. Only twenty years later, women's studies courses in adult, further and higher education became an area of political and educational awakening for many women in Britain enjoying opportunities, which their grandmothers could only have dreamed of.

In nineteenth-century Britain, the majority of girls, particularly if they had come from middle class and aristocratic families, were initially taught at home by their mothers, or perhaps by a governess. Their education sought to equip them for a domestic life, marriage and the administration of a household. Girls learned to play the piano; sing; sew and sketch; to support and amuse their husbands; to raise a family, and to be a 'virtuous influence on men' as mothers, wives, daughters or sisters.[3] Indeed, Sarah Stickney Ellis's guide book, *The Daughters of England*, explained that in 1845, 'the first thing of importance is to be content to be inferior to men, inferior in mental power in the same proportion that you are inferior in bodily strength.'[4] Parents who saw marriage as the most desirable and natural future for their daughter's life did not see any point in spending money on girl's education, and even worried cleverness was a disadvantage in the marriage market. The anti-suffragist writer, Sarah Sewell, suggested in 1868: 'women who have stored their minds with Latin and Greek seldom have much knowledge of pies and puddings.'[5] Doctors even argued brain work could damage women's reproductive organs, whilst Dr Henry Maudsley suggested that educating women would lead to 'a puny, enfeebled and sickly race.'[6]

Notwithstanding such ridiculous pronouncements, the campaign for women's education grew in the second half of the nineteenth century. Not all women wanted or were able to marry, and some sought economic independence, a fulfilling single life, and the chance to enter professions, such as law and medicine. Campaigns by Sophia Jex-Blake (1840- 1912) led to first herself, and six other women, studying medicine at the University of Edinburgh, followed by the setting up of the London School of Medicine for Women in 1874. By 1920, of the 40,000 qualified doctors in Britain, 2,000 were women. These included Mabel Lida Ramsey (1878–1954), who was employed in Glasgow, Leeds and Huddersfield, before moving to Plymouth in 1908. During the First World War, she worked in hospitals close to front line in Belgium, before pursuing an outstanding career in gynaecology, obstetrics and maternity care. Mabel became a consultant at several hospitals and clinics in the west of England.

In 1869, two London based feminists, Emily Davies, Barbara Bodichon, founded Girton College, Cambridge, together with Lady Stanley of Alderley, Cheshire. Newnham College, originally a house in which women could stay so they could attend lectures at the university, was established two years later. Both colleges were deliberately built at a physical distance from the already established colleges for men at Cambridge. As a student noted in 1913, this distance served as a constant reminder that they were 'not merely students but also female ones'.[7] The tiny number of girls who managed to obtain a place at university, often endured hardships as they found their lives framed by numerous rules and regulations. Colleges sought to protect the reputation of both the institutions and their students from the barrage of potential criticism which freely came their way. Anxiety about co-education and the consequences of young men and women being in close proximity to one another continued well into the twentieth century. Hence, as Lucy Delap has pointed out, women's experiences at these elite universities differed significantly from those of men. At Cambridge, 'the first female students were required to ask permission to attend lectures, were not allowed to take exams without special permission and, until after the First World War, usually had to be accompanied by chaperones in public.'[8]

Likewise, at the University of Oxford, when Somerville and Lady Margaret Hall Colleges were founded in 1879, and St Hugh's and St Hilda's in 1886 and 1893, women students were subject to copious restrictions. Joan Evans, who studied at St Hilda's College in 1914, recalled: 'Regulations were numerous and old fashioned, I remember going to the Vice – Principal for leave to go to look at Oxford architecture by myself as there was a rule which said that students should not go for expeditions in the city alone.'[9] In the same year, 'the head of one women's college felt compelled to write to her students warning them of 'a very tiresome complaint that the men examinees are disturbed by the way our students sit in their tight skirts and show their legs.'[10] Universities across the country reflected the fears and social expectations of the era. At the University of Durham, women who illicitly met male students were liable to asked to leave the university, whilst at the University of Cardiff, women students were forbidden from partaking in the dubious joys of joint picnics or drama productions with male students.[11]

The assiduous separation of sexes meant girls were initially denied access to the main University of Cambridge laboratories, which necessitated the construction of alternative laboratories in 1879 at Girton. These facilities were by no means lavish: one student in 1880 recalled 'raw days in the laboratory, barely tempered by a little grate fire in one corner', but they did enable girls to study chemistry and biological sciences.[12] In 1884, the Balfour Biological Laboratory was opened, and it continued to be used by students preparing for the Natural Sciences Tripos at both Newnham and Girton, until 1914. Marsha Richmond argues that it 'offered advanced students the opportunity to engage in independent research, and, most important, formed the locus for the scientific subculture created by women at Cambridge to compensate for their exclusion from the social community of science.'[13] Nevertheless, then and for many years to come, women scientists remained a rarity.

Many newer universities founded in the Victorian era were co-educational from the get-go. In 1878, the University of London became the first British institution to award degrees to women. Hester Millicent Mackenzie (1863–

1942) became a Professor of Education (Women) at the University of Cardiff in 1908, writing books, campaigning for the suffrage, and standing as the only woman parliamentary candidate in Wales in the 1918 general election. Oxford University was slow to follow these examples and Cambridge University even slower; it was to be many years until women could graduate as full members of these universities. Women could sit the same examinations as men at the University of Cambridge from 1882, but were only able to gain titular degrees, mailed to them in the post; their names were excluded from the degree ceremony list. However, such limitations did not act as a disincentive or impede the young women's academic success. In 1880, Charlotte Angas Scott (1858–1931) gained the eighth-highest results in the Mathematical Tripos, whilst in 1887 Agnata Ramsay (1867–1931) came top in Part I of the Classical Tripos, doing better than all the men who had sat the examinations.[14] In 1897, male undergraduates at Cambridge reacted with horror at the suggestion that women should be allowed to receive degrees and become full members of the university. They hoisted an effigy of a 'new woman' on a bicycle above one college; burnt dummies of female scholars; displayed posters with straplines such as 'frustrate feminine fanatics'; pelted women students with eggs and threw fireworks at the windows of women's colleges as a near-riot ensued in the city.

Women who campaigned for access to higher education made some progress in the late nineteenth century. Historians have seen the period that followed, in the first 30-to-40 years of the twentieth century, as a period of growth and consolidation, when the scope for women to enter higher education broadened, and when they also became integrated and accepted in universities. However, as Carol Dyhouse has pointed out, this 'makes it more difficult to account for the conflicts of the 1920s and 1930s' and the very uneven, unique, contradictory, even perverse, approaches taken by different institutions throughout this period.[15] For example, women students at the University of Oxford between 1904 and 1907, gained the dubious pleasure of being allowed to travel to the more liberally minded University of Dublin where they could be awarded their degrees. The mode of transport employed to reach Dublin, led these intrepid campaigners to be dubbed the 'Steamboat Ladies'.

Despite the difficulties women students faced, a growing awareness of university as a possible life-path for some middle and upper-class girls resulted in there being 30 fee-paying boarding schools teaching an academic curriculum and preparation for university entrance by 1900. These schools, which catered only for the daughters of wealthy parents, included Cheltenham Ladies College, North London Collegiate College, and St Leonard's School in St Andrews. These schools combined forward-thinking approaches to girls' education with a sympathetic approach to women's suffrage. From the age of sixteen, Jessie Chrystal Macmillan (1872- 1937), the only daughter of a tea merchant John Macmillan, attended St Leonards. She progressed to gain a First-Class Honours degree in Mathematics and Moral Philosophy at Edinburgh University, the first women to graduate in Mathematics at the University. In 1900, she obtained an MA in Mental and Moral Philosophy at the university, before spending some time studying in Berlin. When Chrystal returned to Edinburgh, she, like many other independent university women graduates, became involved in campaigns for women's suffrage.

One of the quirks of the Edwardian electoral system was that a number of MPs were elected by universities; the four Scottish universities sent two MPs to the House of Commons to represent them. Graduates of the university were members of the General Council of Edinburgh University responsible for voting for these MPs. However, the university denied Chrystal and other female graduates that right. Chrystal became both the honorary secretary and treasurer of the Committee of Women Graduates (Parliamentary Franchise) set up in 1906. Five women – Chrystal Macmillan, Elsie Inglis, Frances Simson, Frances Melville, Margaret Nairn, all Edinburgh University graduates – then took legal proceedings against the university, arguing the case that the use of the word 'person' in 1868 legislation did not exclude them. They took their case through local courts, the appeal court, and finally to the House of Lords in 1908. They were complemented on their rational and eloquent arguments. The *Aberdeen Press and Journal* noted:

> Miss Macmillan, the lady who conducted the hearing before the Lord Chancellor and his colleagues, is of quiet and refined manner, not at all like the representatives of "shrieking sisterhood" who have caused so much trouble recently; and the behaviour of herself and her companions showed the claim to a right, real or supposed, need not be accompanied by a species of female hooliganism.[16]

The campaign was however unsuccessful, although Chrystal Macmillan and Frances Simson's eloquence in arguing their cause made them heroines of the suffrage societies.

The *Aberdeen Press and Journal* reported how on their return,

> A women graduates' lunch was held on Saturday at the Women Student's Union, Edinburgh, in honour of Miss Chrystal Macmillan, M.A. BSc and Miss Frances Simson, M.A. in recognition of their energy, patience

and ability with which they conducted the women graduates' appeal to the House of Lords, and the able manner in which they pleaded the case.[17]

Chrystal went on to become a leading light in the National Union of Women's Suffrage Societies, later the National Union of Societies for Equal Citizenship (NUSEC) and Women's International League for Peace and Freedom (WILPF). She was one of the very first women to train for the bar after the Sex Disqualification Removal Act was passed in 1919, qualifying in 1923. As a barrister, she assisted women and women's organisations campaigning for justice.

Women who went to university in the early years of the twentieth century sought not only to benefit from an academic education, but also to take advantage of the other opportunities that higher education offered. They increasingly participated in sport, debating clubs, rag weeks and drama clubs. They also undertook social work in the settlements in urban working-class areas, and involved themselves in suffrage politics.[18] Nevertheless, it was only a tiny minority of women who were able, like Chrystal Macmillan, to go to an academic school or university; many parents of middle-and upper-class parents continued to see an academic education as a waste of time and money for girls in the first half of the twentieth century. The writer and feminist campaigner, Virginia Woolf (1882–1941), was denied the University of Cambridge education seen as natural for her brothers. Instead, she was educated at home by her parents, with the added benefit of free access to her father's extensive library. She was strongly aware of the discrepancy in the access to higher education between girls and campaigned against this and for greater funding for the relatively new and poorly endowed women's colleges at Cambridge.

In the years leading up to the First World War, Vera Brittain also had a struggle on her hands to persuade her parents to pay for a university education for her as well as her brother. Like many other women in the era, Brittain gained her first taste of academic study by attending a course of University Extension lectures which were held across the country. The course she took, held in Buxton Town Hall, Derbyshire, focused upon 'the problems of wealth and poverty.'[19] Vera followed this up by winning an essay competition, which enabled her to attend a Summer School at St Hilda's College, Oxford, where she soon discovered that the education she had so far received, lacked the academic rigour to prepare her to attempt the Oxford University entrance exam.

Brittain embarked upon a programme of self-study, 'an uphill grind…getting up every day at six o'clock and working steadily until lunchtime in a chilly little north-west room.' Over several months she mastered History, English

Literature, and Latin whilst also undertaking tuition in Mathematics. Her efforts were rewarded, when in March 1914, she was awarded an exhibition to study at Somerville College, Oxford. This would provide her with £20 towards the costs of her study for three years. By the time she began her degree, the First World War had started and her fiancé, Roland, like many young men, had abandoned the prospect of university study describing it as 'a secluded life of scholastic vegetation'.[20] The recruitment of so many young men, like Roland, into the armed forces, did however offer new opportunities to women seeking to study at universities across the country, and restrictions around chaperoning and the separation of the sexes began to be eased.

By the end of the conflict, women at the University of Cambridge were finally able to work alongside men in the main university science laboratories.[21] Cecilia Payne-Gaposchkin (1900 – 1979) was one of the young women who benefitted from these new opportunities. After studying for a year at St Paul's School for Girls in London, she was accepted to study science at Newman College, Cambridge in 1919. Like many women at the time she initially chose to study botany, but having been inspired by a lecture by the head of the Cambridge Observatory on Einstein's Theory of Relativity, she transferred to physics and astronomy. Cecilia continued her study in America, where she became the first woman to receive a PhD from Radcliffe College, and become an astrophysicist and the first woman to receive the American Astronomical Society's lifetime of eminence award.[22]

Progress for women seeking to undertake higher education or study in these elite British universities was not however guaranteed in the inter-war years. The University of Oxford did begin to award degrees to women in 1920, but operated a quota system which limited the total number of women studying at the university, a system which remained in place until 1957.[23] Dorothy Hodgkin (1919 – 1994) was one of this new crop of women undergraduates who gained an Oxford degree in the 1920s, completing her studies in Chemistry at Somerville College in 1928. In the 1930s, she moved to carry out doctoral research at the University of Cambridge, where in 1924, Katharine Margaret Wilson had become the first woman to complete a PhD at the University.[24] Two years later, Hodgkin returned to Oxford where her research on the structure of penicillin led to her election to the Royal Society in 1947. Hodgkin had the rare privilege of being financed by her aunt, Dorothy Hood, who paid all her college bills, while financial constraints prevented most other women from even considering applying for university.

Many at the University of Cambridge continued to remain wary of women's place in an institution with over 600 years of history of male domination, which they were reticent to overturn. A further vote on whether women should be allowed to receive degrees and become full members of the university was held in December, 1920. The small but influential feminist women's magazine, *Time and Tide*, supported campaigners at the university, noting 'feeling runs high and the majority either way is expected to be a very narrow one.'[25] They poured scorn on those who opposed equality for women at the university, including Professor of Archaeology, Sir William Ridgeway (1853 – 1926), whom they described as still looking 'upon every women as a cross between a neurotic invalid and an irresistible Cleopatra.'[26] A 'note written by undergraduates apologising for the damage that had been done to Newnham College during the riot' provides further evidence that Ridgeway was not alone in his antipathy towards women at the university.[27] *Time and Tide* also expressed outrage, when in the 1920s, some of the London medical schools likewise began to close their doors to women students, which they had admitted enthusiastically during the First World War. Some of the hospitals claimed 'teaching co-educational classes causes embarrassment; that the experiment of co-education having been tried for ten years has been found unsatisfactory; that 50 per cent of women doctors and these the most brilliant abandon their profession on marriage.'[28]

It took the social upheaval of another war for real progress to be seen, with the University of Cambridge finally awarding women degrees in 1948. By then, Gloria Carpenter had become the first black woman to matriculate at the University. She had emigrated to Britain from Jamaica at the age of thirteen, and after attending a London grammar school, studied Law at the university, completing her degree in 1945. A pioneer of women's education, she helped to set up the University of West Indies Law department. Two years later, Efua Theodora Sutherland graduated from Homerton College, becoming a Ghanaian educator, publisher, artist, dramatist and writer.[29] Full equality between the sexes at the university was not able to be achieved, while most of the colleges, and all those with rich endowments to fund them, continued to take men only. But change was on its way.[30]

Joyce Reynolds, former Director of Studies in Classics at Newnham College, Cambridge, pointed out, 'prejudice against women was a serious problem at Cambridge in the 1960s …. Discrimination was so ingrained at Cambridge that it was almost erased by the distance between men's and women's colleges.'[31] Despite such difficulties, individual, trailblazing women at both Oxford and Cambridge universities continued to demonstrate their sex's intellectual capacity, and their right to participate in academic life at the highest levels. Dorothy Hodgkin, who spent much of her working life as Official Fellow and Tutor in Natural Science at Somerville College, Oxford, became a university lecturer and demonstrator in 1946. Ten years later (in

1956), she became a University Reader in X-ray Crystallography. In 1960, Dorothy became a Wolfson Research Professor of the Royal Society, winning a Nobel Prize for her work on penicillin and vitamin B12 in 1964.

Such opportunities and careers did not even enter the imagination of most young women, despite the opportunities offered by free secondary education to all pupils, enshrined in the 1944 Education Act. Teachers and parents continued to assume that most girls, and particularly working-class girls, were destined to focus most of their energies on marriage, home and family. This was because, 'The vast majority of girls left school at 15 and, after, at most, a brief training period, entered employment only to leave once married.'[32] Thus, only 1.2 per cent of women went to university in the 1950s, and a tiny number of these studied science.[33] Professor Dame Athene Donald recalled that when she matriculated in 1971, 'women in physics in the University were a rare breed... there were eight of us in physics in my final year cohort of perhaps 80'.[34] In 1972, however, Churchill, Clare and King's Colleges, Cambridge which were previously male-only establishments, started the process of admitting women. The Sex Discrimination of Act (1975) subsequently banned discrimination on the basis of sex and the practice of prioritising male over female student applications. Nevertheless, it would take many more years for the male-female ratios at Universities of Oxford and Cambridge to become close to fifty-fifty.

It was the expansion of higher education in the 1960s, with the opening of new universities such as Universities of Sussex, York and Warwick, which really benefited women. In these new institutions, and in some of the older-established universities, predominantly middle-class women found that higher education could be a route into the women's movement, as it had been for some suffrage campaigners in the Edwardian era. Sara Maitland (1950-), who grew up in a middle -class family in a small town in Wiltshire, recalls how she 'arrived in Oxford in the autumn 1968, more virginal in more ways than seems credible'. It was in 1970 that she was taken by friends to hear the feminist Germaine Greer speak at Ruskin College, Oxford, when the first Women's Liberation Conference was held there.

> My world was transformed. The sky was bright with colour, I smoked my first joint, lost my virginity and went on my first political demonstration, I stopped attending lectures and my ears unblocked so I could actually hear what was going on around me, I realised that classical education, Whig history and compassionate liberalism were not the only values in the world.[35]

Having discovered feminism, socialism and a new set of priorities in her life, Sara went on to become a writer and intellectual.

In the 1970s, the links between feminism, individual liberation and education in the post-war world began to extend beyond the middle and upper classes, through new institutions including Polytechnics, the Open University (set up in 1969), and a multitude of educational classes, provided by the Workers Education Association (founded in 1907), Adult Education, and University Extra Mural departments, that were orientated towards women. In 1969, the feminist, Juliet Mitchell, taught a short course titled, 'The Role of Women in Society' in what was described as the 'Anti University' and was organised by radical academics supporting student protest movements.[36] This has been described as the first Women's Studies course and it was soon followed by others, which, alongside courses in Black Women's Studies and Lesbian Studies, began to appear across the country. London University Extramural Department, for example, had six such courses in 1975 and twenty-nine in 1988.[37] Throngs of women talked, discussed, debated and found their voice through education. Anna Davin, who taught women's studies and women's history in this era, later recalled,

> I can remember a rather good class on work where I got them to talk, I said, 'What sorts of work do you think of women as doing?' and wrote up on the board their suggestions, but kind of categorised them as I did so that somebody would say, 'Cleaning', and I'd say, 'Yes, well that could be in domestic service or it could also be unpaid work, or...' So, I'd be trying to make them think about how to categorise as we went along, and also commenting on what women, how far women did that particular kind of work, at what point during the nineteenth century or the twentieth century.[38]

Arguably, there were two distinct strands to these women's studies courses. On the one hand, there were those directly linked to the women's movement and political activism, which often led to the setting up women's centres or support groups, these sought to change women's sense of themselves and their rights. Numerous courses in women's health, run by the Workers' Education Association (WEA), were important examples of this. On the other hand, there were also a multitude of courses that paved the way for women who had left school at fifteen, often with few formal qualifications, to return to education. These carried titles such as Second Chance or were badged as access courses. Women increasingly began to take up opportunities to study as mature students through the Open University (founded in 1969) and at new polytechnics and universities. Eve Worth's research on women and adult education in the 1970s demonstrated how returning to education as an adult was a catalyst to social mobility for women who had left school at 15 or 16.[39] As Eve explains:

> The women I interviewed born around the 1940s often re-entered education when they were already married and had children. They told me that when they were younger they had thought they would want to permanently give up work after becoming a mother, or to work part-time in clerical or service roles once their children had started school. But this life-cycle did not stick, and many women expressed being bored, or wanting to be challenged, or simply needing a means of escape – 'it was great not to be constantly asked "where's my socks?"' stated one interviewee, or as another interviewee put it – 'just wanting something different than the life that seemed mapped out for you.'[40]

For many mature students in the 1970s, 80s and 90s, education became a first step towards not only higher education, but also new careers and financial independence, their pathway made easier by the flexibility of distance learning provided by the Open University, or the commitment of some polytechnic courses to accommodate them. When I began my first degree as a young mum in 1981, I chose to study Cultural Studies at what was then Portsmouth Polytechnic, after the admissions officer explained that taught sessions took place between 10 o'clock in the morning and three in the afternoon – an arrangement deliberately designed for approximately one third of their students who were studying while their children were at school. The entry into higher education for many women was not without its costs. Many relationships and marriages struggled, as women gained greater confidence, independence and a more critical perspective on the social roles, which society and families ascribed to them. The film, *Educating Rita* (1983), tells the story of a 26-year-old hairdresser who embarks upon an Open University degree in English Literature, but as she gains new interests, perspective, priorities and confidence, her marriage breaks up.

These new students and their lecturers also challenged and changed the very nature of higher education itself. What should be studied, and using which approaches, became heated areas of discussion. Women's Studies developed as an academic field, and feminism became a legitimate tool of analysis within academia. At the University of Kent, Mary Evans and colleagues introduced the first degree in Women's Studies in 1980. Other universities, such as Bradford and Warwick, followed in this wake, introducing MAs in Women's

Studies, while the Open University developed a course titled, *The Changing Experience of Women*, in 1983. There were tensions around assimilating feminist perspectives into universities that had developed their traditions in an era of male dominance. Students studying for a Master of Arts in Women's Studies wanted, for example, to know why they could not be awarded a Mistress of Arts. In other discussions, the personal and the political overlapped, and heated, emotive discussions took place.

By the end of the twentieth century, mass higher education ensured that women of all backgrounds, with or without parental support or finance, had the opportunity to study for a degree. The staff who taught them were as likely to be women as men, and the perspectives and approaches they used for analysis were often informed by feminism. For most women involved in political activism, a degree was their first step, and the women's political movement and higher education continued to be entwined. Furthermore, a graduation ceremony finally took place at Cambridge in 1998, where all the 900 graduands were female. They were the women who had completed their studies before the university had allowed them to be awarded degrees in 1948. This ceremony was put on to honour their achievements. Women attended from all over the world; the oldest was 97 years old. It was too little and too late for many women, but at least these pioneering women campaigners were not forgotten.

Chapter 7

'We got a little hall and took our children there with their toys' (1961)

In August 1961, unable to find childcare, Belle Tutaev wrote to *The Guardian* women's page seeking signatures for a national petition for 'more nursery schools and play facilities for children under 5.' It led to the formation of the Pre-School Playgroups Association (PPA), the Early Years Alliance, and the rather optimistic demand at the first National Women's Liberation Conference in 1970, for free 24-hour nurseries. Before writing to *The Guardian*, Tutaev and a friend had already hired a local hall to provide space for groups of children to play. Numerous other mothers followed her lead and set up playgroups and nurseries across the country. The PPA became an important women's self-help group, changing the provision of, and attitudes towards, care for young children.

In her letter to *The Guardian* titled 'Do-it-yourself nurseries', Belle Tutaev explained,

> The campaign has two aims. One is to gather names for a large-scale petition to be presented to the Minister of Education asking him for more nursery schools and play facilities for children under 5. The other is to encourage mothers to start their own schools wherever they can find suitable premises, employing trained teachers, especially those who are married with their own small children and want only part time jobs.[1]

These aims hinted at what were three elements of the twentieth-century campaigns to provide social spaces for children, for them to play and learn, and to be cared for with others of their own age. These social forms of childcare, whether nurseries, playgroups, kindergartens, creches or nursery schools, first sought to improve child welfare, second to enable women to work, and third, to develop careers and professionalise the skills of carers of small children. Which of these three different elements was prioritised shifted over time and varied from one campaigning group to another.

Prior to the early twentieth century, young children's care in Britain was shaped by their parents' financial resources, occupation and circumstances.

The very wealthy handed the day-to-day care of small infants over to a nanny or nursery maid. More ad hoc arrangements occurred in families with more limited financial resources, with grandparents, siblings and relations looking after little ones. Children as young as eight found employment caring for babies. Such arrangements prioritised the needs of the parents. Thus, Colonial English families in South East Asia employed local women to look after their children, named *ayahs*, an Anglo-Indian word which stems from the Portuguese *aia* (nurse). Farhanah Mamoojee's research has uncovered how in the nineteenth century, children were often brought back to Britain for their schooling at the age of seven or eight, and the women who had cared for them all their lives were left behind, or having accompanied them on their journey across the ocean, abandoned upon arrival in Britain.[2]

The fate of some children whose parents desperately needed to earn money to support them could be equally tragic. Desperate mothers sometimes left their infants in the care of unscrupulous childminders, who cared for multiple infants, relying upon a variety of rather dubious but easily available opiates to keep their charges quiet. Scandals occurred about what was termed baby farming. The most infamous of these was the case of Amelia Dyer, thought to have murdered up to 400 infants over a 20-year period. When she was found responsible for their deaths in 1896, the government began the process of introducing increasingly strict legislation to regulate childcare.[3] Nevertheless, in 1914, a six-month-old baby, Mary Sophia Bowter, died after having been left in the care of her 10-year-old aunt while her mother was hop-picking in Fladbury, Worcestershire. The coroner was of the opinion that while it was a case for enquiry, 'there was no neglect', and the Jury returned their fees to the bereaved mother with no hint of a suggestion that Mary Bowter's carer was too young to have responsibility for a baby.[4]

By this time, new approaches to infant care, structured around the needs of the child, were emerging; perhaps the most influential of which came from Friedrich Froebel (1782–1852), who invented the kindergarten. He argued that child-care practitioners 'must nurture the ideas, feelings, relationships and physical development of children.'[5] His supporters proposed that 'education was about three things: the child, the context in which learning takes place, and the knowledge and understanding which the child develops and learns.'[6] Social reformers sought to establish nursery provision with outdoor spaces where children could play, thereby counteracting the deprivation experienced by those who lived in impoverished urban environments. Such ideas lay behind the setting up of the St Saviour's Child Garden, which opened in Edinburgh in 1906. It started with only a handful of children but within a few years, had 40 small attendees. It was initially located in the mission hall of the

Episcopal Church of Old St Paul's in the city, and early pictures show the little attendees gardening.[7]

The early staff at St Saviour's Child Garden had been trained and influenced by the Sesame Club, formed in 1895 at Victoria Street, London, founded for members of the suffrage societies who were also interested in literature, art, science and improvements in education. The early feminists who attended events at Sesame House, sought to both improve child welfare and also importantly, to provide training for young women seeking a potential career that did not challenge Edwardian notions of womanliness and femininity. Three years earlier, Emily Ward, another educational reformer influenced by Frobel, founded the Norlands Institute, which fashioned the profession of nursery nursing. Her training system which involved a rotation of practical placements, created a model for the future. Norland trained nannies who were not domestic servants, but were on a par with governesses, and like them predominantly worked for middle and upper-class families, including royal and aristocratic nurseries across Europe. According to Louise Heren, their small charges learnt nursery rhymes, parlour games and to speak English. It is noted that 'Where Norlanders did learn the mother tongue of the family employing them, they did not speak it with the children in their charge.'[8] The benefits of a Norland-trained nanny were reserved for the wealthy, but many of these trained professionals also worked in nurseries and staffed creches in Bethnal Green and Acton, London, looking after youngsters while their mothers worked in munitions industries during the First World War.

The need for working-class women to undertake war work created a conducive environment for nurseries to flourish in a number of urban areas. Sylvia Pankhurst, aware that the outbreak of war brought about a rise in the cost of living, which led many women in the East End of London to seek work, identified the need to organise a nursery. She was one of many women's suffrage campaigners who undertook infant and child welfare activities during the conflict.[9] Margaret and Rachel McMillan likewise established an open-air nursery at Deptford to provide a safe, nurturing environment for the disadvantaged children of the area in 1914. 'The sisters stressed the importance of free play... through craft and water activities', the importance of learning outdoors, and the need for nurseries to provide 'large and varied external areas' for children to explore and investigate.[10] In the inter-war years, other educationalists and psychologists, such as Susan Isaacs, also opened nurseries and an early years training college was also linked to the Deptford nursery in London. McMillan, however, was clear she 'did not deny the importance of maternal forces', but explained that in a nursery school, a child was nurtured by being 'surrounded by diffused love.'[11]

Despite such initiatives, on the eve of the Second World War in 1938, there were only 104 Day Nurseries in Great Britain, providing care for 4291 children.[12] Once again, during this conflict there was a need for women workers. This led to the establishment and support for a range of childcare arrangements by local authorities and the Ministry of Health, including both day and residential nurseries. Women paid for their children to attend, but the costs were usually subsidised. For example, Barking & Dagenham Council opened a day nursery in 1942 in Eastbury Manor, a National Trust property with grounds for children to play. Arrangements to care for the children included constructing an air raid shelter. The 40–50 children arrived daily between 7 and 9 am and stayed until between 5 and 7 pm, to enable their mothers to complete a 10-hour working day at nearby factories.[13] In Uttoxeter, a residential nursery looked after babies in the Staffordshire countryside, safe from the bombing while their mothers worked in Birmingham. Such nurseries were not however widespread or necessarily convenient. Ann Day interviewed women who worked in the Portsmouth Dockyards. They included one mother, a widow with three children, who worked as a wire splicer from 1942 to 1945. She had to walk three miles to deliver her youngest child, who was only two years old, to the government day nursery, which had been set up in the Kingston area of Portsmouth in 1942. After which, she caught a bus to work, repeating her journey in reverse in the evening. She often returned home after dark in the blackout, and unsurprisingly, she had few happy memories of war work.[14]

Many war nurseries survived into the post-war era, in Birmingham and Derby for example, but in peacetime, the cost of running them was often perceived to be an unjustifiable expense by local authorities which argued that there was no longer the same demand for childcare. Those nurseries which did exist, prioritised children with social problems. In time, both the children, and the nurseries they attended, became stigmatised. Most women's organisations, psychologists and politicians saw a woman's place as predominantly in the home, caring for their children. However, this could be isolating for both mothers and children. In the early 1960s, for example, when Belle Tutaev's family lived in a central London flat, at Cavendish Mews just behind the BBC, her son was at school, but her three-year-old daughter had no social spaces in which to play with and meet other children. She saw 'children going past our window and on to school' and consequently had no friends to invite to her a birthday party.[15] Belle Tutaev's response to her predicament was to get together with other local mothers she had met at the school gate, and search for a space for their pre-school children to play. A qualified nursery nurse offered to work with her, but as she later recalled: 'It was difficult to get a place that would accept children en-masse.'[16] Those in charge of the halls and similar places, who they approached appeared to respond by making 'up every excuse under the sun'.[17] Eventually, they 'got a little hall and took [their] children there with their toys.'[18] The group they set up in a church hall in Marylebone, London, was attended by six children for two hours a day. Belle Tutaev then began her campaign to obtain more nursery schools and received funding from the Nursery School Association, Save the Children Fund, and the Advisory Centre of Education. In 1961, she wrote her influential letter to *The Guardian* Newspaper.

The journalist Mary Stott had been the editor of *The Guardian*'s Women's Page since 1957, and as a committed and active feminist, turned the page into the launch pad for a number of organisations including, The National Housewives' Register, the National Association for the Welfare of Children in Hospital, and the National Council for Single Women and her Dependants. The Women's Page, under Mary's editorship, welcomed letters about ordinary women's experiences, which as she pointed out, were the voices with which readers identified. For example, she included one describing the life of Betty Thorne, who lived in a Sheffield two-up, two-down 'squeezed in like sardines in suburbia.'[19] Other letters told of the isolation of mothers, or the limited facilities for their children to play, socialise and learn.

When it was printed in August 1961, Belle Tutaev's letter invited mothers to become involved in her campaign for more nurseries, or to set up a do-it-yourself nursery. Letters of inquiry were welcomed, letters which included a stamped addressed envelope were particularly welcomed. Within a week, 250 letters from mothers of young children had poured in. These responses led to the formation of the Pre-school Playgroups' Association (PPA), which held its first annual general meeting the following year, having gained 150 members, within two years membership had grown to 2,500. Mothers across the country set up playgroups and nurseries, in scout huts, chapel vestries, sports clubs, community halls – anywhere they could find a room to hire. Thousands of children attended the new playgroups. Isabella Outen recalled how, in her London childhood of the 1960s, she went to a 'children's playgroup in the mornings' and that she retained for many years, 'clear memories of "The Wheels on the Bus", "Incey Wincey Spider", and "I Hear Thunder", as well as painting and drinking orange squash.'[20]

Belle Tutaev became the first President of the PPA, which was later renamed the Pre-school Learning Alliance (PLA). The organisation developed and became a registered charity, but its campaign to obtain educational, social spaces for children's play was not easy. Tutaev later recalled:

> We were trying to get more nursery education because that was what was needed....It was hard work achieving anything because all the government ministers I met were men. All the politicians I met were men, all the vicars who had the church halls were men, too. They seemed to be saying: 'Why do you need this? Can't your children just play at home like everybody else?'[21]

She left her role as President of the PPA in 1966, to train as a teacher. In later life, she become the headmistress of an infant school in Bristol. The participation in the running and organising of playgroups through the PPA, empowered many mothers, helping them to acquire the confidence and inspiration to start new careers. Reverend Dr Jean Prosser later recalled how having read Belle Tutaev's 1961 letter to *The Guardian*, she started a playgroup for her own small children, which kickstarted a career as a vice-principal of several further education colleges, as an adviser to the Department of Employment, and as a senior civil servant. She explained,

> In 1967, without any qualification other than being a mother, I approached the local vicar for use of the village hall for a playgroup. After assurance that this was not a drama group, he became our strongest supporter. When a legal requirement for qualifications came in, the principal of the local college agreed to offer training and 46 mums enrolled on the first night. Then via the Open University and a PhD at Surrey, my career developed. I believe it could not have happened without that letter.[22]

Whole communities also benefited from campaigns to provide a local playgroup and safe play spaces. The determination of women in Armagh, thirty-five miles from Belfast, to establish a playgroup was reported in the feminist publication *Spare Rib* in December 1975. The article, titled 'A Playgroup called Freedom,' described the problems faced by young mothers living on a modern estate, served with only one expensive shop and few safe places for their young children to play. The women's experience was set against the thirty years of ethno-nationalist violence, unemployment, poverty, and armed British troops patrolling the streets of Northern Ireland. The community hall built on their estate lay empty and unused. Unable to persuade the Protestant council to reopen the hall, the women took action. They moved into the hall and took it over, clearing it up and raising funds by holding events there. Despite getting caught up in the sectarian tensions and being accused of being linked to terrorist groups, such as the provisional IRA (the Irish Republican Army), the women set up youth groups, discos and keep-fit classes. Eventually,

'We got a little hall and took our children there with their toys' (1961)   73

the Department of Education agreed to pay for the centre's renovation, and to support the creation of a playgroup. The women explained how they 'put in plans for small toilets, washbasins… [to] have a purpose-built room for a nursery.'[23] On reflecting on the project, they noted it had 'started to break down the isolation felt acutely by women living in a family set up on estates like this.'[24]

The PPA grew in size and influence. By the mid 1970s, it provided safe, creative spaces for more than a third of a million three and four-year olds to play. Although playgroups sought to have a trained and paid leader, there was also an assumption they would rely on volunteers. Mothers whose children attended playgroups were expected to help out on two or three mornings per half term, which kept the cost of running playgroups down. The PPA organised and ran courses in people's houses, halls and local colleges, to inspire and help mothers to the obtain skills needed to manage, run and work in playgroups. Anyone who already had relevant skills was seen as a godsend. One ex-primary school teacher with two under-fives in Emsworth in Hampshire popped out during a meeting to make the coffee in the early 1980s, only to discover on her return, that she had been made chair of the local PPA group.

As the PPA grew, it needed to employ tutors for its courses, area organisers, and people who were also in great demand as speakers at Parent-Teacher Associations in schools, Women's Institutes, Townswomen's Guilds and Young Wives' Clubs. The PPA also began to develop a shared ethos around childhood, motherhood, education, play and learning. Some of these were articulated by Brenda Crowe, the national advisor to the PPA, in her book first published in 1973.[25] *The Playgroup Movement* explained the organisation, its aims and ethos, and also provided guidance to those setting up and running playgroups. The tone followed that of many of Victorian social reformers and proponents of infant and child welfare: the writer was the expert, mothers needed educating in how to look after their children, and the needs of the child – not their mothers – were the key concern. The tone seems condescending towards ordinary women and it echoed the assumption of many of those involved in the PPA: that mums would and should be the primary carers of pre-school children. It did however acknowledge that 'there is a very real need for mothers to go off duty for a couple of hours occasionally.'[26]

Playgroups are idealised in Brenda Crowe's book, yet the rather ad hoc rented accommodation in which they operated had its limitations. All the equipment had to be got out and packed away at the end. This could have disastrous consequences, as one young mum in Emsworth, Hampshire in the 1980s found, when she had to return to the church hall in which the playgroup operated and unpack and then re-pack all the materials when she realised her son had left his bit of blanket, which he needed to go sleep, amongst the dressing up clothes. Rented halls rarely came with outdoor spaces for children to enjoy the fresh air, seen as so vital by early nursery school campaigners. Inadequate security, and doors and locks not purpose-built to ensure small children were contained, also had their disadvantages. Mothers in Chichester, West Sussex in the 1980s, were scandalised to discover that one small lad had escaped from the playgroup housed in the local rugby club; he was found wandering down the main road on his own.

The main limitations of playgroups being housed in temporary, rented accommodation, and heavily reliant upon volunteers, were children usually only being able to attend for two to three hours at a time, and then only for two or three times a week. This was of limited use to mothers who wanted to undertake paid work. Mothers in employment continued to have to rely on relations, friends or childminders to look after their young children. From the 1970s onwards, groups of women, predominantly in urban areas, began to seek more comprehensive facilities to care for their children. The first women's liberation conference, held at Ruskin College, Oxford from 27 February to 1 March 1970, provided an impetus for these needs to be included on the national agenda at last. The conference was attended by a number of women with young children for whom childcare was a pressing concern. Many brought their little ones with them to be cared for by groups of men, who supported the conference by organising and running a creche. Cath Hall, whose husband, a sociology lecturer, was one of those volunteering in the creche, later recalled, 'We weren't at that point working women in full employment. We'd had educational opportunities. So, the thing that hit home most with us was about the importance of childcare provision.'[27] Much discussion and debate led the conference to adopt a demand for twenty-four-hour childcare for all children from nought to five, which became one of four key demands made by the British women's liberation movement.[28]

This demand 'proved unrealistic and unworkable.'[29] Something acknowledged at the time and in retrospect. Cath Hall, who became involved in the Birmingham Women's Liberation Playgroup in the seventies explained,

> Of course it's a ridiculous demand, twenty four hour childcare, but we certainly did believe in the importance of proper provision of childcare and spent a lot of time talking about that and working on that, and setting up first – what we called the baby playgroups and then a playgroup, which became the Women's Liberation Playgroup, which survived for many, many years and moved from one premises to another.[30]

She remembers that the Birmingham group 'was all very organised' with 'a regular rota. I think we probably did it three days a week and we did it for a long morning including lunch so that they had their lunch and we had our lunch.'[31] There was a paid helper and volunteers, including the fathers who all took turns in helping out. Those involved met regularly, and running the playgroup became 'a very sociable activity. We all became very close friends.'[32] The political commitment of those running the group fed through to the creation of stories and games, which sought to challenge male and female stereotypes; they rewrote fairy tales with girls as heroines.

Likewise, in 1977, a group of local women organised a drop-in playgroup in Harmony Hall, Walthamstow, London, and following 'lots of fun, laughter and hard work a unique childcare project was born'.[33] The First Neighbourhood Co-operative Nursery opened on Verulam Avenue, London, in 1986. It was run by parents and paid staff, 'who worked together to provide high quality childcare and education for their children.'[34] The co-operative was based on feminist principles and created a unique experience for both parents and children. Alternatively, the Kingsway Children's Centre, London which opened in September, 1977 was a trade union initiative. It was organised by the staff of a number of local firms. Employers covered two thirds of the fees for children who attended; their parents paid the remaining one third. At the time of its opening, Angela Phillips, writing for the feminist magazine *Spare Rib* argued: 'Kingsway proves that it is economically possible for even small firms to provide childcare facilities. It should provide a useful example for all those of us trying to negotiate with employers for creches.'[35]

Co-operative nurseries were scarce and there were few enlightened employers like those in Kingsway. Furthermore, cash-strapped local authorities closed some already existing nurseries. South Oxford nursery was shut down, despite an occupation by irate mothers. Local members of the County Council Education Committee commented that there should be 'no baby minding on the rates.'[36] In this, they echoed the views of the Conservative Party Social Services spokesperson, that mothers were the best people to look after young children and mothers should stay at home full-time to do so.[37] It required more organised and formal structures to challenge government and public opinion. In 1986, the Daycare Trust was established, with a mission to 'secure access to high quality affordable childcare for all children in Great Britain, where and when they and their parents want and need it, at a price their parents can afford.'[38] The trust was a product of the feminist movement, and it acknowledged that many women wanted both a family and a working life. The Daycare Trust led the way in campaigning for nurseries to be set up in workplaces, colleges and universities, and for better professional training for nursery staff. Despite their efforts, childcare was still considered a private matter in 1990, at which time private providers offered just 59,000 nursery places. They were usually expensive and scattered unevenly across the country.

An inquiry set up into the quality of the educational experience offered to 3 and 4-year-olds was chaired by Angela Rumbold MP. Known as the Rumbold Report, and published in September 1990, it pointed the way towards more formal, regulated and uniform provision. Stating 'while diversity of provision can be healthy, there must be better local co-ordination of services, with central government setting a national framework within which local development could take place.'[39] The inquiry also pointed out that the demand for education and childcare for the under-fives far outstripped the supply of places, and suggested childcare and education were competing aims, although there was an overlap between them.[40] In 1996, the Conservative government introduced a nursery education voucher scheme to fund part-time pre-school education for four-year-olds. The Labour Government, which took office in 1997, pledged to go further and to provide a nursery place for every three and four-year-old whose parents wanted them to have one. This resulted in five two-and-a-half hour sessions a week (12.5 hours) for 33 weeks of the year, free for all four-year-olds. The provision was later stretched to 38 weeks a year, the equivalent of 15 hours a week, and then extended to all three-year-olds. There were just 100,000 places in nurseries and creches in 1997; twenty years later there were 1.7 million.[41]

By the end of the twentieth century, attitudes to childcare, pre-school education and the expectation that young children should spend almost all of their time with their mothers were shifting. The benefits of safe, nurturing spaces for children to play outside their home was accepted. Local authorities, libraries, religious groups and mothers themselves, organised mother and toddler groups. Families were much smaller than they had been at the beginning of the century, and more mothers wanted or needed to work. So, provision for the under-fives in nurseries and playgroups expanded, beginning at last to meet the aims of the campaign Belle Tutaev had initiated thirty years earlier. Nurseries and playgroups, though much more common, were still, of course, a long way from the demands of the 1970 Women's Liberation Conference. Indeed, for most working mothers, childcare still relies on ad hoc arrangements with relatives and childminders; full-time nursery care is for most, prohibitively expensive.

Chapter 8

Avoiding Unwanted Pregnancy for the Young (1964)

In the 1960s the first Brook Advisory Centre opened, providing birth control advice to young, unmarried women. Its founder, Helen Brook (1907 – 1997), was a mother of three children, and an artist – just one of many women, who, from the 1920s onwards, actively campaigned for women to have access to reliable birth control. Nevertheless, in 1980, the Brent Women's Centre, when explaining why and how they had set up a ten-week course on women and health, stated their belief: 'women are always on the receiving end of male-dominated health care, for period problems, birth control, pregnancy, childbirth, menopause and depression.'[1] Their course included sessions on issues such as: contraception, abortion and sexuality, because these were fundamental for women's health and wellbeing. Throughout the twentieth century, campaigners had faced an uphill battle as they sought to ensure that all women had access to reliable contraception and safe abortion. When discussing topics and practices which were not considered respectable, they often had to contend with prejudice and moralising, particularly when, like Helen Brook, they sought to acknowledge and address the issue of young women's sexuality.

The lives of many married women in the nineteenth century were punctuated by multiple pregnancies, some ending in miscarriage, others in a new addition to their every-growing families. Mechanical methods of contraception were neither affordable, particularly reliable, nor widely available, although rubber condoms made their appearance in the mid-1850s and spermicidal suppositories followed in 1885. The withdrawal method of contraception (coitus interruptus) was the most common method of preventing pregnancy; it had been promoted in sex manuals published from the 1820s and was still widely practised in mid-twentieth century Britain. It however relies upon male cooperation. In the twentieth century, the contraceptive cap, spermicides, the safe period or abstinence, were also utilised by some women, with or without their partner's consent. Maggy Fryett, who was in her eighties when she talked to Mary Chamberlain in the 1970s, explained: 'I had three children. And I didn't want no more. My mother had fourteen children and I didn't want that.

So I stayed up mending, my husband would be asleep when I come to bed. That were simple weren't it?'[2] For some women abstinence was not an option: assumptions that women were available for men's pleasure, fear of physical abuse if they resisted their husband's advances, or concern their husbands would find their pleasures elsewhere, meant that a number of women risked the health and financial implications of multiple pregnancies.

Understanding how to prevent unwanted pregnancy and how to access birth control, however crude and unreliable, was more readily available to wealthier women, as was the accurate information about human reproduction. Middle-class parents were able to afford to use some of the limited publications available to educate their children about sex in the nineteenth century, and by the early twentieth century, schools occasionally included a smattering of sex education in lessons for girls. Badged as 'hygiene', these encouraged youngsters to adhere to principles of 'self-reverence, self-control and true modesty.'[3] Alternatively, organisations such as the Social Purity League and the Girls Friendly Society sought to address the perceived absence of moral guidance for working-class girls by strongly encouraging sexual abstinence. Given the haphazard approaches to sex education, it is hardly surprising that some young women understood little of the physical side of married life when they walked down the aisle, while many others were already pregnant.

In 1877, Annie Besant and Charles Bradlaugh published *The Fruits of Philosophy*, subtitled 'An Essay on the Population'. The subsequent legal case suggested that information about birth control was obscene and should not be made readily available to the population. For Annie Besant, involvement in the case had personal consequences: she lost the custody of her daughter because of her involvement in the promotion of contraception. The Malthusian League was set up in response to the Besant and Bradlaugh case, and was informed by the ideas of the economist, Thomas Malthus (1766–1834). He had argued that the population growth outstripped the earth's ability to produce an adequate food supply. The Malthusian League advocated contraception as a way to prevent overpopulation and poverty, and argued that families of all social class should have only two children. In 1913, the league published a pamphlet titled, *Hygienic Methods of Family Limitations*, which provided contraception advice to married couples. Family limitation was becoming more acceptable by this time, as Pat Thane has pointed out, 'between the 1770s and the mid nineteenth century the average number of children born per woman was around six. From the 1870s the number fell gradually to an average of two by the 1930s.'[4] Many factors contributed to these changes, including that women getting married a little older reduced their active childbearing years. It was also increasingly understood, the health of the mother and her children could be enhanced by having a smaller family. Couples began to see that having fewer children would improve their standard of living and to obtain greater economic security.

In the 1920s, birth control campaigners established clinics for working class women in urban areas. The most well-known of these campaigners was Marie Stoppes (1880 – 1958), who set up the very first clinic in Holloway, then a working-class district of London. She became founder and president of the Society for Constructive Birth Control and set up further clinics in conurbations such as Manchester and Salford; she also organised mobile clinics to visit other areas. The Malthusian League clinic opened The Walworth Women's Welfare Centre at 153a East Street, Walworth on 9 November 1921, the first clinic to provide advice from a medical doctor. Numerous women helped at the clinics, interviewing women about their circumstances before they saw a doctor. Many of the attendees were nervous and anxious and had been referred by their GPs, midwives or health visitors. Others heard about the clinics from friends or relatives, and most could not afford to pay for the service. Women campaigners had to organise fundraising activities or gave money to cover the financial costs of running the clinics, which included purchasing or renting buildings, the fees doctors were paid to cover sessions, and medical supplies.

In 1930, the National Birth Control Council (NBCC) was set up. It involved doctors and campaigners such as, Marie Stoppes, Eva Hubback, Dr Helena Wright and Margery Spring Rice, and it was chaired by Lady Denman, who was also Chair of the National Federation of Women's Institutes. The organisation stipulated that their aim was 'that married people may space or limit their families and thus mitigate the evils of ill health and poverty.'[5] They sought to have clinics set up in cities across the country, to publicise birth control, to make it more respectable, and enable midwives and nurses to provide birth control advice in maternity and infant welfare clinics. Support and opposition to such proposals came from all quarters: the following year (1931), the Church of England publicly declared its moral objection to the use of contraception. The motivations of the campaigning women who sought to provide working-class women with the means to achieve a smaller family were varied. Some were concerned about the deterioration of race and held objectionable views that the British nation was being damaged by indiscriminate breeding amongst the working classes. Many original members of the NBCC, such as Eva Hubback and Marie Stoppes, were eugenicists, aiming to improve the genetic quality of the population. The links between the NBCC and Eugenics are underlined when the group, which initially met in Lady Denman's Mayfair house, moved its base into the Eugenics Society's headquarters at Ecclestone Square, London.

The political views of campaigners like Marie Stopes were exemplified by her clinic, which supplied rubber caps to be placed over the cervix, acting as a barrier to sperm entering the uterus. These were emblazoned with Marie's trademark RACIAL, or PRORACE – which is deeply unpalatable to contemporary readers.[6] She however remained in the NBCC for only three years, and by the 1930s her behavior seemed increasingly erratic. Her views particularly in relation to eugenics became more extreme; she apparently objected to her prospective daughter-in-law because she wore glasses. Eugenics was a complex and varied movement, with supporters from across the political spectrum and included social reformers such as the economist, John Maynard Keynes, and William Beveridge, who is seen as the founder of the Welfare State in Britain. Some 'believed people inherited mental illness, criminal tendencies and even poverty and that these conditions could be bred out of the gene pool.'[7] Feminist and leading birth control campaigner, Eva Hubback, wrote in *The Woman's Leader*, that sterilisation was the only method of birth control for that 'section of the population too degraded mentally, morally and physically' to be able to use contraception methods. This group was producing 'a far larger number of children than are the classes where offspring inherit qualities of value to the nation'.[8] Many birth control campaigners did promote voluntary sterilisation, a reflection of the inadequacy and unreliability of methods of birth control available, and of the difficulties that women living in substandard housing encountered with fitting and caring for the contraceptive cap.

The prime motivation of most birth control campaigners seems to have been their deep commitment to help working-class women escape the financial and physical consequences of multiple pregnancies. They argued that smaller, more spaced-out families, were beneficial to the health of both mothers and their children, whilst unplanned pregnancies led to maternal mortality for those women who already had underlying health problems. As Lady Denman, chair of the NBCC explained to the *Daily Mirror:*

> The aim of those who advocate birth control is the proper spacing of families so that every child born shall have a chance of health and happiness...
>
> Recent cases at birth control clinics include a woman who had fourteen children in eleven years, another with tuberculosis who had four children under four, another who had thirteen children of which only four were living, a girl of twenty-four who had seven, six of whom were alive, and a woman who had six children – and both she and the children had tuberculosis.[9]

Mary Barbour, Scottish political activist, local councillor, bailie, magistrate and leader of the Rent Strikes on Clydeside. (*The Vote 1924-12-12*)

Mary Macarthur, trade unionist and parliamentary candidate in 1918. (*Women's Library, LSE, London*)

Helen Crawfurd, secretary of the GWHA and peace activist. (*Women's Library, LSE, London*)

Officers and members of the National Union of Societies to Equal Citizenship after Royal Assent to the Equal Franchise Act, on 2 July 1928. The group includes Millicent Garrett Fawcett, Ray Strachey, Philippa Fawcett, Agnes Garrett, Chrystal Macmillan, Miss Macadam, Catherine Marshal, Miss Courtney, Miss Ward. (*Women's Library, LSE, London*)

Women's Freedom League's *Victory Breakfast* celebrating enfranchisement of all women over twenty-one. Hotel Cecil, London on 5 July 1928. (*Women's Library, LSE, London*)

Chidham WI meet at Cobnor Lane in West Sussex in the 1920s. (*Women's Library, LSE, London*)

Members of the National Federation of Women's Institutes (NFWI) Executive Committee and others, 1937. (*Women's Library, LSE, London*)

Radcliffe Hall C 1930s. (*Wikimedia Commons*)

National Birthday Trust Fund Flags for 'Help our Mothers' appeal, 1930. (*Wellcome Collection*)

Maggie Wintringham and Nancy Astor, the first women to sit as MPs and campaigners for women on a number of issues including equal pay in 1922. (*Women's Library, LSE, London*)

Ray Strachey, campaigner for equal pay. suffrage campaigner, and author of *The Cause*, a history of Suffrage. (*Women's Library, LSE, London*)

Group of Lady Margaret Hall students, 1879. (*Women's Library, LSE, London*)

Group of Newnham students with Anne Clough, c.1880. (*Women's Library, LSE, London*)

A birth control clinic in a caravan, with nurse. (*Wellcome Collection*)

Racial Synthetic sponge, London, England, 1940–1960. (*Science Museum, London*)

Rubber vault cap, London, England, 1915–1925. (*Science Museum, London*)

Rubber vault cap, London, England, 1915–1925. (*Science Museum, London*)

Lady Denman, Chair of the National Birth Control Council and the National Federation of Women's Institutes (NFWI), in uniform of the Women's Branch of the Board of Agriculture. (*Women's Library, LSE, London*)

Outwrite
women's newspaper

SSN 0265 8429

ISSUE 65, MAY '88

50p

FAWCETT LIBRARY
-9 MAY 1988

Outake

The Dykes go marching on!

Clause 27, 28, 29 and then 28 again, is set to become Section 28 at the end of May when the Local Government Act comes into effect. On the 30th April, over 50,000 people marched through London, ending a month of protest. See pages 8 and 9 for more actions against the Clause.

Outwrite Women's Newspaper – an example of women's self-publishing in the 1970s and 1980s. (*Women's Library, LSE, London*)

lesbians rule - OK?

I WANNA BE A LESBIAN-OK?

```
*************************************************************************
* WELCOME to the first ever "LESBIANS RULE - OK?". This new Women's Group magazine *
* isn't meant to replace the Gay Alliance Newsletter, just to do things that the G.A. *
* Newsletter doesn't. Things like provide a place where gay women in Manchester can *
* write things and express their opinions, without being bound in any way by any of *
* the other groups in Manchester. It's sent free to all Women's Group members. The *
* cast list of people helping to put together this first issue is on the last sheet. *
* But if there's going to be a number 2, all the people who promised to help with this *
* one in some way had better get themselves along to the next meeting to produce it. *
* This will be on SATURDAY JANUARY 9TH 1977 in the FRIENDS' MEETING HOUSE. And so *
* - start writing now! Don't forget - ANYTHING about being gay and a woman: articles, *
* news, views, opinions, jokes and cartoons (and anything else you can think of). *
* *
* P.S. We particularly need some women who can TYPE to come to this meeting. *
*************************************************************************
```

manchester women's group newsletter no 1

Manchester Women's Group Newsletter - an example of women's self-publishing in the 1970s and 1980s.

Eleanor Rathbone campaigning in 1922. (*Women's Library, LSE, London*)

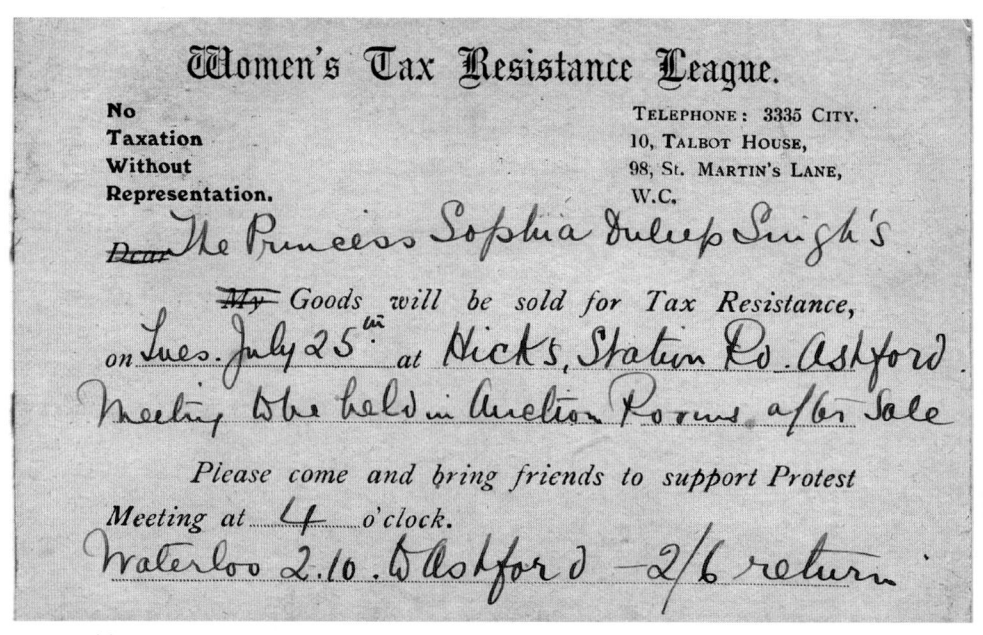

Women's Tax Resistance League – the protest against Sophia Sale of Duleep Singh's goods in lieu of tax. (*Women's Library, LSE, London*)

Black Women for Wages for Housework

King's Cross Women's Centre, 71 Tonbridge St., London WC1   tel. 01-837-7509
Mail to P.O. Box 287, London NW6 5QU

TRINIDAD - LONDON - VIENNA: COUNTING WOMEN'S UNWAGED WORK IN THE GNP

You are invited to a PRESS RECEPTION for Bernadette Rambarand and Clotil Walcott on *Monday, 19 February, 5 pm at the King's Cross Women's Centre.*

Ms Rambarand and Ms Walcott will be in London on their way from Trinidad & Tobago to the **Extended Session of the United Nations Commission on the Status of Women** in Vienna, Austria. Before the Commission meeting they will speak in two workshops at NGO Consultation 1990: **Making the Forward Looking Strategies Work** - a conference organized by non-governmental organizations (NGOs) affiliated to the United Nations. Both the Commission and the Consultation will be tackling the question of how to speed up implementation of Forward Looking Strategies, the final decision document of the UN Decade for Women, agreed by governments - including the UK.

Ms Rambarand's and Ms Walcott's contributions to these meetings will focus on Forward Looking Strategies Paragraph 120 - which calls for women's *unwaged* work in the home, on the land and in the community, to be counted in the GNP of every country. Both women have a long track record of campaigning on this issue, both in the West Indies and in Britain. Vienna will be an opportunity for them to share their personal experience and their expertise as community organizers among unwaged, low-income and non-professional women, with NGOs and government delegations from the industrialized countries of Western and Eastern Europe, and from the Third World. In particular, their participation will bring a crucial message from the Black and Third World grassroots to the Commission's discussions about the negative effects on women of the present international economic situation.

Ms Rambarand is a mother of three grown-up sons, and worked as a nurse in Britain for many years before returning to Trinidad. In 1976 she appeared in the BBC television film "All Work and No Pay". She also contributed her experience as a Black nurse in the NHS to the book *All Work and No Pay.*

Ms Walcott is the founder of the National Union of Domestic Employees (NUDE), which brings together domestic workers and housewives, and a member of International Black Women for Wages for Housework. A mother of five and a grandmother, until her recent retirement Ms Walcott worked at Cannings multinational poultry processing factory. As a trade union organizer she defended the interests of women workers, impressing on the company, union and government alike their responsibilities to women who do a double day of waged work outside the home and unwaged work in the home.

BWWFH particularly welcome the example of Afro-Asian unity shown by Ms Rambarand and Ms Walcott working together to get women's enormous unwaged workload recognized.

Housewives in Dialogue, the educational charity which runs the King's Cross Women's Centre and has consultative status with the United Nations Economic and Social Council, did the fundraising to enable Ms Rambarand and Ms Walcott to go to Vienna. HinD will lead two workshops at the NGO Consultation: *Counting Women's Work in the GNP* and *Crossing the Divides of Race, Nation and Poverty: Counting Women's Work in Immigration.*

Ms Rambarand and Ms Walcott are available for interviews, and to speak to community groups, and can be contacted at the King's Cross Women's Centre.

14 February 1990

Black Women For Wages For Housework news-sheet. (*Women's Library, LSE, London*)

Gertrude Paul's blue plaque.
(*Leeds Archive Trust*)

GERTRUDE MARETTA PAUL
Born in St Kitts, she came to England in 1956. She taught at Cowper Street School and in 1976 she was appointed here (then called Elmhurst Middle School) as the city's first black head teacher. She was one of the founders of the West Indian Carnival and a Commissioner for Racial Equality.
1934–1992

Claudia Jones, black women's activist.
(*Wikimedia Commons*)

Chrystal Macmillan, early graduate, suffrage and peace campaigner. (*Women's Library, LSE, London*)

Embracing the base, Greenham Common December 1982, near to Greenham, West Berkshire, Great Britain. (*Wikimedia Commons*)

British WILPF members arriving in Geneva with their Disarmament petition, 1932. (*Women's Library, LSE, London*)

Spice girls in Toronto Ontario 2008. (*Wikimedia Commons*)

In her speeches, Lady Denman frequently drew attention to the detrimental cost of paying privately to see a birth control doctor; one of the well-known experts in the field was Dr Helena Wright, who had a lucrative private practice in London.[10] Lady Denman also described how working-class women, unable to afford birth control 'in order to remove unwanted children from the world before birth adopted illegal practices.'[11] She was not alone in linking the campaigns for birth control and abortion, when she suggested that contraception could reduce illegal and dangerous abortions. Many of the campaigners and volunteer workers who staffed the clinics also supported the Abortion Reform Society, set up in 1936.[12] Women often kept their support for both campaigns quiet. As Dora Russell, who was one of the founders of the Workers' Birth Control Group in 1924, said, 'We were trying to get birth control on the way and we didn't want a disturbance to our work.'[13]

The nineteenth century had seen an increasingly punitive approach taken by the British legal system towards women who sought to abort an unwanted foetus. Prior to 1837, terminating a pregnancy before the quickening – that is, when a mother first felt her baby move – was not illegal. However, the 1868 Offences Against the Person Act made women liable for prosecution for procuring an unlawful abortion and they were potentially given a sentence of life imprisonment. There was some scope for medical practitioners to undertake an abortion, perhaps to save the life or mental stability of the mother. How widespread these medical abortions actually were, is open to question, and anxious doctors often sought a second opinion before performing the procedure. Nevertheless, Gynaecologist Dugald Baird, for example, was understood to perform social abortions in Aberdeen for disadvantaged women.

In 1929, Stella Browne gave a lecture titled 'The Right to Abortion' at the World Sexual Reform Congress in London. Born in Canada in 1880, Stella Browne campaigned for women's suffrage, birth control, divorce reform, socialism and pacifism, but is most well known for her work as one of the founders and proponents of the Abortion Reform Society. In feminist circles her belief that women had the absolute right to decide whether or not they wanted to bear a child, marked her out as well ahead of her time. When Stella Browne went before the parliamentary committee set up to explore some relaxation of the abortion laws, she said, 'I have…the knowledge in my own person that, if abortion were necessarily fatal or injurious, I should not now be here before you.' [14] By admitting, as a single woman, that she had had illegal abortions, she not only shocked her audience, but also sacrificed her social position and respectability for the campaign she believed in.

The illegality and unreliability of the wide variety of actions undertaken to terminate pregnancies and the significant number of pregnancies which spontaneously aborted, make it both controversial and difficult to judge how common abortion was in the first half of the twentieth century. Anecdotal evidence from memories and oral histories suggests it was commonplace. One working-class mother, facing another pregnancy she could ill afford in 1915, explained she had taken 'strong concoctions to purge me of the little life that might be mine. They failed as such things generally do and a third baby came'.[15] Estimates have suggested that there were between 37,000 and 60,000 illegal abortions per year; many of which led to serious illness and some to fatalities.[16] Many feminists and doctors were horrified by the consequences of backstreet abortions and supported the gynecologist, Aleck Bourne, when he performed an abortion to preserve the mental health of a fourteen-year-old girl in 1938. His caution over the case involved observing the girl, who had been gang raped, for two weeks before the termination took place. Immediately after the operation, he went to his local police station and reported his actions. His subsequent trial was closely followed by campaigners across the country, to whom he was a real hero. When a jury failed to convict him, important case law was established, and increasing numbers of women who knew the right doctors and could pay them, began to have 'legal' abortions.

The NBCC was renamed the Family Planning Association (FPA) in 1939, but its campaigning work was dramatically curtailed during the Second World War. It began to work with the newly formed National Health Service in the late nineteen forties. In Sheffield, Dr Libby Wilson recalls that the 'local branch of the Family Planning Association was run by a group of highly committed Non- Conformist and Quaker ladies, who, against the political correctness of the time were prepared to champion the cause of birth control, especially for the mothers of the poor.'[17] Nevertheless, unwanted pregnancies continued to be a key part of many women's lives due to the unreliability of the contraceptive methods that were readily available, as Dr Libby Wilson discovered when she 'conceived and carried to term three children in under two years' – the third, despite her husband using a condom alongside her use of the Dutch cap.[18]

To those struggling with mechanical means of birth control, condoms and caps, spermicides and safe periods, the introduction of what quickly became known simply as 'The Pill' was the greatest scientific invention of the twentieth century. This new chemical contraceptive, a combination of the hormones, progestogen and oestrogen, became available on the National Health Service in Britain in 1961. It offered women reliable control over their fertility, as the novelist Margaret Drabble, recalled:

By the time the Pill was available I already had three children; I think I would have had a child a year if I hadn't started taking it. So, yes, it made a very considerable difference to one's life. You were able to make a choice, you were able to look after yourself, and I was pleased to do so.[19]

The introduction of the pill contributed to the mythical status that surround the so-called swinging sixties. For many women, married or single, the pill offered to reduce the association between sex and anxiety about pregnancy, something many found liberating. It enabled women to combine careers, education and small families with a sex life.

Historians, however, question how liberal attitudes in this decade really were. The government eased legal restraints on personal behavior, and suicide and homosexuality were decriminalised.[20] The death penalty was also abolished, and there was a relaxation of the laws on gambling, alongside divorce reform, introducing divorce by mutual consent, or after 5 years without the consent of an ex-partner. Nevertheless, Geoff Gorer's survey of sex and marriage in England, which was published in 1971, suggested that a double standard still continued in attitudes to men's and women's sexuality.[21] At the beginning of the decade, he proposed, people's morals were more conservative than their behaviour and that by 1970, the position had reversed. It was married women who made up the vast majority of the one million women who took the pill in the 1960s. It was their lives that the new drug changed and the rise in the birth rate, seen in the 1950s, was 'again curtailed'.[22] But concerns over the side effects of the new wonder drug were expressed by some women, and Barbara Seaman published *The Doctors Case Against the Pill* in 1969, drawing attention to the risk of blood clots, heart attack, stroke, depression, weight gain and loss of libido for those taking the pill. However, as Jane, a married woman who went on the pill in the 1960s after having had two children and a late miscarriage within three years, recalled: 'It changed my life... I felt in control, I felt free, if I had known then what know now about how dangerous it is I don't think I would have cared.'[23]

This new contraceptive did offer the possibility that women could engage in recreational sex on the same terms as men and not necessarily within long-term relationships. This caused alarm amongst some religious groups and those who wanted women's sexual activity limited to within marriage, as well as to those who remained opposed to contraception in any circumstances. They questioned the morality of separating sexuality and procreation, whether in marriage or not, and feared that the widespread availability of the pill would lead to promiscuity. In 1968, Pope Paul VI published *Humanae Vitae*, a letter to the millions of Catholics across the world, which started from the assumption that, 'The transmission of human life is a most serious role in which married people collaborate freely and responsibly with God the Creator. It has always been a source of great joy to them, even though it sometimes entails many difficulties and hardships.'[24] *Humanae Vitae* promoted chastity and self-discipline, and concluded that Catholics should not use any artificial form of birth control, including the pill, even if they were married – a controversial position which Pope Paul's successors have maintained ever since.

For young women, as the fashion designer, Mary Quant recalled, the pill: 'was hellishly difficult to get hold of at first. There was a lot of pretending one was married when one went to the doctor, and a minor disadvantage was that the early pills made one put on a couple of pounds. But that was nothing! Who cared? The other forms of contraception were so hellish.'[25] Pat Thane has pointed out, sex 'appears to have been a normal part of the courtship for many over the past 250 years…There is clear official evidence of this from the late 1930s. It was not an innovation of the 1960s'.[26] Yet there was constant concern, even what might be termed an obsession, around the perceived promiscuity of young people and this restricted them obtaining access to information or advice about sex and contraception. Young girls were unwilling to ask their family doctor for contraceptive advice, fearing that their sex lives might be discussed with their parents. They turned to the anonymity of FPA clinics, with varying degree of success.

In 1952, the Family Planning Association AGM, following advice from the Medical sub-committee, approved the provision of contraception advice to those about to be married. In the 1960s, FPA official policy continued to be that birth control advice should only be given to the married or to those within 4–8 weeks of their wedding. In 1964, a packed AGM discussed giving information on contraceptive techniques to the unmarried at the doctor's discretion. After a heated debate, it was agreed to refer the unmarried seeking advice to Youth Advisory Centres, the formation of which, the FPA would encourage. The policy was shaped by many in the higher echelons of the FPA, such as the chair from 1955–1966, Margaret Pyke, who wanted to present the FPA and contraception as respectable. At a personal level, many supported widespread availability of contraception to all women, but they had experienced first-hand the opposition and criticism that the organisation faced in its early years and knew how fragile the progress they had made was.

Whatever the views of religious groups or their parents, many young girls circumnavigated the FPA policies and claimed to be engaged. Other teenagers loaned each other cheap Woolworths wedding rings and pretended to be married to obtain a coveted prescription to the pill and freedom from unwanted pregnancy. The opening of Brook Advisory Clinics changed the need for this subterfuge. Helen Brook had joined the FPA in the late 1940s, becoming first an interviewer at the Islington Clinic and then for 12 years, its chairman. After the death of Marie Stopes in 1958, she took on the role of organiser of the Marie Stopes Clinic at Whitfield Street. As Stopes and her clinics had not been part of the FPA, she was not restrained by their policies. So, by 1962, she began introducing advice sessions for unmarried women. Brook was a pragmatist, aware that sexual attitudes and practices were changing. She felt 'shock and moral attitudes are not what is needed, but a recognition of the struggle the girl is going through.'[27] The Board of the Marie Stopes organisation quickly decided it was preferable to separate their provision for the married from that of the young, so with an anonymous donation of £5,000 for three years, the Brook Advisory Centres were born. The first clinic opened in London in July 1964, with other clinics set up in Cambridge and Birmingham in 1966; Bristol and Edinburgh followed in 1968. By then, the 1967 Family Planning Act allowed, but did not compel, local authorities to provide birth control to unmarried women.

Brook Centres provided services for 16–25-year-olds with the stated aims of 'the prevention and mitigation of the suffering caused by unwanted pregnancy and illegal abortion by educating young persons in matter of sex and contraception and developing among them a sense of responsibility in regard to sexual behaviours.'[28] There were varied reasons women campaigned to provide clinics for the young people, with some seeking to reduce the number of illegal abortions and 'illegitimate' births, and to inculcate a sense of sexual responsibility in the young. An obituary of Helen Brook explained:

> Brook was motivated by fervent belief that children should be born to mothers who wanted them and could care for them. She also believed that women should enjoy equality with men and that to achieve this they needed to be able to avoid unwanted pregnancy. In an interview to mark her 79th birthday she explained: "I felt that, until women were free of the fear of unwanted pregnancy, they would not be able to take up the equal opportunity of work."[29]

Helen Brook wanted the centres to be staffed by 'non-moralising mother-figure doctors'[30] and for those who worked in the clinics, to take a non-judgement approach to young people's sexuality, albeit within an expectation of heterosexual monogamy. Consequently, as Caroline Rusterholz has pointed out, the work in many of the Brook Advisory Centres, as in the early family planning clinics, required a significant amount of emotional labour.[31] In the Birmingham Clinic every client was interviewed by a social worker, and it was hoped their approach, listening and building a trusting relationship, helped to move away from the doctor-patient hierarchies.

Some girls were actually referred to the clinics by social workers, concerned by rising illegitimate rates. Pat Thane has pointed out that even in the nineteenth century, 20% of first births were illegitimate and over half of all first births were probably conceived outside marriage. However, in the 1960s, the number of illegitimate births was rising rapidly and by the 1980s, one third of all births in England and Wales occurred outside marriage. It also meant that whatever Helen Brook's intentions, a whiff of the eugenics ethos of the early birth control movement was still around alongside a re-occurring moral panic about working-class girls' sexuality.[32] The working-class girls and especially Irish and West Indian immigrants who came to the clinics, were often seen as needing to be educated to become responsible. Concern was also growing about different attitudes expressed towards the increasing number of white, middle and upper-class girls unable to marry for financial reasons.

A number of youth advisory centres, separate from, but with similar motivations and approaches to the Brook clinics, were also formed. Dr Libby Wilson was amongst those who campaigned for and organised the 408 Clinic in Sheffield, which opened in September 1966, accompanied by some unexpected but very welcome publicity. Splashed across the front of the *Sheffield Telegraph* was the headline 'Bishop condemns sex clinic'.[33] The media interest continued with coverage on local radio and television and included an interview with an unmarried woman who was expecting her sixth child, who refrained from explaining that she was visiting the clinic to check if she had caught 'a dose' from one of her clients. Reflecting on the records she had kept many years later, Dr Libby Wilson noted:

> Half of the young women were engaged and a further quarter regarded themselves as 'going steady'. Most of the remainder were in relationships where one or other partner was married, separated or divorced. Many were students and a few came from wealthy or deprived backgrounds.... It soon became obvious that many of them were stressed, not only about their need for contraception but also by the circumstances of their lives and their relationships.[34]

Some women came to see Dr Wilson too late, including a 15-year-old girl who had been left in the care of her eighteen-year-old sister while her parents went on holiday to the Bahamas for six weeks. On examination, it turned out she was pregnant: 'She had conceived without penetration which was really the most appalling bad luck but not without precedent.'[35]

By the 1960s, many young women understood that those with sufficient funds could access abortions in private clinics. Alternatively, working-class girls had to rely on a very few sympathetic doctors, or on what were termed 'backstreet abortions' – a procedure which carried significant risk of damage to their insides or even death. Women campaigners once again sought to publicise the problems of this, in books such as Nell Dunn's collection of short stories *Up the Junction* (1963). This portrayal of working-class life in Battersea and Clapham, which was later made into a television play, included protagonist, Rube's, visit to an abortionist. The 1965 television documentary *A Law for the Rich* (1965) contrasted the experience of wealthier women able to see a private doctor or clinic for an abortion, with the experiences of a working-class married woman with 10 children, who felt she would go mad if she had another child. She could not afford the £20 (the equivalent of £432 in 2022) for an illegal abortion. With approximately 35 women a year dying as a consequence of illegal abortions, a private members bill was introduced in parliament in 1967 to legalise abortion. The Labour government eased the passage of the bill, whilst keeping their distance from it to avoid antagonising any of their voters who were Catholic.

The 1967 Act legalised abortion during the first 24 weeks of pregnancy, when authorised by two doctors. Grounds for an abortion included risk to the physical or mental health of the pregnant woman or her family. It did not apply to Northern Ireland, nor offer abortion on demand and access to safe abortions was geographically varied. Women continued to seek assistance from private organisations and charities such as the British Pregnancy Advisory Service. For feminists, access to abortion and birth control was a fundamental right for women; they felt that no woman should be forced into motherhood. The 1970s women's liberation movement adopted the slogan 'A Woman's Right to Choose', and thereby side-lined debates about the circumstances around which women made choices about continuing a pregnancy, including poverty, abusive relationships, health issues, age and limited childcare provision.

Family planning clinics finally began to prescribe the pill to single women again in the late 1960s and early 1970s, and in 1974, the government finally made contraception free to all. Nevertheless, the FPA Clinic in Chichester in West Sussex continued to call everyone Mrs throughout the 1970s, whether or not they wore a wedding ring, even when they were teenagers. Those unable to access a clinic claimed that they needed the pill to alleviate painful, heavy and irregular periods. Nevertheless, many youngsters in the 1960s and 1970s continued to rely upon practices such as having sex standing up, or even girls douching their vaginas with Coca-Cola, in a vain attempt to prevent pregnancy. Whilst there was some agreement amongst campaigners that youngsters needed more reliable advice and information – who should do it, how and what it should include – remained a topic of debate.

As early as 1944, the National Union of Teachers (NUT) committed itself to support a 'healthy, frank climate in the discussion of sex' but oral histories suggest that this is not what occurred in the post-war era.[36] Embarrassed and ill-equipped teachers with reticence to actually mention or describe sexual intercourse, instead resorted to euphemisms and discussion of the reproductive habits of animals, leaving pupils confused and misinformed. Brook Clinics, girls' magazines' authors, educationalists, social and welfare workers, all campaigned for more accurate, sex education for youngsters.[37] Films, books, problem pages in girls' magazines and the Brook Clinics, all tried to give supportive information to the young. The Marriage Guidance organisation 'offered small informal discussion groups in schools and youth clubs for young people from about thirteen years of age upwards' in the 1960s.[38] They provided the facts of life to youngsters but took a very clear line: sex was 'placed firmly within a loving relationship, preferably within marriage, but at the very least with someone you knew well and to whom you were committed.'[39]

Others sought to place an emphasis on 'informative', rather than 'morals' or 'values'. In 1978, Jane Cousins' unpatronising book, *Make it Happy*, was published by the feminist publishing house, Virago. It aimed to inform teenagers of 'what sex is all about', and from the first page, acknowledged that 'sex is a natural part of our lives whatever our age.'[40] The book was criticised for its apparently non-judgemental approach to what were considered taboo subjects, including bestiality and voyeurism. It had been written in consultation with youngsters, and received praise for its straightforward, no-nonsense discussion of topics such as contraception, puberty and homosexuality. Such freely available down-to-earth sex education was not welcomed by everyone. Those who did not want youngsters to engage in sex before marriage regarded the frank discussion of sexual matters as pornographic and responded to the book with horror.

The appropriate age for girls to be given the pill was also surrounded by controversy. In the 1980s, the Catholic campaigner, Victoria Gillick, herself a mother of ten children, fought a long and unsuccessful campaign to prevent teenagers under 16 being prescribed the pill without their parents' consent. Some GPs were anxious about assisting young girls, whilst others were determined to continue assisting girls in a non-judgmental way, in order to prevent unplanned pregnancies. The Brook Centres and clinics orientated towards youngsters offered safe spaces where teenagers could go for help and advice. Dilys Cossey recalled 'my first visit to Brook was a light hearted one. In the late 80s, when I was at Wimbledon high school. 70% of our school went to Brook (under the pretext of going to the cinema) in order to go on the pill.'[41] Thus, the journalist, Susan Pearce, noted at the end of that decade, that Brooks had: 'done a very good job. It has done a job that nobody else has been doing in quite the same way. Teenage pregnancies have gone down since the Brook opened.'[42]

Chapter 9

The Miss World Protest (1970)

On the evening of November 20, 1970, what was referred to affectionately as Women's Lib, 'gate-crashed the public's consciousness in the UK.'[1] As millions of television viewers watched on, a group of feminists caused mayhem, throwing flour bombs at the stage and releasing clockwork mice amongst the audience of the Miss World competition. They were protesting against the objectification of women, and in the years that followed, this sort of direct political action was mimicked by other women who defaced degrading adverts, demonstrated outside porn shops and, in time, ran campaigns against the topless pin-up models on Page 3 of the tabloid newspapers. Such campaigns sought to encourage debate about women's portrayal in the media and to challenge the media's complicity in exploiting women.

Concerns over the way women were expected to dress, and the detrimental impact of their objectification on health and wellbeing, go back to the latter part of the nineteenth century. Restricting tight-fitting corsets which deformed the body, crinolines that were a fire risk, tightly fitting skirts and high heeled shoes preventing ease of movement, were all objects for criticism at various times. In 1881, the Rational Dress Society was formed requiring all women 'to dress comfortably, and beautifully, to seek what conduces to birth, comfort and beauty in our dress as a duty to ourselves and each other.'[2] The selectivity of images of women in society, where and how they are included or excluded from the media, how women are expected or allowed to dress, and ideas of beauty by which women judge themselves, became important areas of campaigning in the last third of the twentieth century. Simultaneously, groups such as the Women in Media Group in the 1970s challenged the discrimination and limited opportunities for women to work in the media industries.

Pornography and saucy images of large busted women were by no means invented in the twentieth century, but new modes of publishing and distribution made them more readily available. The first pin-ups in newspapers appeared in the 1930s and were, as Richard Hoggart has pointed out, an integral part of working-class male culture by the 1950s.[3] Pin-ups and calendars featuring semi-naked women increasingly came to adorn not only the inside of men's lockers and bedrooms, but also many male-dominated workplaces and workshops. A relaxation of censorship in the 1960s saw many of the last vestiges of Victorian middle-class prudery abandoned.[4] In the swinging sixties, culture became more sexually explicit, and there was an explosion of images of scantily clad and supposedly sexually available women in a diverse range of media, including James Bond films and car adverts. *Playboy* magazine went on sale in Britain, and a linked club opened in London, in 1966. On November 17, 1970, *The Sun* newspaper launched its first Page 3 images, making the viewing of pin-ups of semi-naked women part of many family's breakfast routine. It was in the same year, in February, that the first Women's Liberation Conference was held at Ruskin College, Oxford, and the year in which the Miss World Contest was scheduled to be held at the Royal Albert Hall. For some, page 3 images, the Miss World beauty pageant and other media portrayals of women as sex objects, were light-hearted and harmless fun, where the models were liberated, confident women, in control of their sexuality. To others, these portrayals objectified and degraded women.

The origins of the Miss World beauty pageant lay in an international bathing beauty contest organised by Eric Morley as part of the Festival of Britain in 1951. It was apparently intended to add some pizzazz and to spice up the more sedate attractions of the event.[5] Many of the girls who entered the competition wore bikinis, including the 1951 winner, Kiki Hakansson, from Sweden. This recently introduced mode of attire was still regarded as rather daring and risqué, ensuring that the event received significant media coverage. The competition was dubbed Miss World by the press and led to Eric Morley making the pageant an annual event – the Miss World Competition. Women initially took part in beauty pageants in their own country to win a national title, before coming together to compete to be crowned 'the most beautiful woman in the world'. The popularity of the Miss World beauty pageants increased in Britain once the BBC began broadcasting it in 1959. It became one of the most watched shows in their schedule of family viewing and at its peak, was watched by over 18 million British viewers, with a worldwide audience of many millions in over 155 other countries.

The competition gained a veneer of respectability and backing from multinational corporations, by raising money for charity. When the American comedian and movie star, Bob Hope, began his tours of USA troops fighting in the Vietnam War in 1964, the newspapers carried reports of how the reigning Miss World accompanied him to add some glamour. The rising popularity of Miss World did not, however, go uncontested. Criticisms from religious groups resulted in the swimsuit replacing bikinis as the girls' attire. Objectors describing the competition as a 'cattle market' were responded to by the introduction of slightly uncomfortable, staged question-and-answer sessions, with each girl being quizzed about their ambitions and intellectual achievements. There was further controversy surrounding the 1970 London competition: South Africa had decided to send a Miss White South Africa and a Miss Black South Africa. Anti-apartheid campaigners objected and they were both banned from the competition until racial segregation was abolished.

The assumption of the Miss World competition, that women should be judged primarily on their looks, was insulting to many feminists.[6] They sought to challenge the need for women to be beautiful to get noticed, as well as the perceptions of a Disney-style princess as the ideal of womanhood.[7] The Miss World competition's large television audience offered a unique opportunity to stage a protest, which would create impact and reach thousands of women across the country. Sally Alexandra was a student in her twenties with a young daughter at the time, who had been involved with the Women's Liberation Conference at Ruskin College, Oxford and later mused:

> I really don't know where the idea came from – except Miss World, women being judged by their looks and their bodies …. and when we heard it was Bob Hope compering and he'd just come back from Vietnam and we were all anti-Vietnam, or a lot of us were because – particularly those of us involved with the left… – And it was television spectacle, family viewing. So, we knew that to demonstrate against Miss World … if we could disrupt the spectacle, as we called it, the visual spectacle of a television programme going into everyone's homes, it would make an impact.[8]

Meetings were held by a women's group in Pimlico and word of mouth soon spread news about the protest much further afield, to women's groups across the country. The protest required careful organisation, where one protestor stated, 'loads of us who had children had to be careful about who was going to look after them and that sort of thing.'[9] Many were motivated by their desire to create a better world for their children to grown up in.

Both feminist and anti-apartheid protesters assembled outside Albert Hall, the youngest participant, Carole Vincent, was 16 years old and had gone with an older group of peace activists. About 50 women had bought tickets to go inside the hall; they had dressed up smartly and individually entered and took their seats. The protestors did not openly acknowledge one another, but surreptitiously settled down and waited. Sally Alexandra remembered:

> we were terribly nervous, incredibly nervous. I mean, none of us had ever done anything like that before…I did think: what on earth am I doing

here, it is terrifying. It is so silly to say that because, you know, what you were doing. You were just inside the Albert Hall. But it was frightening. And we weren't quite sure how we'd react when the signal came.[10]

One of the organisers, Sarah Wilson, carried a football rattle in her handbag, to notify others when to begin the protest. She soon found herself enraged by Bob Hope, when he acknowledged the protests outside and attempted to make a joke about the competition being likened to a cattle market. When he commentated: 'I love cattle. I've been out there, feeling their calves' she 'jumped up and waived her rattle. It took a bit of time for the action to get going because the other women had to light cigarettes so they could light the smoke bombs, I felt a bit like a general waving on the troops and then they didn't appear.'[11] Mayhem soon ensued.

Yelling the slogan 'We're not beautiful, we're not ugly, we're angry!' the protestors retrieved items from handbags and threw them at the stage. These included, leaflets, vegetables and flour bombs, which when they exploded made it look as though the stage had been covered in snow. Toy mice were released amongst the audience, water pistols fired and whistles blown. Jo Robinson, another of the organisers, a member of the radical print-making collective Poster Workshop and the Grosvenor Avenue Commune, was four months pregnant at the time. She later recalled:

> I didn't know exactly what I was going to do when I heard the signal. But I did have an arsenal in my bag of flour bombs, smoke bombs, a water pistol and rotten veg ....
>
> I just held my belly, thinking this is the moment! ... I looked around and thought well all these people are nice around here, so I need to go and find a target. I walked down towards the stage and saw lots of press. The sexist, male press had never written anything about women that we liked, that we could identify with, so I thought, right, and I got out some big old lettuces and tomatoes and started lobbing them at the press saying "take that! take that!" I got some leaflets out and threw them saying "read about us!" The leaflet was addressed to all women – read why we're here.[12]

For many of the protestors, participating in direct action was thrilling. 'There was a sense of exhilaration and excitement that we were making a mark and making ourselves heard.'[13] Protestors clambered over other members of the audience and rushed towards the stage, mounting the barrier which surrounded it. In the ensuing chaos, the compere, Bob Hope ran from the stage and the broadcasters cut the transmission. Scuffles occurred between the protestors and the venue's security staff and the police began to make arrests, sometimes carrying women out of the hall. Jo Robinson 'escaped a bouncer by spraying him with blue ink, but was arrested later for discharging a smoke bomb and ended up on trial, spending a night in Holloway Prison.'[14]

With difficulty, Bob Hope was persuaded back onto the stage and the event and its broadcast coverage resumed. The competition was won by Jennifer Hosten, from Grenada, the first black women winner. She worked as an air hostess but went onto become Grenada's High Commission to Canada, a Canadian diplomat to Bangladesh and a technical adviser on trade to the Organisation of Eastern Caribbean States. At the time she was uncertain what the protest was all about, because her participation in the pageant was about challenging ideas of feminine beauty which were linked to being white. She later mused: 'for me it was about race and inclusion – for them, it was about female exploitation'.[15] At the end of the event, the TV personality, Michael Aspel, accompanied the contestants to the Coronation Ball at the Café de Paris nightclub. He remembered as they left: 'People were shouting and jumping in front of the bus and hammering on the glass ... And the girls were getting a bit defiant, so 'We shall overcome' was being sung on both sides of the glass.'[16]

The protest was seen by over 10 million British television viewers creating headlines in local and national newspapers the next day. This, and the ensuing public trial of five women, provided a wealth of publicity for the Women's Liberation Movement, although not all of it was sympathetic or very detailed. *The Birmingham Post*, for example, discussed events under the heading 'Miss World Contest disrupted by demo' without mentioning the women's liberation movement, or even that the protestors had been women. Miss World continued to be a worldwide phenomenon and rebranded itself in the 1980s under the slogan 'Beauty with a purpose', giving a supposedly greater emphasis to intelligence and personality. However, thanks to women's campaigning activities, the pageant began to look increasingly outdated on British television, although it continued to be broadcast on ITV between 1980 and 1988 and then on Channel 5 from 1998–2000. However, as controller of BBC1, Michael Grade announced in 1984, that it no longer merited national air time. He argued that such pageants were 'an anachronism in this day and age of equality and verging on the offensive.'[17] By that time numerous campaigns over media images of women were taking place, in many respects, these were spawned by the Miss World protest.

Advertising and billboards became another area for direct action: women's groups objected to the copious images of naked women selling everything from typewriters and printers to cars and films. Armed with stickers saying 'this advert degrades women', they set about making such adverts a space for feminist action. Others used spray cans to subvert the advertising rhetoric, which suggested that women were first and foremost sexual objects. A Fiat car advert in 1979, with the slogan 'If it were a lady, it would get its bottom pinched', received the added retort, 'If this was a lady she'd run you down'. Laura Posener, who photographed this early example of what was referred to as a culture jamming campaign, explained how the advert was opposite her place of work. With a colleague, she had added the graffiti as a 'way of taking over the poster.... making the point that ad agencies don't have the monopoly of wit.'[18] In a similar vein, a local punk collective in London known as the Deptford Dykes supplemented their own particular take to an advertising poster with a pin-up girl accompanied by a slogan suggesting that a certain beauty product made her 'feel like a new man'. A 'speech bubble in the same red paint countered, 'I've obviously never met the right woman.'[19]

For some women's groups the problem with media images lay not only in the selective portrayal of women in the media, but also in the limited roles women had to work in the media industries. Joan Bakewell, who by the 1970s was a mother of two children and a co-presenter with three men on BBC Two's chat show *Late Night Line-Up*, asked the BBC's head of news, 'Might a woman one day read the news?' only to be told 'absolutely not.' She recalled:

> Somewhere along the line, I had been tagged "the thinking man's crumpet" and Fleet Street editors never let me forget it. Meant as a compliment, it labelled me as frivolous and, I suspect, kept me out of serious BBC programming for a decade. Unaware of what was happening, I did PR for the programme, always articles about fluffy stuff: makeup and clothes.[20]

In 1970, the Women in Media group was formed. It brought together women who worked in all areas of the media: broadcasting, book publishing, advertising, film, theatre, public relations. They sought to use their professional skills to improve both the position of women working in the media and women's portrayal in the media. They held seminars on discrimination and stereotyping, images of women in advertising, and produced videos entitled 'Super-Soft Quick-Mix After-Eight Women' and 'Female Stereotypes in Television Advertising.'[21]

One of the key Women in Media campaigners was the journalist, Mary Stott. Born in Leicester in 1907, she joined the *Leicester Mail* in 1924. In 1926, at the age of only 19, Mary was made editor of the Women's Page of the *Leicester Mail* – not something she greeted with enthusiasm. Rather, as she told the Radio programme *Desert Island Discs* in 1994, 'I didn't want to be a woman's journalist. I wanted to be a journalist...I wanted to be on the same terms as men.' She thought her chances of being a 'real journalist was over.' After a time working with the Co-Operative Press, the *Bolton Evening News* and the *Manchester Evening News*, she became editor of the *Guardian*'s women's page in 1956. The women's page acted like a community launching pad for a number of campaigning organisations. She changed the face of women's journalism in Britain; the woman's page ceased to be regarded as light relief amidst the 'serious news.'[22] Three years after she died, in 2002, Stott was posthumously included in the Press Gallery's 40-strong gallery of the most influential British journalists; one of only five women to be found there.

Women in Media picketed and lobbied, went on deputations and marches, and in February 1973, Stott led a group of representatives to Downing Street, where a duty policeman received their petition. The group campaigned for anti-discrimination legislation – something that finally came to fruition in 1975 with the Sex Discrimination Act. In 1977, Stott edited a book with Josephine King, titled, *Is This Your Life: Images of women in the media*. Many other women, exasperated with the poor portrayal of numerous different women's campaigns by the media, sought to create their own publications. Local women's groups produced newsletters, and a number of newspapers, magazines and journals were set up, often run on not-for-profit lines by a co-operative. It is said that, 'These were often useful in organising local campaigns, underpinning networks and breaking down isolation'.[23]

Shrew, (1969–74), for example, was the London Women's Liberation Workshop's newsletter; *Women's Voice* (1972–1982) was published by International Socialists;[24] and FOWAAD! was the newsletter of the Organisation of Women of Asian and African Descent (OWAAD). *Sappho* (1972–81), a small-scale subscription magazine, was set up to support lesbian and women's causes. The most famous and long-running feminist campaigning magazine of this era was *Spare Rib* (1972–1993), set up by Rosie Boycott and Marsha Rowe, who later explained,

> We called ourselves an alternative women's news magazine. I adored magazines and their visual aspect, but we could only afford two colours, to go with black and white. I wanted *Spare Rib* to have all the traditional elements of a women's magazine, but with a different spin. Our first fashion spread was a double page on jeans. No one in fashion ever mentioned jeans back then.[25]

The magazine sought a wide readership and was available in the high street shops enabling it to achieve national circulation. But its finances were always rocky, advertising was hard to come by, and the editorial board went through many changes as the magazine sought to reflect the diversity of the women's movement. In 1981, the collective that ran the magazine confirmed that their approach was to ensure *Spare Rib*,

> should be challenging in content yet accessible in its form and available in every newsagent... reflect women's lives in all their diverse situations so that they can recognize themselves in its pages. This is done by making the magazine a vehicle for their writing and their images. Most of all, *Spare Rib* aims to bring women together and support them in taking control of their lives.[26]

One of the many controversies with which *Spare Rib* struggled to contend, was the divergent experiences and priorities of different ethnic and racial groups within feminism. There were heated debates about who had the right to speak for which minority group, and accusations of racism against *Spare Rib* and white feminists. The mainstream media's portrayal of black women was particularly sexualised and demeaning. In 1984, the Black Women and Media Conference (14–15 April) was held at The Factory in West London, attended by 150 women. Black women and women of colour shared their skills, explored access to the media and sought to understand the media's role in perpetuating racism and sexism. In 1979, Women in Media held a seminar on women's writing, which led to the formation of Women in Publishing to support women in the profession. A number of different feminist groups in the 1970s and 80s were also involved in setting up theatre companies, film groups, artist collectives and publishing houses, to give a voice to their campaigns. It was Virago, set up in 1973, which first published the Brixton Black Women's Group's book, *The Heart of the Race: Black Women's Lives in Britain* (1985). The book discussed Afro-Caribbean immigration, as well as the experiences of Black British Women and their anti-racist campaigns.[27] However, mainstream media and its problematic portrayal and exploitation of women continued to remain a key area of campaigning in the 1980s and 90s.

Whilst many campaigners were keen to draw attention to the exploitation of women in Miss World Competition, to deface adverts, critique the portrayal of women in the media, or search to find ways of creating their own alternative images of women in the media, some campaigners sought to alter the laws around obscenity and censorship. Feminists in women's groups and universities debated, with much emotion and little evidence, about what could be defined as obscene or pornographic, whether such materials were harmful and whether they could or should be restricted. Campaigners seeking greater regulation or even the banning of pornography, were influenced by radical feminists in the

USA, such as Andrea Dworkin, Robin Morgan and Catherine MacKinnon. They argued that pornography is implicated in violence against women, using the slogan 'pornography is the theory – rape is the practice'.[28] Some women lobbied against the opening of sex shops and a few stood outside existing shops with placards registering their disapproval. Other women saw the iconic photoshoot of actor, Burt Reynolds, naked on a bear skin rug in the April 1972 edition of *Cosmopolitan* magazine, and the launch of *Playgirl*, a soft-porn magazine with images of naked men as signifiers of women's equality.

As debates became more heated, there was concern amongst many women about who would or could define what was obscene or pornographic, and also anxiety that censorship would restrict women's right to sexual self-expression. In 1986, such problems were emphasised, when the Conservative MP for Davyhulme, Winston Churchill, the grandson of Britain's wartime leader of the same name, attempted to introduce an Obscene Publications Bill. His proposed bill included a list of images that would be regarded as obscene and therefore illegal, wherever they appeared. Medical and biology text books, sex education materials and some war reporting would have been outlawed. Claire Short, who had been elected as a Labour Party MP for Ladywood constituency in Birmingham three years previously, leapt to her feet objecting to the bill and suggested that it would be more useful to introduce a tightly written piece of legislation to remove Page 3 images from tabloid newspapers.[29]

Short has since described how on entering House of Commons, she had encountered the racks of national newspapers in numerous rooms in the house. This afforded her the opportunity to look at newspapers she had not really concentrated on before. *The Sun*, the *Daily Mirror*, the *Sunday People* and the *Daily Star* all included Page 3 pin-ups and she was 'struck by these pictures and how inappropriate they are in newspapers' and how 'degrading they are to everybody.'[30] Despite a lukewarm response and some sniggers in the House of Commons, her unprepared speech proposing legislation on Page 3 images in tabloids sparked a campaign supported by women of all walks of life across the country. She received 'an avalanche of enthusiastic letters from women' and created a debate about the 'difference between sexual openness and pornographic degradation.'[31] For many women, it was the everyday depictions of women as sex objects that they disliked – images which pervasively seeped into every area of culture. In one of the letters Clair Short received, an infant school teacher from Northampton described how it upset her when spreading out newspapers, sent in by helpful parents so the children could do art work, as she was confronted by 'pouting naked women between the paint pots.'[32] Little boys sniggered, little girls were perplexed and uneasy. Other women were appalled by how young, just 16 or 17 years old, some of the models were, or how they were dressed to appear even younger.

On the 12 March, 1986, Claire Short sought to introduce a private members' bill in parliament, which would 'make illegal the display of pictures of naked or partially naked women in sexually provocative poses in newspapers.'[33] Whilst many readers of the tabloids may have regarded Page 3 as harmless fun, the campaign influenced many other women and led them to question this, to voice their disquiet and anger, and to discuss pornography. In introducing her bill, Short was able to express the views and concerns of the women who had written to her. She explained how:

> They stressed time and again that they did not consider themselves to be prudes but objected very strongly to such pictures. One letter came from a young woman who worked in an office. She was writing on behalf of quite a few young women. They considered themselves to be young and attractive, but every day they were subjected to men reading such newspapers in the office, and to them tittering and laughing and making rude remarks such as 'Show us your Page 3s then.[34]

Despite sniggering, laughter and ridicule from those who opposed the bill, it gained the support of 97 MPs, whilst 56 opposed it. However, as it was introduced under the 10-Minute Rule, it only required one MP to shout 'object' for it to be put back for another date. After this happened a number of times, the parliamentary session ended and the bill died. In the 1987–88 parliamentary year, Claire Short was able to introduce her bill again. On the 13 April, 1988, 163 MPs supported it and 48 opposed it, despite her having added an extra clause to ban the display of soft-porn in workplaces. As with many private members bills, it was not however allocated the parliamentary time to go through the necessary stages to become law. It took another campaign, the No Page 3 campaign, launched in 2012, before the daily tabloids eventually removed these images. *The Sun* finally abandoned Page 3 in 2015. The *Daily Star* followed suit in 2019, two years after the Me-Too movement served as a reminder that what some consider a bit of light-hearted fun, others see as an exploitative abuse of power.

The campaign which took place outside the House of Commons in the 1980s and 1990s, was much more important than the discussions and votes in the chamber; it was the campaign that changed public opinion. Some big supermarkets withdrew their advertising from the tabloids that had the most blatantly sexualised images of women. It was concerns about profits and offending their readers, which ultimately led to daily newspapers to drop the pin-ups. Although Clare Short was vilified in some sections of the press, her bill and speeches in the House of Commons empowered women. Some signed petitions of support that were sent to MPs; large numbers of women wrote letters to her and the local and national press. A selection of the letters that Short received were put together in a book, *Dear Clare*, published in 1991. Women's anger had been further fueled by the response of some MPs to the bill. Mr Robert Adley, the right honourable member for Christchurch, Hampshire had been concerned that if the bill were passed, it would deny him one of his few pleasures: 'sitting in an underground train watching the faces of people who are pretending not to be looking at Page 3 of the newspapers.'[35] However, women who wrote to Short described how Page 3 images in newspapers had been used to harass them on public transport, as male passengers deliberately pushed the images into their faces, or sniggered and compared the young women to the Page 3 models they were looking at.

Seeking a 'constructive outlet for the strength of women's feelings', Claire Short cooperated with other MPs to launch the Campaign Against Pornography in 1987. Its aims included 'undertaking research into the links between pornography and violence against women and children and their position in society and to publish the results of such research.'[36] It set up a helpline, training events, and worked with the University of Bradford's Violence Abuse and Gender Relations Research unit. Its two most significant campaigns were 'Off the Shelf' (1989–95), and Red Hot Dutch (1993), the latter seeking to prevent the launch of a hardcore porn satellite channel. The Off the Shelf Campaign aimed to challenge the selling of soft porn in local newsagents, by encouraging women to use their voices and buying power to convey their objections to shopkeepers.[37] It gained active support from numerous organisations including the National Union of Students and the Townswomen's Guild.

The Off the Shelf Campaign was launched in January 1990, when a number of women entered the Kingsway branch of W. H. Smiths, in London, and removed all the porn from the shelves, 'dumped it by the cash till and explained their objections to the material.'[38] Women across the country were invited to use similar tactics. W.H. Smiths was chosen as a target for activities, as it was the leading high street retailer and was also a wholesaler of newspapers and magazines at the time. Some campaigners wrote to their local managers of W.H. Smiths branches and explained that they would withdraw their custom if they did not stop selling porn. One elderly lady in Wales, 'filled up her basket with goods, waited in a long queue, then after the items has been rung up asked if her branch of W. H. Smith's sold porn.'[39] On receiving a positive response, she refused to pay for the goods and enjoyed the chaos that ensued.

This campaign of direct action once again created debate, women argued about what should or should not be sold, and where and how it should be sold. Women discussed the embarrassment caused by men leafing through porn magazines as they waited to buy a pint of milk in their local newsagents. Once again, practice eventually changed and porn began to be sold in cellophane covers, which prevented the pages being viewed before purchase. Shoppers of all ages were not subjected to casual porn-browsing by fellow customers and the sellers of porn avoided it being handled, sampled and potentially damaged before it had been paid for.

As the twentieth century drew to a close, women continued to debate critically the media images of women, pornography and censorship. Feminists Against Censorship, a large network of women seeking to explain feminist arguments opposing censorship, and to defend individual sexual expression, was set up in 1989. Although they did not bring about changes to the law or censorship, the direct action of those involved in the Miss World protest, Off the Shelf, cultural jamming, and the quieter campaigners who wrote letters and joined organisations, had a significant influence. By the end of twentieth century, far fewer workplaces were adorned with soft porn calendars and posters: advertising, films and numerous other media outlets no longer casually used titillating images of women in the way they had done in the 1960s and 70s. Media images became more varied and women had very different roles in the mainstream media. They read the news and even commentated on various sports, including football. However, as the 1990s drew to a close, the internet was just beginning to be established. While it undoubtedly provided vast scope for women to create their own media, the lack of almost all regulation also meant that demeaning and demoralising images of women, which the Miss World protestors had sought to eliminate, once again proliferated.

Chapter 10

'We appreciate the cards and flowers but they are not enough' (1972)

Over 100 women met in London's Gate Cinema on Mothers' day in 1977 to demand financial remuneration for their domestic labour. The meeting heard from the Bristol Wages for Housework Campaign, that although flowers and chocolates were all very well, housewives wanted more, many were fed up, unable to get any time off even on Mother's Day. 'All of us are housewives and mothers – we do the work of mothering other people. We're tired of doing it for free', explained Suzie Fleming of the Bristol Wages for Housework Campaign.[1] Campaigns like this, which drew attention to women's poverty and to the domestic, physical and emotional labour they undertake as mothers, carers, wives, partners, friends and colleagues in households received a mixed reception within the feminist movement and wider society, yet they addressed important issues which shaped many women's everyday lives.

Selma James, who founded the International Wages for Housework Campaign in March 1972, was born into a working-class household in the Brooklyn district of New York in 1930. She had experience of working in factories, getting married at seventeen and becoming a full-time housewife and being a mother to her young son. She saw motherhood and housewifery as necessary work – not just a role, but fundamental, important, basic work which produced wealth and welfare. Women who did this work, she argued, deserved to be valued and economically rewarded; yet very many, perhaps most of them, lived in poverty. When she spoke at the Women's Liberation Conference, held in Manchester in 1972, Selma James put forward the idea of wages for housework in a pamphlet titled, *Women, the Unions and Work*, which she wrote specifically for the conference. However, her campaign was not met with enthusiasm from all feminists, as she later recalled:

> The dominant voice at the conference (which was white and largely middle class) was that wages for housework would institutionalise women in the home and that going out to work was the beginning of liberation – no reference to wages or working conditions. As a young mother, I had

waitressed, packed sweets, and wired and soldered TVs on an assembly line. Liberation didn't look like that![2]

Many of the issues raised by Selma James about women's caring and domestic work were not new: they had been discussed during the suffrage campaigns, explored in the inter-war years by those proposing the introduction of family endowment (which is now known as child benefit), and were a concern amongst some women's organisations during the Second World War, before resurfacing in the 1970s.

Well before the twentieth century, the expectation was established in many societies, that because some women were the biological mothers of babies, all women were natural carers, not just of the young, but also of the sick, the old and most importantly perhaps, of men. The physical and emotional labour women undertook as a result of such expectations did not go unquestioned. As early as the 1890s, American social reformer and feminist Charlotte Perkins Gilman's book, *Women and Economics: A Study of the Economic Relations Between Men and Women as a Factor in Social Evolution*, had argued, 'wives, as earners through domestic service, are entitled to the wages of cooks, housemaids, nursemaids, seamstresses, or housekeepers' and providing women economic independence is key to their liberation.'[3] Gilman was principally addressing middle-class feminists, perhaps problematically encouraging them to hire housekeepers and cooks, so that they themselves could escape domestic labour. Instead, she suggested, they should 'participate in the workforce and lead a more worldly life.'[4] Despite initially being published in the USA, her book was read by British suffrage campaigners, who also discussed marriage and ways of reducing the burden of domestic labour for women – although perhaps for some middle-class suffrage campaigners with servants, housewifery and domestic labour were not necessarily pressing concerns. Their households relied upon the army of cooks, housemaids, nursemaids and housekeepers who kept many British homes functioning in the first half of the twentieth century. In the Edwardian era, domestic service employed more women than any other industry – a position it retained during the First World War. Nevertheless, under the influence of Dora Marsden and Mary Gawthorpe, the radical suffrage journal, *Freewomen*, began to explore the possibilities of collective housekeeping.[5]

The introduction of the National Kitchen scheme, during the First World War, was at least a nod towards this idea of collective housekeeping. Kitchens were set up in many large towns to enable the families struggling to deal with wartime food shortages and price rises, to get a cheap meal. Wartime food shortages meant that housewifery became nationally significant: women's roles as housewives, cooks and housekeepers were important to the war effort just as their employment in the factories and fields was. Propaganda posters portrayed women in their kitchens while announcing 'the key to victory lay in her cupboard.' The inter-war years saw the heyday of domesticity, when there was talk in some women's organisations and middle – class women's magazines of the new citizen – housewife.[6] Married women increasingly chose, or were forced by employers or husbands, to give up paid employment once married. Some women welcomed this, seeing it as positive to be able to focus on one job – in the home – rather than undertake a double shift made up of both paid employment and unpaid domestic work.

Organisations such as the Women's Co-operative Guild and the Women's Institute emphasised the significance of domestic labour, whilst also pointing out the need to improve housewives' everyday working lives.[7] Women were involved in a multiplicity of campaigns to alleviate the consequences of poverty in this period. Many feminist campaigns, as Sheila Rowbotham has argued, focussed on 'housing, health care, unadulterated food and fresh milk, better education, free milk and school dinners for children, as well as clothing and shoes. "Boots for Bairns" became part of the struggle to improve the conditions of working-class women and children.'[8] Alternatively, a foretaste of the Wages for Housework campaigns can be seen in the ideas expressed by the suffragette and feminist, Lady Rhondda. She argued, according to Angela John, 'any wife should be able to go to court while still living with her husband, and if she could prove that she did all the house management and/or housework she should be entitled to a proportion of her husband's income – up to seventy-five percent.'[9] Whilst Lady Rhondda's suggestion did not gain much purchase, the campaign for Family Endowment led by the formidable feminist from Liverpool, Eleanor Rathbone, did obtain significant support.[10]

Eleanor Rathbone (1872–1946), was the daughter of a Liberal MP, brought up in a family dedicated to philanthropy and social reform. After completing a degree at Oxford, she spent many of her formative years working to help the poor of Liverpool. She helped establish a District Nursing system in the city, and was the first woman to be elected to Liverpool City Council, representing the Granby ward from 1909 to 1934. Having witnessed the poverty endured by many working-class mothers, she was convinced of the need to recognise the immense amount of work involved in raising children, and the malnutrition experienced in many large families. At that time, it was assumed working men would be paid a wage sufficient to provide for their families. However, many workers had no dependent children, whilst wages were unable to increase to a level necessary to provide for the larger families. The answer, Rathbone argued, was for the state to contribute to the cost of bringing up children; for motherhood to be endowed. She campaigned for more than twenty-five years for this. Her tactics were reasonable, restrained and polite: she sought to argue, cajole and persuade people to share her viewpoint, by carefully explaining the reality of many mothers' everyday lives.

Rathbone's lucid arguments were supported by the detailed social investigation of the conditions in which working-class women lived. In 1924, she published *The Disinherited Family*, in which she stated, 'nothing can justify the subordination of one group of producers – the mothers – to the rest.'[11] They should not be deprived, she claimed, of the 'wealth of a community which depends on them for its very existence.'[12] This book, and Rathbone's determined political campaigning, were often sympathetically received, and together, were the catalyst for the formation of the Family Endowment Society having support from across the political spectrum. *The Scotsman* reported on one of her speeches, where she argued that the principal work of a married woman was 'to bring up her children, to be a competent citizen.'[13] She continued to explain that the Family Endowment Society's aim was for all wives to have sufficient income. As Rathbone noted 'the real basic difficulty in the normal home was not any defect in the goodwill of the husband, but the fact that the income of the family did not expand with its size. The service of motherhood, although a whole-time job for most women, did not entitle them to any share of the world's wealth.'[14] The article went on to elaborate on Rathbone's suggestion for family allowances paid to mothers at a rate of 6s 1½ d (31p) a week for each child under the age of 14. Acknowledging that this would cost the government £179,000,000 per annum, she had apparently reminded her audience that it was some £32,000,000 less than the country spent on alcoholic liquor.[15]

Eleanor Rathbone had been a strong supporter of women's suffrage, and in 1919, when the National Union of Women's Suffrage Societies became the National Union of Societies for Equal Citizenship (NUSEC), she became its first president. In the years that followed, there was controversy over the priorities of the organisation: for Rathbone, political equality was not an end in itself, but a means to bring about social reform. In 1929, she was elected as an independent MP, representing the Combined English Universities, and she used the national platform this provided to speak, write, and to seek to bring the idea of family endowment to those with influence. In a turbulent economic and political era, she continued to campaign in and out of Parliament to win Family Allowance for all mothers. She received support from women in the Labour movement and the Women's Co-operative Guild, but not in the end from the Trade Union Movement. They were concerned any introduction of a specific payment to wives and mothers, would undermine unions' campaigns for men to be paid a family wage sufficient to support their wives and children.[16]

Those who discussed Family Endowment in the 1920s and 30s assumed children were provided and cared for by their biological parents, as approximately ninety per cent of them were at the time. The outbreak of the Second World War brought about a significant change in this; approximately three million children were evacuated from towns, cities and coastal regions of Britain to protect them from aerial bombing and potential invasion.[17] Parents could decide whether or not to have their children evacuated to safety. Housewives in areas deemed to be safe, mostly in the countryside, had no choice over accepting evacuees into their home. They were legally required by the government to care for them, to cook, clean and look after children, thanks to a policy which the social reformer, Margaret Cole, described as 'nationalising hundred and thousands of women.'[18] They received a regular payment to cover their expenses and were excluded from other, often lucrative war work. Some took to their role enthusiastically, others did not. Many found the task of looking after traumatised children difficult and exhausting, particularly as it was usually carried out in rural homes lacking electricity and an inside water supply.

Only the National Federation of Women's Institutes spoke out about the financial burdens, exploitation and lack of support for the women who looked after evacuees. They correctly identified it as a consequence of the low status of domestic labour; one writer in *Home and Country* pointed out:

> the planners of the evacuation scheme could – and did – calmly assume that the housewife need not be paid anything for the time, energy, labour and skill spent in cooking, washing, ironing, mending and 'minding' and doing housework for three or four extra children. They did not ask school buses to run free services with unpaid drivers; or farmers to charge nothing for milk and vegetables, or cobblers not to send in accounts for mending evacuated children's shoes.[19]

The desire for housewives' work to be rewarded and for wives to be recognised as equal partners with men, continued to shape the demands of many women's organisations in the 1940s. When the Beveridge Report was published in 1942, some thought they were at last making progress: the Women's Institute's magazine, *Home and Country*, proclaimed: 'Housewives have come into their own at last! The Beveridge Plan for social security ... puts in its own words a premium on marriage instead of penalising it.'[20]

The Beveridge Report, a blue print for the post-war welfare state, included proposals for the introduction of family allowances and health care, and for all married women to be included in the National Insurance system.

It also sought to ensure that housewives, like other workers, would have a state pension. In 1945, a resolution was passed at the National Federation of Women's Institute's AGM, requesting sickness pay for all housewives, widows, and those who were not technically speaking 'gainfully employed.' However, while it did not gain wider support, it did draw attention to the limitations of the Beveridge report's proposals.[21] The idea of Family Allowances had gained the backing of public figures, such as the economist, John Maynard Keynes and Seebohm Rowntree, author of a number of reports on poverty in the 1930s. Parliamentary support for Family Allowances grew and a white paper on the topic was published in May 1942. The coalition government, led by Winston Churchill, dragged its feet over the implementation of any of Beveridge's proposals, and there were suggestions that family allowances, when introduced, might not be paid to mothers. Rathbone, by then in poor health, rallied the press, women's organisations, other MPs and her own strength, to oppose such ideas.

Eleanor Rathbone lived long enough to see the Family Allowance Act passed in 1945, a year before she died. It provided payment of five shillings (25p) a week for the second and subsequent child until they reached fifteen years old – the equivalent of approximately £12 in contemporary currency. Beveridge had suggested subsistence levels of payments should be set at nine shillings and adjusted as the cost of living increased. In time, the rates did rise to eight shillings (40p) in 1952, whilst in 1956, the rate for the third and subsequent children became ten shillings (50p) per week. Furthermore, as the school leaving age went up and further education became more common, the payments increased in duration to cover children until they were eighteen. Shifts and adaptions continued to be made to the payment; the most significant of these was the phasing in of child benefit paid for all children between 1977 and 1979. By this point, attitudes to domestic labour, childcare and the conditions in which domestically focused women worked, had changed significantly.

As Pat Thane has pointed out 'after the Second World War marriage, at least once, became almost universal' and within marriage it continued to be assumed that women would take on the domestic responsibilities of a housewife.[22] These were responsibilities many women found less than fulfilling. The BBC daily radio programme, *Woman's Hour* (1946 -), saw its audience as lonely housewives 'unwilling to communicate to their neighbours and families' and even considered featuring anonymous letters, which would lift the lid on a range of emotional problems behind the supposed ideal of family life and domestic contentment portrayed in advertising and women's magazines of the era. Their archives suggest that women did not need anonymity to write in and describe the dubious joys of 'spending 2 hours at each meal trying to feed a 3-year-old.'[23]

The lives of domestically – orientated women were, however, changing. Many of the women who wrote into *Woman's Hour* had to cope with the challenges of motherhood and domesticity in substandard and overcrowded housing conditions. In the 1950s, housebuilding, the increasing introduction of water, drainage and electricity, all improved domestic women's working conditions. Increasing levels of new technology entered the home from the mid-1950s, supposedly to reduce the burden of domestic labour in the era of never-had-it-so-good consumerism. Fridges were often brought into the house as a gift for the wife or children, reducing the necessity for women to undertake frequent visits to the shops. Inside bathrooms and toilets, washing machines, gas fires and cookers alleviated some housework. For middle-class housewives, this equipment helped to assuage some of the realities of the steady disappearance of servants and domestic help, as did the employment of au pairs and daily cleaners.

New technology was also accompanied by new assumptions of the amount of domestic work housewives could and would provide. For example, whilst in the 1920s and 1930s clothes were expected to be washed and changed weekly, by the 1970s and 80s, they were tossed into the laundry basket each night with gay abandonment, for housewives to wash, dry, sort, iron and return to drawers. Despite the wonders of new appliances, there was little reduction in the number of hours women actually spent on domestic labour. Post-war domesticity turned out to be less than ideal for many women, who often felt bored and isolated. No wonder then, as Carol Dyehouse has pointed out, 'the stereotypical image of the 1950s housewife [...] a happy – looking woman, apron-clad, content in her kitchen' slipped 'into parody or pastiche: the woman begins to look demented as she beam[ed] ecstatically over kitchen devices, spongy cupcakes, and whiter than white washing piled high in her laundry basket.'[24] More sinister images of discontent, isolation and misery began to appear, on television, radio and in films such as, *Woman in a Dressing Gown* (1957), whilst novels of middle -class life in the 1950s began 'to probe the dissatisfactions of housewives whose lives revolved around house and home, however well-appointed and materially secure.'[25]

The 1950s Sociologist, Richard Titmuss, argued that demographic changes also reshaped women's lives. Families were smaller, and childbearing began to be regarded as a phase, rather than a long-term and debilitating life sentence. Within twenty years, however, motherhood had expanded to encompass all manner of new demands on housewives, including running a taxi- service, to numerous after-school activities providing educational support and counselling troubled teenagers. Women who had fewer children often discovered in their forties their youngsters were grown up and wondered what to do with the rest of their lives.[26] The initial stirrings of American feminism came from across the Atlantic with Betty Friedan's book, *The Feminine Mystique* (1963) which struck a chord with many women. She asked why the suburban housewife, materially comfortable and secure, apparently envied across the world, was so tired and miserable. Their discontent, stress, anxiety and unhappiness made up 'the problem with no name', which she termed the feminine mystique. Women, she suggested, saw their misery as a consequence of their own failings, but it was actually a structural, societal problem.

In the 1960s and 70s, discontentment around housewifery was being articulated in a number of different places, as were solutions to the problem. The heroine in Carla Lane's sit-com, *Butterflies* (BBC 1978 – 1983), was a disgruntled housewife and mother of two teenage sons, who was well aware of her central caring role in the family. She declared early in the series. 'I devote my entire existence to this family ship, I am the cook, the laundry maid and the captain.' She felt suffocated by this life of housewifery and domesticity. This is emphasised by images accompanying the theme tune of her husband catching butterflies, smothering them and pinning them onto a display board. Some women were portrayed as seeking, and sometimes fighting for, new freedoms: in the long-running BBC Radio drama, *Mrs Dale Diary* (1948–1969), the heroine responded to Dr Dale's refusal to let her have driving lessons by going on strike and not cooking his meals.

Although, the media began to portray women's discontent with some sympathy, many areas of society continued to see housewives' misery as their own failure. Pharmaceutical journals carried adverts for tranquillizers for 'the stressed, depressed housewife with erratic moods swings and outbursts.'[27] Promotion for the tranquilizer, Serax, was explained to doctors, 'You can't set her free, but you can help her feel less anxious'.[28] The widespread use of chemical solutions to alleviate housewives' discontent was enshrined in the 1966 hit by the Rolling Stones, about Valium which included the lyrics: 'Mother needs something today to calm her down and though she's not really ill, there's a little yellow pill.'[29]

Feminist campaigners questioned the use of drugs to silence women's complaints about housewifery. In 1981, Virago Press published a book charting the fictional life of East Anglian housewife, Jane, who struggled with the mind-numbing tedium of her daily life of cooking, cleaning and caring for two small children. The response to her discontent had been a visit to the doctor and a prescription. Indeed, as the first page of Diane Harpwood's book, *Tea and Tranquilizers*, explained, 'I start my day the Valium way, at 7:20 am when my departing husband brings me a mug of tea and a Diazepam tablet...I need Valium to numb my rebelling mind into insensibility...I hate taking it but am a dependent, nervous, miserable wreck without it.'[30] Some argued that women should seek jobs. Some saw this as a double burden, whereby women would be expected to undertake paid work, as well as housework in the evenings and at weekends.

Many rebellious women, uninspired by a life of housewifery, were unprepared to be controlled by tranquilizers. Then the growth of second-wave feminism and community groups, gave a voice to women who found housework abhorrent. Members of the Peckham Rye One o'clock Club in London, argued that 'our window on the world is looked through with our hands in the sink and we have begun to hate that sink and all it implies.'[31] Such views did not necessarily sit comfortably with those of Wages for Housework founder, Selma James. She recalled how, in 1972, at the Women's Liberation conference in Manchester, she had articulated six demands: the right to work less; the right to have or not to have children (rather than just abortion); equal pay for all; free community-controlled nurseries and childcare (rather than 24/7 state childcare); an end to price rises; and the right to a guaranteed income for women and men, and wages for housework.[32]

Yet, in the wake of the Manchester Conference, James and three or four other women formed the Power of Women Collective in London and Bristol, to campaign for wages for housework. It was a grass-roots organisation, which by 1975, had bases in London at the Crossroads Women's Centre in Kentish Town, and in Bristol, Cambridge and Manchester. Their actions were part of the wider International Wages for Housework Campaign (IWFHC), formed in 1972, by Marianrosa Dalla Costa, Silvia Federici, Bridgitte Galtier and Selma James. Across the world, women sought, as Silvia Federici explained, 'to redefine in the public consciousness of what this work is.'[33] As a pamphlet by the New York Wages for Housework campaign explained, 'wageless work in the home – is the same in every country of the world and so is our struggle against it'.[34] In Iceland, women left workplaces and homes to strike on 24 October, 1975. 90% of the country's women apparently participated in the event, entitled a 'day off' by the organisers. The demand of wages for housework was seen as symbolic by some. Louise Toupin has argued the movement provided 'opportunities to politicise housework issues such as family allowances and welfare; abortion and women's health .... Overall, Wages for Housework remained more of a general perspective on struggle than a formal demand.'[35] For many who joined the campaign, wages were an economic necessity, a fair payment for their contribution to society.

Many in the women's movement agreed that the unpaid housework, cooking, cleaning, looking after children, the sick and elderly, made a huge but unrecorded contribution to the economy, arguably more than retail, or even perhaps, manufacturing. Why, some feminists asked, was the man or woman who worked in a bakery categorised as working, an economically active member of society and therefore entitled to receive a wage, when the women who baked bread and cakes at home was not? Debates raged amongst feminists in the 1970s, over the low status of domestic and caring work, and the degree to which this was intimately entangled with the poor economic rewards that housewives received for their seemingly endless toil. However, many argued the answer to these problems was for women to seek to escape domesticity, to go to work, and to get men or the state to take greater responsibility for chores in the home and caring roles. This was perhaps a solution that was more appealing and realisable for middle-class women who had more education or training and consequently employment opportunities. For working class women, black women and many single parents, those areas of employment open to them had limited appeal. The work was often alienating and depressing, offering a new area of drudgery to be undertaken alongside domestic labour.

A number of middle-class feminists were appalled by the very suggestion of wages for housework and the campaigners who apparently 'harangue conferences, shout from soapboxes, gesticulate on television, burn with a strange fever.'[36] Nevertheless, Jill Tweedie, writing in *The Guardian,* acknowledged, 'On the street corner they go down well. Within the movement ... they set up a high level of irritation.'[37] Tweedie abhorred housework and admitted that her only way of engaging with it was 'either to ignore it, shut off my brain and try to do it like a robot, or pretend to myself that I love to do it and I am therefore good. What do I feel? The horrid resentment of a mind bred to slavery and faced with freedom.'[38]

In women's groups across the country, women explored ways of shifting the burden of the uneven share of the housework that they undertook. Why, women asked themselves, did they almost unwittingly and unthinkingly, clear up and look after the men they lived with? In April 1976, Wendy Whitefield, a married mature student, wrote to *Spare Rib* to describe the struggle she had undertaken to renegotiate domestic responsibilities in her household:

> I went on strike, I announced from now on I would do only my shopping, cooking and cleaning. I would not clean up, nor would I keep up my incessant tidying, writing lists, washing and returning milk bottles, putting away dishes he left to drain instead of drying them, defrosting the fridge or cleaning the cooker, clearing away coffee cups or writing to

his relatives. In short, I would do no more than a man would do. Dave thought I was joking.[39]

The response was humour, admonishment and then finally negotiation; her standards of cleanliness came from the idealised images of homes in women's magazines, her husband's were somewhat lower and more realistic. However, in the weeks that followed, despite tensions, cursing and irritations, a new division of domestic labour was worked out. Such solutions were not open to all women.

The feminist sociologist, Anne Oakley, who undertook research on housewifery and questioned its low status, revealed a widespread perception of feminism as unsympathetic towards the traditional housewife, and that it was only really supportive of middle-class women.[40] Oakley's interviewees, despite experiencing monotony and loneliness, also felt autonomy and the satisfaction that could be found in housework – in part through women specifying and adhering to their own standards, routines and rules.[41] Sally Jordon, living in a three-bedroom council house explained to Oakley, 'I think of myself as a housewife, but I don't think of myself as a cabbage. A lot of people think they're housewives and they're cabbages. I don't like to think I'm only a housewife ... I wouldn't like to work full time and run a home as well.'[42]

Wages for Housework opposed the Conservative government's proposal to replace some family allowances with more tax benefits[43] and their campaign to maintain family allowances appealed to women, like Sally Jordon, in the 1970s and 80s. Women signed petitions in front of post offices arguing 'this is the only money I can call my own' and their campaign had a number of allies, including the Child Poverty Action Group and the feminist Labour party politician, Barbara Castle. She became Secretary of State for the Department of Health and Social Security in 1974, and the following year, she introduced the Child Benefit Bill in the House of Commons, explaining that it offered:

> a long overdue merger between child tax allowances and family allowances into a new universal, non-means tested, tax-free cash benefit for all children, including the first, payable to the mother. In this way it ensures that the nation's provision for family support is concentrated first and foremost where it is needed most on the poorest families; and that it goes to the person responsible for caring for the children and managing the budget for their food, clothing and other necessities.[44]

Mother's Day was seen as an ideal day to promote women's campaigns for Wages for Housework and increases in the benefit payments paid to all mothers, and most specifically family allowances. On March 20, 1977, the rally held at the Gate Cinema in London discussed mother's unpaid labour. The slogan for the day was 'when women stop, everything stops'. Impressed by the militant actions of Icelandic women, some called for a housewives' strike. Others argued that because women's domestic work was seen as a labour of love, it was unpaid and low status. Some questioned the assumption that housework was 'naturally' women's work. Others felt that demanding a wage for housework was a tacit acceptance of the home as women's primary role. At the end of the day, a giant Mother's Day card with 10,000 signatures was delivered to number 11 Downing Street. It was addressed to the Chancellor of the Exchequer, Dennis Healey, from the Wages for Housework Campaign, requesting an improvement to family allowances.[45] Over the next two years, the new child benefit scheme was introduced. It became known as a transfer of money from the wallet to the purse, as it ensured that £4 child benefit (the equivalent of £28.50 in 2022) would be paid to the main carer of all children. This was a contribution towards the high cost of bringing up children and gave many mothers a new level of control over at least some money. But it was not the introduction of wages for housewives.

The rally in the Gate Cinema was attended by a BBC camera crew, and the media continued to be interested in the ongoing campaign to draw attention to the very real contribution housewives made to both society and the economy, and how poorly women were rewarded for this work. They received support from Jennifer Simon, a journalist writing for a Scottish daily newspaper, who pointed out that a man with two children might give his wife £35 a week housekeeping. This should be compared, she said, with the 'figure he would have to pay to look after himself for a week – it might be £75 or £375. He could expect to pay about £339 for bed and breakfast and an evening meal in an Aberdeen guest house; £14 for luncheon; £1 for a laundry service wash; and from £10 to £110 for the services of a prostitute, which he may require on average three times a week.'[46] She went on to point out, 'Housewives are not paid. The situation is taken for granted, or not fully appreciated, though the "Wages for Housework" campaign sought to alter that.'[47]

In 1989, *Sunday Life* magazine pointed out that housewives' labour was worth £370 a week to households – £19,000 a year – and suggested, 'an increasing number of women are finding that being at home is a rewarding and full-time job in itself.' Whilst Wages for Housework spokeswoman, Ange Neil, pointed out, 'At the moment many women are forced out to work by financial pressures and end up doing all the housework as well – twice the work for half the pay.'[48] However, with an ageing population, by the 1980s and 90s, it was clear that for many, women's domestic caring roles were multiplying. More women looked after the elderly or ill than the under-fives. Judith Oliver, a carer for her disabled husband, founded, the Association of Carers in 1981. In 1986, the European Court ruled that the refusal to pay Invalid Care Allowance, introduced in 1976, to married women was unlawful sexual discrimination.[49]

In the 1990s, the Women's Institute launched their 'Caring Campaign', first undertaking a survey on carers, to explore the conditions under which they cared for others; the help that they did or did not get from social services; and their financial problems. They publicised their results by holding a conference on the issue in 1993. Nearly twenty years later, when Carers UK gave evidence to the Women's Budget Group Commission on a Gender-Equal Economy, it drew attention to the 2011 Census, which revealed that 3.2 million women provided unpaid care for older, disabled, or chronically ill friends or relatives. Women continue to make up the majority of carers. 20% of women aged 45 to 54 gave unpaid care to someone with a disability or illness, or who is older; women gave up jobs and faced poverty to fulfil these caring obligations.[50] This burden has curtailed many women's working lives and seriously impinged upon their potential to enjoy any leisure time.

At the end of the twentieth century women's labour-saving devices, such as washing machines and dishwashers, began to be seen as necessities rather than luxuries and generally, men took a more active role in parenting, cooking and housework. Few men would dare to respond to their wives' suggestion that they make a cup of coffee, with a retort of 'why should I keep a dog and bark myself', as some had experienced in the 1970s. In 1995, the United Nations undertook to measure and value unwaged work in national accounts.[51] Yet, women continued to take more responsibility for housework and dedicated more hours to it than men, and being a housewife was often aligned with poverty and low status. The demands and issues raised by the Wages for Housework Campaign were still very much alive in Britain and elsewhere. On March 8, 2000, the campaign called a global women's strike in which women from over 60 countries participated. Their demands included payment for all caring work – in wages, pensions, land and other resources – demands which seem unlikely to be fulfilled, despite 50 years of campaigning.[52]

Chapter 11

Airport Protest against Virginity Tests (1979)

On 24 January, 1979, a 35-year-old teacher from India arrived at Heathrow Airport. She was travelling to Britain to marry her fiancé who was a British resident of Indian descent, and as the marriage was due to take place within 3 months, she did not require an entrance visa to come into the country. However, to her shock, like a number of other Asian women who entered Britain in similar circumstances in the 1970s, she was subjected to a humiliating gynecological examination to ascertain whether or not she was a virgin. Given her age, immigration officials apparently thought that she might already have been married and had been attempting to enter the country illegally.

Subjecting migrant women to virginity testing was an abusive, discriminatory and humiliating procedure; neither men nor white women entering the country to marry their fiancé(e)s experienced anything like it.[1] The tests occurred, as Evan Smith and Marinella Marmo have argued, neither as a consequence of race or gender alone. Instead, they were intersectional, 'shaped by a combination of factors', which included 'race, gender and nationality, as well as marital status, age and socio-economic status.'[2] Cultural prejudices about Asian women worked in tandem with legal regulations, because, as Pratibha Parmar has pointed out, virginity tests were 'based on the racist and sexist assumption that Asian women from the subcontinent are always virgins before they get married.'[3] They relied upon a belief that Asian wives would be meek and submissive, embedded in the traditions of another country and continent. On the February 1, 1979, the Asian Women's Collective, Awaz, and the Organisation of Women of African and Asian descent (OWAAD), began their picket of Heathrow Airport to express their horror and opposition to the virginity tests, which were considered by many to be a form of sexual assault carried out at the request of immigration services.

OWAAD, which was formed in 1978 and ran until 1983, brought together a number of different groups of Black and Asian women who had a multitude of divergent interests, focusses and priorities. OWAAD and the Awaz were examples of the success of Black and Asian women working together to get their voices heard. Simultaneously, Melanie Phillips, at the time a feminist journalist on *The Guardian*, wrote an explosive front-page article titled, 'Virginity tests on immigrants at Heathrow.'[4] After *The Guardian* printed a front-page feature on the virginity tests, the campaign became worldwide; many Indian newspapers discussed it. Despite an initial claim by the Home Office that the experience of the 35-year-old teacher on 24 January, 1979, was an isolated incident, it soon became clear that this was not the case. The practice had been going on for 11 years and sometimes took place at British immigration posts on the Indian subcontinent.[5] The campaigns and controversy which followed these actions led, two months later, to an end to virginity testing for any Asian women entering Britain. Awaz and OWAAD's campaign against virginity testing was one of many political campaigns carried out by Black and Asian women's groups in the 1970s and 80s.

The long history of Black and Asian women in Britain has always been like that of white women framed by social class. Princess Sophia Kuldeep Singh (1876–1948), was the daughter of a deposed Maharajah, who lived in an apartment in Hampton Court Palace and became an enthusiastic suffragette in the Edwardian era.[6] She frequently appeared on the stage with Mrs Pankhurst and participated in suffrage rallies and demonstrations, including a raid on Parliament on November 18, 1910. She joined The Women's Tax Resistance League (WTRL), that advocated no taxation without representation and made a number of court appearances due to her refusal to pay tax on her dogs, carriage or servants. A supporter of the Women's Freedom League's Boycott of the 1911 census, Princess Sophia returned her census form with the words: 'If women don't count, neither should they be counted' written across it.[7]

Princess Sophia's involvement in the suffrage campaigns provides evidence of women of different races, ethnicity, class and nationality, campaigning simultaneously or together for shared objectives. Such histories are both rare and often forgotten, although the successful campaign to stop virginity testing relied upon both independent and co-ordinated campaigning of numerous different groups and individuals. This chapter provides a snippet of some of the Black and Asian individuals, campaigns and groups active in the 1970s and 80s that were concerned with issues including immigration, racism, domestic violence, policing, education of children, workplaces, and health. They rarely receive the attention they deserve in histories of women's politics in the twentieth century, although they shook up and changed the women's movement.

For all women, life events and cultural identity, including factors such as class, ethnicity, race, age, sexuality, economic and marital position, have shaped which political campaigns they prioritised. Black and Asian women's experience of welfare, educational provision and the health service differed significantly from that of white women. Consequently, as one contributor to the book, *The Heart of the Race: Black women's lives in Britain,* pointed out, 'We didn't want to become part of the white women's movement. We felt they had different priorities to us.'[8] Their priorities were intrinsically tied up with histories of imperialism and experiences of migration and racism, particularly since the Second World War. Thus, Black and Asian political groups have owed as much, if not more, to the 'revolutionary struggles in places like Angola, Mozambique, Eritrea, Zimbabwe and Guinea Bissau' than the white women's movement.[9]

In the 1940s and 50s, labour shortages in the developing British economy were addressed by encouraging immigration from English-speaking British colonies such as the Caribbean (particularly Jamaica), India, Pakistan and Bangladesh. This led to a significant increase in the Black and Asian communities in London, Bradford, Leicester, Birmingham, Manchester and some other cities.[10] Whilst there had been a Black and Asian population in Britain for hundreds of years, many of these new immigrants who worked in manufacturing industries and the newly created National Health Service were regarded with fear and were treated as inferior, second-class citizens. They were frequently subjected to racist abuse, economic exploitation, and faced racial prejudice when they searched for housing. By the 1950s, unscrupulous landlords, such as Peter Rachman, had taken over a number of spacious Victorian family residences in the Notting Hill area of London and turned them into multiple-occupancy accommodation, which he rented to Black and Asian tenants. By the 1950s, Notting Hill had the largest Caribbean population in Britain, all living in cramped, over-crowded, and poorly maintained, shared houses.[11]

Much of the Caribbean population had seen living in Britain as a temporary phase in their lives, and had therefore not become involved in politics; for many, their church provided a social hub and source of support.[12] However, as racial tensions escalated with disturbances, riots and mobs of white youths attacking houses of Caribbean families between 23 August to 5 September 1958, this changed. One of the most influential women campaigners, fighting racism in housing, education and employment, was Claudia Jones (1915–1964). She was born in Trinidad and came to Britain in 1956, after being expelled from the USA. As an active member of the Communist Party, she was a key campaigner on behalf of Black women and their communities, and in 1958 founded the *West Indian Gazette*, Britain's first Black newspaper. She was also involved in setting up the very first Notting Hill Carnival held in St. Pancras Town Hall on 30 January, 1959. The event was attended by approximately 50 people, and was filmed and broadcast by the BBC. It was 'envisioned as a way of showing solidarity and strength within the growing Caribbean communities and to soothe the ongoing tensions.'[13] Similar events were held in other halls across London in the 1960s, supported by the *West Indian Gazette*, and: 'taking inspiration from the carnivals of the Caribbean islands.'[14]

A further influence upon the formation of the Notting Hill Carnival was the community activist, Rhaune Laslett (1919–2002), who had set up a Children's Play Group in Tavistock Square, London, which was visited by Muhammad Ali before his world-title boxing fight against Henry Cooper in 1966. In the mid-1960s, The Notting Hill Fayre and Pageant took place each September and featured a parade with children dressed as Charles Dickens characters, along with a host of performers reflecting the area's cultural diversity.[15] As Rhaune Laslett explained, 'We felt that although West Indians, Africans, Irish and many other nationalities all live in a very congested area, there is very little communication between us. If we can infect them with a desire to participate, then this can only have good results.'[16] It was the involvement of Trinidadian musician, Russell Henderson, who introduced the processions and the steel bands which made the carnival very much part of the community of the area. By 1966, a local newspaper was reporting the event in positive terms, and talking about how 'children in colourful costumes parade through the streets.'[17]

Carnivals were set up in other cities in Britain: in Leeds, Gertrude Maretta Paul (1934–1992), became one of the founders of the Leeds West Indian Carnival; in time, it became one of the longest running carnivals in Europe. Gertrude Paul, who was born on the Caribbean Island of St Kitts, came to Britain in 1956, becoming the first Black teacher in Leeds in the 1960s. In 1975, when she was appointed head of Elmshurst Middle School, she was the first Black headmistress in the city. This was significant because at the time, as Lyttanya Shannon has explained, teachers were revered, and pupils spoke when they were spoken to.[18] Lyttanya recalled 'I think there were a lot of cultural misunderstandings and assumptions that if a child was silent in the classroom, it was because they didn't have the capacity to participate.'[19] Some Black and Asian children were labelled educationally subnormal or stereotyped by teachers as badly behaved, poorly disciplined and aggressive – when they were perhaps showing signs of alienation or trauma as a result of migration to Britain.

The trauma created for children and parents when Black and Asian children experienced racism in education, was summarised in an interview with a woman called Ingrid, who after coming to Britain in 1961, lived in Brixton for many years. She later states, 'The way the children got treated at school was also an issue – because they were black, they were treated in a certain way, put into certain streams.'[20] Children undertook intelligence tests designed in

Europe, which involved identifying household objects, such as a tap, when in some Caribbean countries, a tap was known as a pipe.[21] Noel Gordon was sent to a boarding school for the educationally subnormal at the age of six, after an anaesthetic triggered a severe reaction to his undiagnosed sickle-cell anaemia. He spent the next ten years at the school, receiving limited education and no qualifications, and noted, 'Leaving school without any qualifications is one thing, but leaving school thinking you're stupid is a different ball game altogether. It knocks your confidence.'[22]

The education of their children became a priority for many black mothers in the 1960s and 70s. As Mia Morris, a member of the Organisation of Women of Asian and African Descent recalled big campaigns around education and how when 'you get a group of black women together, inevitably they talk about education and how they're poorly served by it, you know, the schools don't understand them, and it's all very, very difficult and fractious really.'[23] Gertrude Paul's commitment to children's education led her to organise Britain's first Saturday School to teach cultural history, literacy and numeracy to help Afro-Caribbean children realise their potential. Saturday schools were set up in other cities and groups, such as the newly formed Brixton's Black Women's Group that also campaigned against racism in education provision. Gertrude Paul's campaigning work continued when she was a co-founder and President of the United Caribbean Association in Leeds and when she served on the Commission for Racial Equality in the 1980s.[24] Her daughter, Heather Paul, in assessing of her legacy, states,

> She had a lifelong career of rallying Black parents' activism on their children's behalf in schools and in the communities across West Yorkshire and nationally – challenging legislation, the hidden curriculum, ESN campaigns, the rights of young people throughout the decades as a head-teacher, commissioner for the CRE, community member, wife, mother, granddaughter, daughter, sister, friend and extended family member.[25]

Gertrude Paul's successful career in education came after she attended James Graham Teacher Training College in Leeds to obtain a teaching qualification, although she had already successfully completed the qualification at a Teacher Training College in Antigua. Teaching was not the only area in which Black and Asian women faced discrimination or a dismissive attitude to the qualifications they obtained in other countries. Many nursing schools and hospitals operated quota systems to limit the number of black nurses in training or employment; others insisted that trained nurses redo their training.[26] Many Black and Asian women were nevertheless recruited to work in the National

Health Service as nurses, health visitors, midwives, community health workers and allied health professionals, as well as auxiliaries and cleaners in the 1950s and 60s. These were not well paid, and many had no career prospects. Finally, in the economically turbulent 1970s, 55,000 hospital auxiliary workers who were predominantly black women, went on strike. They demanded an increase in wages opposing the government's wage restraint policy.

What were perhaps the most well publicised and widely supported strikes occurred in the summer of 1976, at the Grunwick Factory in North London. The majority of the workers were of South Asian origin and received low pay, compared to workers in similar factories. They also experienced an oppressive working environment and were not allowed to join a trade union. The barrister, Helena Kennedy, recalled that the factory owner thought many of the women, who were recent immigrants to Britain:

> would be docile and compliant and would do his bidding. He paid them very little money and it was really horrible, the conditions. Really there was no dignity in it. They had to put their hands up to go to the lavatory, at an hours' notice they would be told that they would be expected to do overtime, they would be sacked at the drop of a hat; they were treated in the most abysmal ways and spoken to in the ugliest of terms.[27]

On 20 August that year, Jayaben Desai (1913 – 2010), was asked without warning to work late into the evening, to undertake unplanned overtime just at the moment when she was getting ready to go home. She and her son walked out, addressing the manager with what have become infamous words: 'What you run here is not a factory, it is a zoo. There are monkeys here who dance to your tune, but there are also lions here who can bite your head off. And we are the lions, Mr Manager! I want my freedom!'[28] She and her son joined four other workers who had left the factory earlier in the day; working with local black political groups they started a picket outside the factory. A further 137 workers joined the strike protesting against their poor working conditions, pay inequality and the company's institutionalised racism.

Mrs Desai, as she liked to be called, led the strike which lasted two years. She was an inspiring speaker, who addressed meetings of workers across the country and appeared on television seeking backing for the Grunwick workers. She described a situation in which employees were humiliated by management they feared.[29] Supporters from across the country, sometimes as many as 20,000 at a time, travelled to march in solidarity with the Grunwick workers, joining the pickets of the factory. Lord Justice Scarman was appointed by the government to settle the dispute. However, despite his view that the strike was justified, and his recommendations that the workers who had been sacked for striking should be re-instated and a trade union recognised, he was ignored by the Grunwick factory management. On 22 November. 1977, 'Mrs Desai and 3 others went on hunger strike outside the headquarters of the Trade Union Congress (TUC) to try to get the trade unions to take militant action to support the Grunwick workers.'[30] With increasingly aggressive legislation brought in by the government to prevent picketing, the TUC gave little support, and within 6 months, the strike had ground to a halt. Mrs Desai went on to work in the sewing industry, and later became a teacher at Harrow Collage.

Although numerous Black and Asian women worked in the health service, it was not meeting the needs of their communities. It was in many ways institutionally racist: attitudes and treatments administered in relation to birth control, abortion, and mental health, differed from those administered to white women. Many Black and Asian women's groups and organisations challenged the high incidence of mental health problems in their communities and questioned why they were being misdiagnosed and treated very differently by the NHS. One of the most problematic issues, which left a significant legacy of distrust for the NHS amongst Black and Asian women, was the use of the Depo-Provera contraceptive, which was administered by injection every three months. The drug had been problematically trialled in Jamaica in 1963 before being licensed for limited use in the Britain in 1976. It was expected to be administered to women who had recently had a Rubella inoculation or those whose husbands had recently had a vasectomy, although there was also scope for doctors to use their own clinical judgement in prescribing the drug.

Research carried out by the feminist gynaecologist, Wendy Savage, who worked at the London Hospital in Mile End and Whitechapel, examined the records of 200 women given the Depo-Provera injection in 1977. She found that this form of contraception was used disproportionally on Asian women. She questioned whether receivers of the injection had given informed consent, especially those for whom English was a second language. Depo-Provera, it seemed, was often administered alongside other injections with little discussion or explanation.[31] Across Britain as Jenny Douglas points out:

> it appeared that DP was being prescribed to large numbers of black women without their knowledge or consent in London hospitals and in hospitals serving populations of white working class and black and minority women across the UK. It was certainly being administered to black and minority ethnic women in hospitals in Birmingham.[32]

Concerns about some of the side effects of Depo-Provera, such as heavy bleeding, amenorrhea, weight gain and depression, seem to have been given little weight in comparison to racist assumptions that Black and Asian women were too fecund, unreliable, or too ignorant to use other forms of birth control, and that their children were undesirable, a threat to 'white Britain.' Such views did not just belong to a few eugenicist doctors or supporters of racist organisations like the National Front. In 1978, the leader of the Conservative Party, Margaret Thatcher, infamously stated, 'people are really rather afraid that this country might be rather swamped by people with a different culture … people are going to react and be rather hostile to those coming in.'[33] A year later, she led her party to a general election victory and became Britain's first woman prime minister. At this time, Jenny Douglas argues, 'Black women and white working-class women were targeted for abortions and long-term contraceptives by health professionals and policy makers who had a view that they should not reproduce.'[34] Whilst for many white women in the women's movement at the time 'abortion was the number one issue', for Black and Asian women 'abortion wasn't something they had any problem obtaining'.[35] Instead, they frequently felt pressurised into having abortions.

The use of Depo-Provera was, for Black and Asian women, another example of what the Brent Community Health Council, Greater London, in 1981 described as the NHS accepting 'uncritically ruling assumptions – in this instance the desirability of reducing the black birth rate and the assumed ignorance and unreliability of black women….whatever the suffering this may cause.'[36] Consequently, the Brixton Black Women's Group – which opened the Abeng Centre, the first centre for Black women in London – participated in demonstrations against the drug, and wrote about its impact in their newsletter *Speak Out*.[37] Mia Morris, a leading member of OWAAD, recalled the involvement of the organisation in the campaign against Depo Provera, which,

> encourag(ed) women not to take it. Because during that particular period there was also a situation where a black woman would go into hospital and she's got fibroids and they would just say, that's it, we couldn't do anything, we've just taken your womb away. You know, you'd just have a hysterectomy at twenty-five. So it was quite vicious, all that really.[38]

Black and white women campaigned against Depo-Provera in the late 1970s, seeking to get the drug banned.[39] The administration of the drug, along with more readily available abortions and hysterectomies, became a focus for discussion and action across a number of women's groups, which sometimes brought together Black, Asian and white feminism. For example, 'Rowena Arshad remembers the issue of Depo-Provera provoking sympathies across borders and races.'[40] A national group – the Campaign Against Depo-Provera (CADP) – was established in 1978. This was, as Caitlin Lambert argues, spearheaded by Janet Hadley, a white, middle-class and privately educated woman involved with the wider Women's Liberation Movement from its first meetings, and who had 'helped to establish the highly influential *Shrew* magazine.'[41] She had 'experiences of the Black Power movement in the late 1960s and early 1970s, following her relationship with a West Indian man.'[42] Over five years, CAPD sought a ban on Depo-Provera, to expose how it had been administered without consent, and instead campaigned for free, safe and reliable contraception. CAPD collected information about the administration of the drug on women who had not been able to give informed consent and it also produced information and leaflets on the dangers of Depo-Provera. The group's successful media campaigns garnered support and led, in 1982, to the drug's makers not being given a long-term licence to administer the Depo-Provera in Britain.

CAPD's campaign relied, according to Caitlin Lambert, on an 'understanding that different forms of oppression are interconnected and mutually reinforcing, meaning they cannot be examined separately from one another.'[43] CAPD worked with the Organisation of Women of Asian and African Descent (OWAAD), but many other campaigns that this organisation was involved in highlighted the failure of the predominantly white women's movement to understand Asian and African Women's actual experiences. As Amrit Wilson, a member of Brixton Black Women's Group and the Indian Workers' Association later recalled, it was felt that there was 'a real need for solidarity between people like us of South Asian origin and people of African origin – because of our history of imperialist exploitation, which is still continuing, and because of the racism we faced.'[44] Racism ran through most police forces. Hence, in 1979, Awaz collaborated with Brixton Black Women's Group and the Indian Workers' Association GB, to organise a large national demonstration against police brutality.

Olive Morris (1952–1979), who had experienced police brutality first-hand as a teenager, was, along with Stella Dadzie (1952–), key to the formation OWAAD. Morris was born in Jamaica, and had been a member of the Black Panthers and founder of the Brixton Black Women's Group, as well as the Manchester's Black Women's Co-operative when she was a University student in the city. Dadzie was born in London, where her father was a Ghanaian diplomat; she was part of the Tottenham-based United Black Women's Action Group. OWAAD brought together a number of already existing Black and

Asian women's groups, including the North West London's Southall Black Sisters, and the Black Women's Mutual Aid Group. It also stimulated the formation of a multitude of local satellite organisations. As an organisation, OWAAD challenged mainstream feminism, causing white women to question their priorities, assumptions and their own racism. As one of the OWAAD organisers explained,

> We're not feminists – we reject that label because we feel that it represents a white ideology. In our culture the term is associated with an ideology and practice which is anti-men. Our group is not anti-men at all ... We're working together by different routes. We want to show people sisterhood in operation, something that's a forward movement, not a divisive one.[45]

During its four-year life, OWAAD published a bi-weekly newsletter, *FOWAAD!*, and from 1979, held an annual national conference. The first conference, a gathering of 300 Black and Asian women, discussed health, education, the law and immigration. From the 1950s, both political parties in Britain had competed to show how effectively they could prevent the migration of people from Britain's former colonies. The 1971 Immigration Act, although it did not use explicitly racist language, was yet another example of how the state attempted to limit immigration of non-white Commonwealth citizens into Britain.[46] Immigration regulations and officials made visits to and from relations in Commonwealth countries increasingly difficult for Black and Asian women, and created divisions within families which were split across different continents. The experience of immigration regulations shaped Black and Asian communities' engagement with the legal system, but were not a priority or even a consideration for many white members of the women's movement. Issues around women's immigration status and racism were fundamental to many South Asian women experiencing domestic violence. Women who had migrated to Britain to get married, could find themselves not only isolated from their families, but also facing the possibility of losing their right to remain in Britain if they left their abusive husbands.

Amrit Wilson (1941-), who was born in India, campaigned through Awaz to establish women's refuges, which would specifically cater for South Asian women, prioritising women's safety and assisting them to navigate the complicated immigration laws. She later recalled how they 'had to explain that traumatised women and children not only need familiar food and kitchen arrangements but safe spaces free of racism.'[47] By the end of the twentieth century, she recalled, 'an amazing network of refuges and services for South Asian women' had been established which provided 'facilities for mental health counselling, help with immigration cases, outreach work which was a lifeline for women trapped in their homes.'[48] The specialist help and knowledge which such refuges provided enabled them to guide women through welfare and housing systems, immigration laws, the threat of deportation and possible separation from their children.

Southall Black Sisters was set up in 1979, in the same year as OWAAD. Its initial focus was to help Asian women's struggle against racism, but it increasingly became involved in helping women who were victims of domestic violence and opposing religious fundamentalism. As the writer and activist, Ruahila Gupta, explained, Southall Black Sisters ran 'campaigns to highlight and bring about changes in the social, political economic and cultural constrictions which have led women to our door.'[49] The organisation campaigned for Kiranjit Ahluwalia, an Indian born woman who set fire to her husband after ten years of physical, psychological and emotional abuse. She was convicted of murder in December 1989. After a three-year campaign by the Southall Black Sisters, the conviction was overturned on appeal, as it was argued that she had been unaware that she could plead guilty of manslaughter on the grounds of diminished responsibility. She was suffering from severe depression at the time she set fire to her husband. The case raised problems for the Southall Black Sisters, as they sought to explain how 'culture does have a bearing in terms of the strategies available for Asian women to escape violence', without re-enforcing cultural perceptions and prejudices against Asian communities.[50] They politicised 'the issue of battered women who kill,' to broaden understanding of the provocation that battered women experienced.[51] As Pragna Patel has pointed out, the slogans that they campaigned about, on 'Women's tradition, struggle not submission', and 'Domestic Violence is a crime, self-defence is no offence', were adopted by all feminists.[52] In March 1986, 3,000 women demonstrated against male violence in London. The event was organised by, and included, Southall Black Sisters, Women against Violence Against Women, and Women's Aid.

As Jenny Douglas has argued, Black and Asian women's groups had by the 1990s, established a multitude of political campaigning activities which met with varying degrees of success.[53] Hundreds of women like Claudia Jones and Gertrude Maretta Paul campaigned around education, health, culture, housing and racism. However, OWAAD and organization which brought 'together lots of different groups with divergent interests and focuses' discovered 'these differences were both a strength and a weakness'.[54] OWAAD no longer existed at the time of the Southall Black Sisters' successful campaign on behalf of Kiranjit Ahluwalia.[54] Many of those involved in OWAAD had moved on to different phases of their lives and different spheres for their political campaigning.

Black and Asian women's campaigns and struggles occasionally overlapped or were co-ordinated with those of other women groups, as had occurred in relation to Depo-Provera. But in the histories of women's political campaigning in twentieth century Britain, there were also many clashes and tensions. For whilst white women are often blind to racism, for Black and Asian women racism has remained an ever-present factor. They have continued to contend with prejudice and oppression based on both gender and race and this shaped their political priorities at any given moment.

Chapter 12

Prostitutes Sit-in at Holy Cross Church (1982)

In November, 1982 a number of women from the London Collection of Prostitutes staged a 10-day sit-in at the Holy Cross Church in Kings Cross. The media were fascinated by what they saw as a slightly bizarre protest by sex-workers objecting to police harassment and violence. The sit-in was one of an increasing number of political protests and practical activities undertaken in the 1970s and 80s by campaigners seeking to end physical and sexual violence against women occurring both in public spaces and behind closed doors, and in the private sphere. Campaigns also sought to bring about changes in both the police and the court's treatment of victims of physical and sexual violence. Women sought to ensure that those subjected to sexual and physical violence received support from voluntary agencies run by women, such as Women's Refuges and Rape crisis centres. The political motivation of most of the women involved in these activities lay in the feminist movement; they were committed to the idea of working together in non-hierarchical, grass roots, women-only organisations. Consequently, rather than a few well known leaders, there were hundreds and thousands of anonymous women whose practical actions sought to change attitudes to all forms of violence against women.

Women sought the respect for and control over their own bodies – they adopted slogans such as: 'My body, My choice' and 'Whatever We Wear, Wherever We Go, Yes Means Yes And No Means No.' However, despite a multitude of innovative and publicity-catching political activities, including Reclaim the Night Marches, the success of these campaigns can be regarded as patchy. The aim of all women to go out safely when and where they chose, was hard to achieve. This was emphasised by the activities of Peter Sutcliffe, known as the Yorkshire Ripper, who between 1975 and 1981, killed 13 women and attempted to murder a further seven. His reign of terror and the response to it by the police, politicians and media, galvanised even more women to argue forcibly that violence against any woman was never justified or acceptable.

In the 1960s and 70s, women came together and shared their experiences and histories in formal and informal groups. They lifted the lid on the oppression and violence women faced within their homes and families; what many women saw as an individual problem or failure was demonstrated to be endemic throughout society. Early women's shelters had opened in Canada in the 1960s, but much of the impetus in 1972 to set up refuge in Britain – Chiswick Women's Aid – to help women escape from domestic violence, came first from Erin Pizzey (1939-). Erin was married with young children, and her involvement in local women's groups led her to perceive that there was need for a refuge for women seeking to escape domestic abuse. When local authorities refused to provide accommodation, she adopted a pragmatic approach to the problem, and with colleagues, started squatting in an unused house in Belmont Terrace, Chiswick. When this and other early women's refuges for battered wives opened in the early 1970s, further extensive evidence of brutality and violence was uncovered. The stories women told each other and the injuries that their bodies carried, indicated that domestic abuse was widespread, but largely unreported and not prosecuted.

Chiswick Women's Aid placed adverts in newspapers offering 'battered wives refuge, legal advice and moral support, 24 hours a day, Applicants must ring first.'[1] In 1973, Jenny Smith read such an advert in the *Daily Mirror*. She was the mother of two young children who had been subjected to a two-year period of terror, which included, beatings, knifings, burns, bites and an attempted drowning. Jenny rang the refuge after being ignored by a doctor and a psychiatrist, and told to go home and make peace with her husband by a priest,

> this time a woman's calm, soft voice, said: "Can you make your way here? We are in Chiswick, 2 Belmont Terrace. Can you get here? Just try to get here."…..
>
> Within 48 hours of that call, with the help of a neighbour, she had left her home in Hackney, east London, and was standing outside an ordinary terraced house in west London – her seven-month-old daughter in one arm, her 23-month-old at her side.
>
> When the door swung open, she was enveloped in a woman's embrace. "Come in, love," she said. "You're safe now."[2]

18 women and their 46 children were living at the refuge. Jenny Smith recalled 'mattresses snaked out of the bedrooms and up the hallways in any space that we could get them. It was a bit like a refugee camp.'[3] The early refuges were run along communal lines, where women voted on important decisions. In addition to the safety they provided, they gave women the space not only to think, but to begin to sort out their lives. The demand for spaces in the Chiswick refuge grew exponentially: it moved to a bigger house, took over

other houses and even squatted in the 47-suite Palm Court Hotel, Richmond in 1975, ensuring that 'no new arrivals were ever turned away'.[4] Erin Pizzey later recalled 'The police couldn't do anything because it wasn't illegal then – and no council would want to have to re-home 15 mothers and their children.'[5]

Pizzey was media savvy, and while the feminist magazine, *Spare Rib*, was the first national publication to discuss the refuge and its work, other areas of the media were soon falling over themselves to explore this 'new' social problem. The Chiswick refuge was featured on BBC 2's Open Door programme, and a documentary entitled, *Scream Quietly or the Neighbours will Hear* (1974) was made about battered wives; a book of the same name followed five years later. Despite such publicity, the refuge relied heavily on fundraising activities and volunteers. In 1974, for example, 130 people attended a fashion show at Victoria Hall, Harrow, organised by the Get Set boutique and the Harrow Ladies Circle, and reportedly raised £110 for the refuge (approximately £1,100 in modern money).[6] Women in other areas were sometimes luckier in gaining the support of local authorities when they set up refuges. Acton Women's Aid was formed in 1973, after a visit to the Chiswick refuge, but had the good fortune to secure a house from Ealing Council alongside a grant of £2,000 per annum towards their running costs.[7]

By 1974, there were nearly 40 refuges across Britain. Most, like Chiswick, had been brought about by local grass-roots women's groups tenaciously lobbying local authorities for houses to use as refuges, or squatting in empty properties. As Women's Aid campaigner, Dickie James, argues 'They had little in the way of funding and faced considerable hostility because they were challenging one of the most deeply rooted institutions of western society – The Family.'[8] The National Women's Aid Federation gave these refuges a campaigning voice, and in 1976, created the *You Can't Beat a Woman* campaign. The slogan appeared on T-shirts, mugs, leaflets and posters at a local and national level for many years. It was accompanied by an image of a refuge: a house with women hanging out of doors and windows, welcoming others into the women-only space, supporting each other in their opposition to domestic abuse. 'We wanted to change the world, to make it safer for women and children', recalled Anna who was a founder member of one of the early refuges in Staffordshire. 'We were a sisterhood. We wouldn't be silenced and we wouldn't be beaten.'[9] Their actions had some success: the Domestic Violence and Matrimonial Proceedings Act was also passed in 1976, giving new rights to those at risk of domestic violence. The following year, the 1977 Housing Act (Homeless Persons) acknowledged that women and children fleeing domestic violence were homeless and entitled to receive local authority housing support.

By 1976, Erin Pizzey's loose and sometimes fractious relationship with the women's movement had come to an end. Over the years that followed, she increasingly came to see domestic violence as 'a family issue, usually intergenerational, with men and women both having responsibility for it, addicted to the adrenalin high of fear and being feared.'[10] Such a view was not supported by the statistical evidence in, for example, the British Crime Survey. Pizzey was not, however, alone in expressing her concern that some feminists saw all men as a threat. Differentiating between the very real danger some men posed to some women, why and how this occurred; and how it could best be stopped remained thorny issues in the Women's Liberation Movement for many years.

Women who worked in women's refuges, the anti-rape movement and Rape Crisis Centres drew upon their experience to try to understand the possible impact legislation, institutional change (for example in the police and public prosecution service), or shifts in women's cultural and economic roles could have in preventing violence against women. According to Alison Diduck this led to a change in the ways 'rape was understood socially and legally. These centres helped to influence police, medical and criminal justice procedures and substantive law. They have assisted and supported millions of individual women. They are a truly remarkable example of women working together to improve women's lives.'[11]

The Rape Crisis network was inspired by activities which occurred in the USA, where women had begun to share their experiences of rape, as part of what was known as the consciousness raising movement. Women were encouraged to speak out and to relate their personal stories. By doing so, the taboo and victim blaming that surrounded this violent act diminished. In Britain, and many other countries, there was no anonymity for women in court, and the police and defence lawyers cross-examined them about their sexual history. Many women felt that they were on trial rather than a witness when rape cases were prosecuted. Consequently, very few women reported rape; estimates suggest that only one in ninety-nine cases went to court.[12]

The first Rape Crisis Centre was set up in November 1976 in North London, seeking to offer 'sympathetic non-judgmental support, advice and information on police and legal procedures for those women who chose to report', and ultimately, 'to help raped women regain their strength as individuals.'[13] A group of ten women operated a 24-hour telephone line, and they also met women and gave legal advice, undertook research, sought to educate the general public about rape by speaking to groups, and trained new volunteers. Unpaid workers slept overnight in the centre office, 'taking calls from women who had just been raped, women who had been raped years ago, and women who had been raped as children'.[14] As the organisers of Bradford Rape Crisis, which opened in 1981, recalled

> All those first women had was a telephone and a determination to give their time to support as many women as they could. They were all volunteers, making proceeds from organising jumble sales and discos, and collecting individual donations to keep going. As the calls flooded in, they listened to what women told them about what they needed in order to recover and take control of their lives, and they steadily grew a service to meet those needs.[15]

By the late 1980s, the ways of operating and the approaches at the North London Rape Crisis Centre had developed, and had become a template for over 60 Rape Crisis Centres across Britain. All were, like women's refuges, grass roots organisations, set up by women to help other women and were predominantly reliant on charitable and local authority funding.[16] For example, Edinburgh, the third Rape Crisis Centre to open, was founded by women involved in the women's movement and funded by private donations. Its first day of operation on 1 July, 1978, was accompanied by a vigil on Princes Street, with press, TV and radio coverage. It sought to 'provide a safe and confidential space for women who had been raped'.[17] Like many others, the centre has refused to use the word victim and sought to 'work towards changing attitudes in society towards rape.'[18]

The public education work undertaken by Rape Crisis centres was often concerned with myth busting, trying to challenge the assumptions people had about when and who was raped, and to make it clear that women were not culpable for the behaviour of male rapists. One of the strongest preconceptions at the time was that rapists were strangers, whereas ninety per cent of women knew their rapist before being attacked.[19] Indeed, 'rapists can be friends, colleagues, clients, neighbours, family, partners or exes or even husbands.'[20] However, until the Sexual Offences Act of 2003, British law did not explicitly acknowledge that rape could occur within marriage. According to a 1736 legal treatise titled, *History of the Pleas of the Crown written*, by Sir Matthew Hale, a former Chief Justice in England, 'the husband of a woman cannot himself be guilty of an actual rape upon his wife, on account of the matrimonial consent which she has given, and which she cannot retract.'[21] This position was re-enforced by the barrister, John Frederick Archbold, in a legal tome called *Pleading and Evidence in Criminal Cases*, published in 1822.

In 1976, the organisation Women against Rape (WAR) was founded, which demanded recognition of the horror and harm caused by all kinds of rape, whoever the perpetrator, whether they be husbands, fathers or friends. In March 1977, a 19-year-old member of the Coldstream Guards, Tom Holdsworth, was convicted of indecent assault, for ripping a 17-year-old girl's earrings off and breaking her ribs, and he was sentenced to three years' imprisonment. When his sentence was overturned on appeal, a member of WAR stormed the court, campaigned outside the Ministry of Defence, and encouraged the young victim to publicise the trauma she had experienced. The group followed this up by holding a mock rape trial in Trafalgar Square in London in 1977. Women testified, telling the assembled crowd about the violence and abuse that they had experienced at the hands of employers, husbands and others who had raped them. Seeing rape within relationships as a form of domestic violence, they argued that all women should have the financial independence to be able to escape abusive domestic relationships. Adopting slogans such as: 'Yes means yes, No means, no. However, we dress; wherever we go,' and 'Rape like Charity begins at home' they worked to change public perceptions about rape and were strong participants in the campaign to make rape within marriage a crime.

WAR took their campaign to the mainstream media, when in August 1977, *The Guardian*'s Women's Page carried a lengthy article under the heading of *Rapist's Reply*, suggesting that although only a small number of women were raped, all men were being tarnished by the assumption, as they were considered potential rapists. WAR held a demonstration outside *The Guardian* offices, and a member of the group wrote a lengthy article, published in the *Guardian*, titled, 'When Rape Like Charity Begins at Home.' She pointed out that women who were financially dependent on a man faced the expectation of sexual service, and drew attention to the treatment of women who had been raped, pointing out,

> When the Woman goes to the police, to the court, to her employer, she faces the inevitable questions: what were you doing out at that time of night (or day)? What were you wearing? Why weren't you with your husband? Why don't you get yourself a man? Why weren't you safe at home in "your" place?[22]

In public and in private, women, she argued, were in fear of rape, and this was used to control and restrict them. The wider women's movement, Women's Aid, Rape Crisis Centres, and WAR were effective campaigners. Together they submitted evidence to the Criminal Law Revision Committee in 1981 and 1984, under the title, *The Rapist who Pays the Rent: Women's Case for Changing the Law on Rape.* This led to a change in public opinion towards rape, resulting in an increasing number of rapes being reported.

One of the most influential examples of a reported rape, which crystallised a change in legal practice, occurred in November 1989. Those involved remained anonymous and were referred to as Mr and Mrs R who had married in 1984. Five years later, when the relationship became difficult, Mrs R moved back to her parents' house, leaving her husband a note explaining that she was seeking a divorce. The following month, when Mrs R's parents were out, R broke into their house, attempted to rape his wife and assaulted her, applying pressure on her neck with his hands. Mr R was arrested and charged with rape, sentenced to three years of imprisonment, and the couple divorced. Mr R repeatedly appealed against the conviction for attempted rape, relying on the by then several hundred-year-old assumption, that a husband cannot be guilty of raping his wife. However, fifteen years of women's political campaigning had had an impact. When the case finally reached the House of Lords, it was dismissed. Both the Law Lords and the Law Commission, which had published a working paper laid before parliament on the matter, were of the view 'that in modern times the supposed marital exemption in rape forms no part of the law in England.' The Lord Chief Justice Lord Lane pointed out, 'We take the view that the time has arrived when the law should declare that a rapist remains a rapist subject to the criminal law, irrespective of his relationship with his victim.'[23]

R versus R, as it was known, marked a turning point in redefining what was acceptable treatment of women in the private sphere, but as WAR pointed out, fear of physical and sexual violence continued to make women anxious about going out into public places, particularly at night. The Reclaim the Night marches, which also began in the 1970s, sought to address this. 'Take Back the Night' marches had already occurred in the USA and parts of Europe. In Britain, a catalyst for these campaigns was the six years of violence against women perpetrated by Peter Sutcliffe (1946 – 2020). Nicknamed the Yorkshire Ripper, Sutcliffe murdered 13 women, and attempted to murder a further seven others in Manchester and a number of towns and cities across West Yorkshire. Sutcliffe's attacks took place in both residential areas and red-light districts; he had correctly surmised that in the latter, the police sometimes took a rather ambivalent attitude towards violence against prostitutes. After a protracted, and in many respects, bundled police investigation, Sutcliffe was arrested for driving with false number plates in January 1981, and the extent of his guilt was slowly unveiled. During his six years of violence, fear stalked the streets, and anxiety was engendered within communities in which women were constantly warned to stay in their homes and keep off the streets in order to be safe.

In November 1977, Reclaim the Night marches took place in Leeds, Manchester, Bristol, York, Brighton, Newcastle, Bradford, Manchester, Lancaster, London and other cities. A number of Yorkshire Ripper killings had occurred in the Leeds area, and feminists were dismayed and angered by the response of the police. The advice to women was to stay out of public places when it was night, which focused on women's behaviour, not on the perpetrator of the violence. On 12 November, 30 marchers set off from Chapeltown in Leeds and converged with a further 85 marchers from the Woodhouse district of the city for a demonstration in City Square. There, women displayed banners demanding 'no curfew on women' and a 'curfew on men.' Such marches became a key tool in women's campaigns against rape and male violence in towns and cities, well into the 1980s.[24] The large torchlight processions enabled hundreds of women to go to places that they had often avoided or only visited accompanied by a sense of fear and anxiety. Women found empowerment and strength in being part of a group of protestors, and it gave them a voice for their cause: media attention. In 1979, for example, a local newspaper recounted how 'Chanting and singing, about 200 young women marched through Liverpool in a torchlight procession, protesting at the lack of safety on the city streets.'[25] A local Liberal parliamentary candidate who accompanied the marchers noted her concern about the safety of women on the city streets at night and pointed out, 'We are paying our rates and taxes like everybody else, but we don't get protection.'[26] The Reclaim the Night marches garnered support from students, housewives, the young and old – and from sex workers, many of whom had little choice about going out at night and were often subjected to violence by both punters and police.

Peter Sutcliffe's two-week trial began at the Old Bailey in London on May 5, 1981. The following month, the feminist magazine, *Spare Rib*, carried an article titled, *Sutcliffe – Its women under attack*, asking who was 'really on trial, Sutcliffe, his wife or the 13 women he murdered?' It went on to deplore the way that the prosecution, when describing Sutcliffe's victims, chose to distinguish the women according to their perceived sexual activity, saying, 'some were prostitutes, some were women of easy virtue, but the last six attacks involved victims whose reputations were totally unblemished.'[27] The article objected to the distinction being made 'between pure and impure woman'[28] Prostitutes, it was argued, needed to be understood as members of society, as they pointed out that those who were murdered also had families who were mourning them. Sutcliffe's murders of sex workers had left twenty-three children motherless.[29] The article was accompanied by a picture taken outside the Old Bailey, which depicted a demonstration by women from the English Collection of Prostitutes. They too objected to the handling of the case by the police, media and the prosecution.

The English Collection of Prostitutes (ECP), which had been set up in 1975, was linked to the prostitute's rights movement in Europe and to the Crossroads Women's Centre in London. The group sought the decriminalisation of prostitution, to challenge the social stigma which surrounded prostitution, and to campaign for sex worker's rights and safety. It also wanted resources provided for women who wished to get out of prostitution. In March 1979, 50 members of the ECP had attended the House of Commons, cheering and applauding from the visitors' gallery when Maureen Colquhoun MP introduced the Protection of Prostitutes Bill. Although unsuccessful, the bill sought to provide prostitutes with better protection from exploitation and victimisation.[30] The assumption of many, that Peter Sutcliffe was principally a prostitute killer, made the case an important area for their campaigning. It was the moment to remind the public, as Dianne Cerresa's article in *Spare Rib* did, that, 'All women are vulnerable to male violence but no one has bothered to stress the specific vulnerability of prostitutes which makes them easy targets.'[31]

The economic crisis of the 1980s associated with Thatcherism, drove many more women into prostitution, with sex workers sometimes nicknamed 'Thatcher's girls'. As one member of ECP interviewed by the press explained, 'We have to remember that there is an economic crisis. That means that Kings Cross station and Euston station and St Pancras station is bringing women daily, young women, single mothers, all kinds of women into Argyle Square to make some money.'[32] The peculiarity of British law, which does not outlaw prostitution, but which makes soliciting and living off immoral earnings illegal, laid these women and their partners open to harassment, abuse and violence from the police. It also compounded the dangers of rape and violence many prostitutes faced, from pimps, clients, and sometimes from the police. A member of ECP argued that sex workers were, 'trying to make a living and are living independently of men. Out of the thumb of the pimps. That's when the police attack them.'[33]

Sex workers felt that they were repeatedly harassed, frequently arrested by the police, and that legal action against them increased the chances of having their children removed by social services. Racial tensions were also escalating and black women who were prostitutes were on the sharp end of this. Tensions in London increased, when a 'woman reported a rape to the police, only to be told that no rape could have happened, as she was a prostitute.'[34] In desperation, the ECP took their campaigning to a new level. In November 1982, they occupied the Church of the Holy Cross in the red-light area of

King's Cross, London. Their protest against police brutality mirrored some of those undertaken by prostitutes in France in the 1970s. The women camped in the church, some accompanied by their children, sleeping on the cold floor on blankets and sleeping bags, making each other cups of tea, and taking it in turns to go outside and explain to a growing group of interested members of the press what they were protesting about.

Individuals donned a mask covering their eyes but which ensured that their mouth and voice were unfettered. They stood next to an ECP banner and explained their criticism of the treatment of prostitutes by police. One explained,

> women are saying– 'No more. We've had enough of that. We're gonna get justice now. We're gonna have the support of serious lawyers. We're not gonna plead guilty when we're not guilty. We're not gonna have our children taken away. We're not gonna be persecuted. We're not going to make jokes with the police in order to not be arrested. [35]

During their 12 days' occupation, the women wrote letters to the House of Lords and to the Greater London Country Council, seeking to capitalise on the publicity and press attention that their campaign was receiving. They had six demands, which were neither met then, nor in the years which followed. These sought,

1. An end to illegal arrests of prostitutes
2. An end to police threats, blackmail, harassment and racism
3. Hands off our children – we don't want our kids in care
4. An end to arrest of boyfriends, husbands, sons
5. Arrest rapists and pimps instead
6. Immediate protection, welfare, housing for women who want to get off the game.

A number of women from other feminist groups across the country came to lend their support to the protest and there was apparently 'a great spirit inside, a great feeling of togetherness.'[36] As one woman recalled: 'An event like that shakes up your life. You see that a whole set of things you didn't think were possible are clearly possible.'[37] The vicar of the church made no attempt to evict the women and in turn, the women ensured that all the regular services continued to take place undisturbed, while the sex workers sat quietly at the back of the church. Whilst one disgruntled parishioner claimed to be 'very bitter. It's not nice when you go to Mass to say your prayers quietly and you've got prostitutes in the way'[38], the vicar stated: 'the Lord Jesus would not want these women thrown from the church.'[39]

What was seen as an incongruous, slightly bizarre protest, brought enormous publicity and support to the plight of sex workers from, for example, Guyana's Working People's Alliance, Labour MP Tony Benn, Black and Immigrant women's organisations, Greenham Common women's peace camp and Sappho, the lesbian women's organisation.[40] Furthermore, in the years which followed, a range of media and film texts began to undermine distinctions between women who were being catagorised by their sexual activity. Ideas of pure and impure, or a dichotomy between madonna and whore, were dismantled in films such as *Mona Lisa* (1986) and *Shirley Valentine* (1989), whilst the television series, *Band of Gold* (ITV 1995), made a group of prostitutes, who lived and worked in Bradford's Red-Light district, the heroines of the plot.[41]

Thus, different but inter-related campaigns sought to put an end to the physical and sexual abuse of women, whether in the public or private spheres; all relied upon the work of a multitude of mostly anonymous politicised women who sought to help other women. They wanted women to control their own bodies and for this fundamental right to be respected by friends and strangers, husbands and partners, pimps and police – in all circumstances. Young women by the beginning of the millennium had a stronger sense of this themselves.

The work of Women's Aid, Rape Crisis Centres, War against Rape and the English Collective of Prostitutes, made significant progress. They changed attitudes, institutional practice and laws. By the end of the twentieth century, rape within marriage was no longer deemed legally acceptable, and there was a growing understanding of how domestic violence involves a pattern of power and control, not necessarily a series of isolated incidents paving the way for coercive control to become a criminal offence in Section 76 of the Serious Crime Act 2015.

Despite these changes, legal prosecutions against the perpetrators of all forms of domestic abuse or rape still remain small in relation to the number of incidents that occur, and 2–3 women a week continue to be killed by partners. Shockingly, in 2021, fewer than 1 in 60 reported rapes were charged, and the number of rape convictions also continued to fall significantly. Only 1,074 convictions succeeded in 2019–20, a decline from 2,991 convictions three years before.[42]

Chapter 13

'How dare the government presume the right to kill others in our name?' (1982)

On the August bank holiday of 1981, thirty-six women, four men and a few children from Llanpumsaint in Carmarthenshire, Wales, set off on a walk 110 miles from Cardiff, to the USA Airforce base at Greenham Common, Berkshire. They were seeking to prevent NATO carrying out its plan to install cruise missiles on British soil; their destination was one of the places where the weapons were to be sited. The organisers, who called themselves *Women for Life on Earth*, were a group of friends: Ann Pettitt and Karmen Thomas, Lynne Whittemore and Liney Seward. They had formulated their plans sitting around kitchen tables in their homes, while they drank coffee, occasionally stepping around the Lego on the floor, and sharing their concerns about the arms race and fears of a nuclear holocaust. Ann later remembered that at the time, the Government was handing out leaflets titled, *Protect and Survive*, with instructions on actions to be taken in the event of a nuclear war. These included, 'get under the table, draw the blinds, get food in the cupboard under the stairs ... advice which is so clearly off the scale of mad... I was wrenched away from my rural life and into the fear.'[1]

The four women recruited other women of all ages, from teenagers to grandmothers, to join in their protest, through chain letters, adverts in local papers and local radio. Sue Lent, a young mother who joined the march after hearing the organisers interviewed on Radio Wales, pushed her one-year-old son Chris all the way to Greenham Common in his buggy.[2] Jill Evans, a 22-year-old researcher at the Polytechnic of Wales heard about the march through her local branch of the Campaign for Nuclear Disarmament (CND). She and four other CND members from Rhondda were inspired by the uniqueness of the event, as she later recalled, 'we could see that it was something totally different. You could feel the passion and the commitment, even though there was a small number of people. It was really inspiring.'[3]

The initial intention was for the march to arrive at Greenham on 5 September, 1981. As they trudged along wearing purple, white and green scarves and clothes, replicating the colours of the suffragettes, the women handed out leaflets, spoke at meetings and were reported on the local news. As they neared Greenham, aware that their actions had not generated the media coverage and impact that they had hoped for, they sought a more spectacular and eye-catching finale. Something that would be reported in national and international newspapers, featured on the evening news, and bring their message to the notice of both politicians and the public. They decided to replicate the methods of Edwardian suffragettes, who had chained themselves to the railings outside 10 Downing Street in 1908. Finances did not stretch to the expense of chains and padlocks for everyone. So, four women were chosen to chain themselves to the gates of Greenham Common Airbase and demand a televised debate with the Minister of Defence. The initial impact of their protest was slightly undermined, when the police assumed that the women were cleaners, who had arrived early to clean the American army base. When their demand was refused, undaunted, the women remained at the base and continued their protest. Days of protest stretched into weeks, months and years, as the Greenham Common Peace Camp became the most high-profile political campaign by women in the 1980s, and the world's most famous anti-nuclear campaign.

The camp was just one in a long line of women's peace protests in the twentieth century, which assumed that women's relationship to war and violence was intrinsically different to that of men. For many, like Olive Schreiner, writing in response to the Boer War, women's maternal role gave them a particular attitude to armed conflict. She suggested,

> There is, perhaps, no woman, whether she has borne children, or merely potentially a child bearer, could look down upon the battlefield covered with the slain, but the thought would rise in her, So many mothers' sons! So many bodies brought into the world to lie there! So many months of weariness and pain while bones and muscles are shaped within.[4]

Some of those involved in the Edwardian fight for women suffrage even argued that women's enfranchisement and political influence would place a greater emphasis on the value of human life and shift the priorities of political decision makers; there would be fewer or no more wars. Sadly, there has been little indication this has happened.

A commitment to internationalism and peace did however lead a number of women to try to prevent the outbreak of the First World War and to continue to campaign for peace during the conflict. Scottish suffragist, Chrystal Macmillan, was one of many members of the National Union of Women's Suffrage Societies (NUWSS) who were horrified to see Europe slipping towards war in the weeks following the assignation of Archduke Ferdinand on 28 June, 1914. She and other suffragists, describing themselves as 'representatives of twelve million women', drafted a last-minute 'International Manifesto of Women', delivered to the British Foreign Secretary and Foreign Ambassadors in London on 31st July. This entreated politicians to avoid 'the threatened unparalleled disaster' of war, and instead, through negotiation and concessions, maintain the peace.[5]

A year later, Chrystal Macmillan was one of the organisers of the International Congress of Women, held in the Hague in April 1915. More than 1,200 women from twelve countries, including Germany, the USA and France were present, but only four women from Britain were able to attend, due to government restrictions on travel in wartime. The conference led to the formation of the Women's International League for Peace and Freedom (WILPF), and Helen Crawfurd, better known for her involvement in the Glasgow Rent Strikes, became a founding member of the Glasgow branch of WILF. As Ann Todd has pointed out, Helen 'learned of acts of sexual violence perpetrated by soldiers, and believed the wartime experience left women in a powerless position… If women could more actively involve themselves in politics, as 'natural peacemakers', they could help bring about an end to the conflict.'[6] From 1916–18, the Glasgow Women's Peace Crusades met, sometimes with as many as 5,000 attendees, and campaigned for both a 'People's Peace', and a commitment to disarmament. Their aims and ideals were summed up in a song Helen Crawfurd wrote, titled *Song of the Women*.

In the aftermath of the first industrialised world war, women across Britain, whether as mothers, sisters or sweethearts, mourned the dead and the injured. Journalist Vera Brittain's autobiographical novel *Testament of Youth*, about the loss of her fiancé, brother and his friends in the First World War, gave a voice to their suffering when it was published in 1933. Novelist Virginia Woolf's essay, *Three guineas* (1938), presented a political diatribe against war. In 1933, the Women's Co-operative Guild introduced the white poppy, to be worn on Armistice Day as a symbol of the wearer's commitment to peace and avoiding another war. Any divergence from wearing the traditional red poppy was considered by many to be dishonouring those who had died during the First World War. Yet even some of these, like Mrs Smee who wrote to the *Birmingham Gazette*, agreed, 'It was women's job to keep peace…. They had got to see that the last war was not forgotten, and if they taught their children what little was to be gained by war there would not be another war.'[7]

Many women's groups campaigned for peace, through their active involvement with the League of Nations Union and the WILF. In 1923, the Welsh Women's Peace Petition, signed by 390,296 women and which was approximately seven miles long, 'implored America to join and lead the

'How dare the government presume the right to kill others in our name?' 141

League of Nations to secure lasting peace.'[8] As the world leaders prepared to meet at the League of Nations World Disarmament Conference in 1932, WILPF circulated a disarmament petition, gaining signatures from members of women's groups such as the Women's Institute movement. Shop fronts all over Britain were taken over and decorated to promote the petition.[9] Once again, women's efforts were in vain: during the Second World War, the horrors of bombing, only glimpsed in the First World War, became all too real. Hundreds and thousands of civilians were killed and injured by bombing raids carried out by both sides. Vera Brittain was amongst those feminist pacifists who campaigned against saturation bombing. However, when atomic bombs were dropped on Hiroshima and Nagasaki in August 1945, they witnessed destruction and death on a totally new scale.

By 1958, the Campaign for Nuclear Disarmament (CND) had been established in Britain. Later that year, the 64-year-old, Dora Russell, and fifteen other women set off from Edinburgh to travel to Moscow in what is now referred to as the Women's Peace Caravan or the Caravan of Peace. They travelled in two vehicles, a coach and an old army truck, in which they loaded tents, cooking equipment and food. Crossing Europe, at the height of the Cold War, they sought to make links with other women as they went. Dora Russell was one of many women who dedicated time and energy to campaigning for peace, continuing to speak at CND rallies into her eighties. In the final volume of her autobiography, completed in 1985, she continued to proclaim the need for love and understanding between individuals and between nations: 'We do not want our world to perish …. Only by learning to love one another can our world be saved. Only love can conquer all.'[10] By the time Dora Russell died in 1986, a growing number of women considered the threat posed by the cruise missiles placed at the USA Air Base at Greenham Common was so great, that CND demanded a determined, dedicated response.

From September 1981, until the camp was finally disbanded in the year 2000, thousands of women came to Greenham, some staying for months or years, some visiting frequently or just for a particular event – but all felt a strong antagonism towards the existence of nuclear weapons capable of obliterating thousands of women and children. The cruise missiles which were finally installed at the USA air base at Greenham Common in November 1983, carried nuclear warheads with 'four times the destructive power of the atomic bomb that obliterated Hiroshima in 1945.'[11] As large superpowers invested in increasing numbers of nuclear weapons, their populations were told that the mutually assured destruction these weapons offered would operate as a deterrent to war. A nuclear conflict would apparently never happen, but the Greenham cruise missiles had a range covering Europe only. This led to concerns that the USA planned any potential conflict to be fought in Europe so Europe alone would be destroyed. Furthermore, as one Greenham campaigner, Sarah, explained, 'A woman in Russia is the same as myself, the same emotions, leading the same sort of life. In no way will I be part of anything that will murder her.'[12] Such sentiments led women from the *Women for Life on Earth* march to remain at Greenham, seeking to disrupt the construction work and to make the camp a focus for women's peace campaigning in Britain.[13]

The transition from a march to a permanent camp happened gradually; a member of the military on the base showed the women where there was a tap they could use, and a few days later, it was suggested they dug latrines in the woods, which could be emptied into a manhole. Local supporters gave them tents and cooking pots; a portacabin arrived from a CND group in Southampton.[14] As news of the camp spread, more women began to arrive to live in makeshift tents and shelters. Some stayed for a week or two, others a year or more, while an increasing number of letters arrived offering support and finance. The women's protests both obstructed lorries going into the base by lying down in front of them, and attempted to persuade the drivers to turn away. Their presence bore witness to women's continued opposition to the camp and its weapons.

The contrast between the informality and femininity of the peace camp and the structured, masculinity of the missiles and the air base, was not lost on the participants. Notwithstanding that Britain had its first woman prime minister, in the 1980s, the military, the arms industry, political power, and indeed the Campaign for Nuclear Disarmament, were all predominantly in the hands of men. As a Greenham Common newsletter argued, 'The military is the most obvious product of patriarchy.'[15] The peace camp became all female in February 1982, although men could visit during the day. In a statement to Newbury Magistrates Court on April 14, 1982, protesters explained:

> As women we have been actively encouraged to be complacent, by sitting at home and revering men as our protectors: we now reject this role. The law is concerned with the preservation of property. We are concerned with the preservation of life. How dare the government presume the right to kill others in our name?[16]

Jane Powell, who spent a year at camp in her youth, and visited regularly at weekends and for events until the camp was dismantled in 2000, recalled: 'The camp itself was made up of nine smaller base camps.'[17] Seven were situated at the seven gates of the military base; each one, named after the colours of the rainbow, had a different culture and style. The original camp by the main gate was Yellow Gate; Blue Gate's focus was more new age; Violet Gate was more religious. The number of women living at the base fluctuated: 'at the Yellow and Green Gates there would typically be around 20 or 30 women, with slightly lower numbers at the Orange and Blue Gates, and down to three, four, five or so at Emerald and Violet Gates.'[18] Some of the smaller groups, for example at Turquoise Gate, 'came and went.'[19]

Those who stayed at the camps were supported by others who visited, bringing supplies and joining mass demonstrations. It is easy to understand how there was sometimes resentment towards these part-timers coming at weekends and then returning to their homes, nice hot baths and comfortable beds. Jean, who visited the base to offer support as often as her studies in Southampton would allow, wrote in her diary in April 1983,

> The women are fabulous, nothing seems to oppress them.
> Took back some washing for Jan, she seemed really pleased about that.
> Some of the women seem resentful of us weekenders, but I can see where they are coming from. I was a bit hurt that they didn't seem pleased to see us – but we're still not into the good weather and they've got more important things to do than play host to part-time peace campaigners.
> I am totally in awe of what they are doing – really in awe.[20]

Greenham residents and supporters were often weighing up multiple responsibilities and demands on their time and energy, according to their circumstances. For example, one of the original organisers of the Women for Life on Earth March, Anne Pettit, felt unable to stay at the camp, as she had two small children and an elderly father to care for. Instead, she visited, attended big events, and helped to support and publicise the camp alongside continuing to campaign against nuclear weapons.[21]

Support for the camp also came from the Religious Society of Friends, known as the Quakers, in nearby Newbury. Their premises provided washing and shower facilities to peace camp residents for a number of years.[22] Local CND groups brought supplies of food and sleeping bags, but the camp did not go unchallenged; their presence was not welcomed by many of the local communities who complained about the loss of a once beautiful picnic and play area and objected to what they described as the 'blatant immoral behaviour' and 'disgusting appearance' of the campaigners.[23] Some nearby pubs were unwilling to serve the women and the hostility meant that peace campaigners were hesitant about entering local towns and villages. The local branch of Women and Families for Defence, which had strong links to the Conservative

Party, campaigned against the camp, utilising slogans such as: 'Peace Women: You Disgust Us' and 'Clean Up and Get Out.'

On 29 September, 1982, the first attempt to evict the residents began. As one of the women, Jane, noted in her diary, 'Soon everyone was packing up tents and bedding and hiding them, looking for places to put things we would need for the next stage of the camp's life. Saucepans, food, cutlery, cash and bedding were packed into cars; we hid our standpipe very carefully. Meanwhile it rained solidly.'[24] In the years that followed, women at the camp experienced repeated attempts to evict them, police brutality, numerous court appearances, fines and imprisonment. They put up with the practicalities of living with little comfort in rudimentary conditions. Equipment was damaged in the evictions, and some, like the stopcocks used to obtain water from the mains, were expensive to replace. Despite determined attempts to keep things clean and hygienic, an outbreak of gastroenteritis occurred in August 1983.[25] The women's determination to maintain their protest was rewarded with publicity and support from across Britain and around the world. For example, in December 1983, the 100 women and children at the camp settling down for a damp and cold Christmas were cheered by sacks-full of donated food and clothing from well-wishers and cash donations to fill their empty bank-balance.[26]

A high security fence constructed around the base, known as 'Our Berlin Wall' became the focus of many of the non-violent, inventive, sometimes funny protests over the years. It was adorned with items of significance to the protesters and wrapped in brightly coloured wool. There were multiple attempts to breach the fence, going over or through it. Wire-cutters became an essential item for many Greenham women, as they repeatedly entered the 'male space' of the American Army Camp. A small group danced around nuclear silos being constructed, having cut through the fence on New Year's Day, 1983. Later in October that year, women dressed as witches for a Greenham Halloween Party and lulled the police into a false sense of security as they cut down four of the nine miles of fence.

No event showcased the oceans of support for the Greenham Common Peace Camp's campaign more than *Embrace the Base*. On the 12 December, 1982, 30,000 women held hands to create a 14-mile human chain around the perimeter fence, decorating it with pictures, mementoes and children's clothing and drawings. The date was chosen, as it was the third anniversary of NATO's decision to place cruise missiles on British soil. Publicising the event in a pre-internet era took the form of chain letters, leaflets and posters, with the slogan *'Embrace the Base On Sunday. Close The Base On Monday'*. A surviving poster from Birmingham inviting women to attend, included instructions on how to obtain coach tickets at the Peace Centre opposite New Street Station, as well as local activists' phone numbers, written in marker pen.[27] Coaches were laid on by groups across Britain: service stations on the M4 and the surrounding roads were clogged up with them, filled with women excitedly waving at one another, as their transport crawled towards suitable drop off points.

It was well into the afternoon before all the women were unloaded and in position. Lynn Rishworth, a student at college in Reading in the 1980s, recalled the moment when she knew the women had surrounded the nine-mile perimeter fence: 'Our sisters across the Common whooped back to us and we knew that we'd done it – there were enough of us to encircle the entire Base....Women were still coming. Lines formed behind lines and we were all full of such joy and a sense of our own strength in unity.'[28] Jill Evans, a student who organised two coach loads of women from the Rhondda to participate, thinks it really changed perceptions of the Peace Camp.

> The most unlikely people came, not women who had been involved in any kind of protest before but women who wanted to be part of it and felt so strongly they wanted to make their voice heard. It was such a special day. The fence was decorated with baby clothes, with photographs, with doves, with ribbons – it was a really symbolic day. It took the media by surprise and attitudes changed after that.[29]

Other mass events also took place over the years: on 1 April, 1983, approximately 70,000 protesters formed a human chain covering the 14 miles from Greenham to the ordnance factory at Aldermaston. The women who lived or visited the camp routinely, were both conforming and challenging traditional ideas of femininity. There was a strongly essentialist idea, in common with early twentieth-century peace campaigners, that women as mothers, carers and nurturers, were natural peace makers. Many of their activities emphasised women's roles as mothers, for example when they dressed in black, mourning the children who would be lost to nuclear weapons. There was also a teddy bear's picnic, when 200 women dressed as teddy bears entered the base. Teddy bears had been chosen as symbolic of childhood and the children whose lives were threatened by the weapons. Yet Greenham women were also seen as having abandoned their homes and families to protest and to protect their children and the children of others in the future.

The women who stayed at the camp lived communally, outside the control of men, and began to re-imagine ways of being and of engaging in politics and protest. They questioned the priorities and limitations of women's lives in a male society, everything from the way women were expected to behave, dress or love, was scrutinised and possibly rejected. This led some women to embrace, experiment with, or to become more open about being in sexual relationships with other women. While women on the original march, or those who arrived in the early months were, as Rachel Johnson explains, initially motivated by their opposition to cruise missiles, many 'stayed for the feminism.'[30] She herself remained at the camp for five years, going on to become the director and founder of the Acronym Institute for Disarmament Diplomacy, co-founder of the International Campaign to Abolish Nuclear Weapons, and vice-president of CND.

The feminism of Greenham women sought to find new ways of organising, negotiating and making decisions; after all it was a man-made political system which had constructed nuclear weapons. The women challenged masculinity, militarism and violence, whether it was the state violence epitomised by cruise missiles, or male violence against women at a more personal level. They learnt techniques of passive resistance, avoiding retaliation even when faced with violence from the police or their critics. The women developed shared slogans, such as 'Arms are for linking' and 'Fight war, not wars'. They found, as peace camp resident Sharon Ross noted, 'Living with women is a wonderful experience. There is strength here.'[31] Borrowing from many of the political processes being explored within the women's movement, they sought, as Lynne Jones remembered, to have 'shared decision-making; non-hierarchical, leaderless groups; cooperation and non-violence…. and to express those characteristics normally devalued in society at large: caring, compassion, trust. Human characteristics which they feel all of us should reclaim if we want to survive.'[32]

Lengthy discussions and debates took place concerning priorities, how to organise protests and the practicalities of living, which were both challenging and liberating. Predictably, at times there were fallings out and failures in living up to the ideals of a shared women's community. Amy Todd has pointed out there were tensions between the different groups, and between the Greenham women and other women's groups in the 1980s. Some feminist groups took issue with actions or slogans that rested on maternal values, and as Amy Todd has suggested, 'campaigners were focusing on patriarchal views of women as natural peace-makers…..They were scrutinised by radical feminist and lesbian groups because they emphasised maternalism and leaned on traditional stereotypes to achieve short term objectives, rather than challenging the patriarchal assumptions which underpinned these stereotypes.'[33]

Yet Rebecca Mordan, whose mother took her to Greenham as a child, recalled, 'Her mind was completely blown and radicalised…. She was at the 'University of Feminism' encountering multiple different versions of feminism.'[34] Outsiders sometimes characterised the women as having 'woolly hats and woolly minds', but this underestimates the various motivations and priorities of different women. The camp residents explored new forms of politics and power, and grew in confidence. As Sarah, reflecting on the camp, noted:

> It is difficult for many women to learn that they can change things on their own, without men, and that is why they feel helpless in the nuclear crisis. We have all changed since we came here. We know we can survive on our own, run our own camp, and we know that we have the strength to stand up for what we believe in.[35]

For Jane Powell and many other women, the experience of spending time at the camp was formative: it began a lifetime of campaigning for various causes including the Campaign against Living Miserably. She reflected:

> Greenham tested to the limit your physical, mental and emotional endurance; your patience, your compassion and every belief and prejudice you ever possessed. And then it tested you some more....
>
> At camp you were at the receiving end of prison, the police, the bailiffs, the vigilantes, and by God, the media – what a nightmare crowd they were! You saw the world from the underside. Newbury police threatening arrest for littering unless we took back the rocks that soldiers had been throwing at us all night. Coming back to a camp systematically trashed by locals – filling 32 bin bags of rubbish they left behind.[36]

Despite differences and divisions, many forms of protest such as keening – a communal noise made to express grief-heightened women's sense of solidarity, against both the military on the base and the police. Songs articulating their protests were used to bring women together, including one by Rib Bulkeley, sung to the popular tune of *A Bicycle Made for Two*, which began with the words: 'Trident, Trident what an insane idea.'[37] It was, however, *Can't Kill the Spirit*, alternatively known as *Like a Mountain*, written by Naomi Morena and adopted by the peace protesters, which came to epitomise the spirit of Greenham and included the words, 'Nobody can stop a woman from feeling. She's gonna rise up like the sun.'[38]

The widespread media attention the Greenham Peace Camp received stretched across the world. It was one of a number of activities sending a message to political leaders to halt the proliferation of nuclear arms. Finally, in 1987, USA's President Ronald Reagan and Soviet President, Mikhail Gorbachev, signed the Intermediate-range Nuclear Forces Treaty. Between 1989 and

1991, the cruise missiles at Greenham Common airbase were dismantled and removed. The peace camp, however, remained until 2000, continuing the women's protest against nuclear weapons. When the camp, now a business park, was handed back to locals, over 70,000 women demonstrated, danced, sang, cut the fence and stormed the watch towers. It had been the largest women's protest in Britain since the suffrage era. In the years that followed, women have continued to take part in peace demonstrations, but have also risen to prominence in the military. Debates about war and peace, violence, and the military, are not perhaps seen to be so obviously divided along gender lines as they were in the 1980s.

Chapter 14

Equal Pay for Equal Value (1988)

The introduction of the Equal Pay Act (1970) and the Sex Discrimination Act (1975) did not herald a new era of equality for women in the workplace, but rather, they opened the door for numerous individual political and workplace struggles seeking to ensure that employers complied with the laws. Industrial unrest in the 1970s was only part of the battle to improve women's wages. For, as the Research team on the *Sisterhood and After* project has suggested, 'at the base of much inequality in women's pay were two assumptions: first, that women's work was less skilled than men's and therefore required less pay; and second, that a woman's wage did not have to support other dependents.'[1] Assumptions that men had to earn a family wage had been challenged by the equal pay for equal work campaigns earlier in the century, whilst the introduction of the post-war welfare state meant the state helped to alleviate some of the financial responsibilities of dependents. Married men's tax allowances and child benefits undermined the idea men needed to earn a family wage, as did the growing realisation there were many varied types of families. Women were increasingly understood to also have financial responsibilities, often as head of a household.

The assumption that women's work is less skilled, proved much more difficult to challenge, and throughout the twentieth century, continued to be used to keep women's wages down. The idea that women's work was of equal value to that of men, was apparently first muted over 100 years previously in 1919 in the Treaty of Versailles, and was finally enshrined in law in 1983.[2] It was at the heart of a number of campaigns by women, initially involving strikes and then later legal action, in the last third of the twentieth century. However, as Heather Wakefield, National Officer for the Trade Union of Local Government employees, UNISON, has pointed out, 'I don't think that the concept of equal value is widely understood. I think the concept of equal pay for the same or similar work is understood but the concept of equal value, I think, is something a lot of people in the trade union movement still struggle with.'[3] Definitions and ideas of skill have often been linked to masculinity, craft unions and apprenticeships. Men, with support from their wives and families, have struggled to protect their skilled status which often justifies higher rates of pay. However, post-war production lines, greater mechanisation and new technology reduced the skill and physical strength needed for many jobs, and resulted in disputes and challenges to definitions and differentiations around the skilled status of women's work. Many successful campaigns took place through the courts, against the industrial turmoil and economic uncertainty of the 1960s through to the 1980s.

Hayward versus Cammell Laird shipyard, which argued the work done by a woman in the kitchens, was equivalent to men's work in the shipyards paved the way for a reappraisal of the value of women's work. Another important, but unsuccessful, earlier campaign about skill was the strike by machinists at the Ford factory in Dagenham in 1968 – a strike which in popular mythology, and particularly since the release of the film, *Made in Dagenham* (2010), is seen as responsible for triggering the Equal Pay Act of 1970. Indeed, four of the women, who led the strike – Gwen Davis, Eileen Pullen, Sheila Douglas and Vera Sime – have been heralded as heroines of the campaign for equal pay, feted at film premieres and voted women of the year by *Woman's Weekly* in 2013. The strike was actually about the value and status of the women machinists' work, and about grading and recognition of their skills making car seats. As such it was, in many ways, a failure.

The car industry was notorious for poor industrial relations during the 1960s and 70s, with numerous stoppages and strikes. As a result, Ford brought external consultants into their factories to develop a new grading system for all the staff's jobs. Before the job evaluation, all hourly paid women at the Ford Motor Company received the lowest grade of pay, lower than the most unskilled man working in the company. Following the job evaluation scheme, 'women were present in the lowest three of the new grades, but at a lower rate of pay to men in the same grade.'[4] As Sheila Douglas explained, it was when 'the new wage structure came in that they found they weren't classed as skilled.'[5] The women had been put on B grade, the same grade given to the factory's janitors, although two women doing sewing machinists employed in the company's prototype research centre were placed on the higher-grade C.[6]

Sheila and the other 186 machinists at the factory considered, 'It was a skilled job. I mean you had to have two years machining experience before Ford would even consider taking you on.... And there's a man going around getting a B grade same as us. We could get up and use his broom, but he couldn't sit down and use our machine, so we felt we was skilled.'[7] Women machinists at the Ford plant at Dagenham put in a claim to the management for re-grading. They met with little success, as Sheila later recalled, 'we just said 'enough's enough. We had a meeting over the canteen and we voted that we should stand up and fight, which is what we did.'[8] Initially, the machinists banned overtime, and then on June 7, 1968, they began an all-out strike.

The 187 women machinists belonged to a number of different unions, mostly the National Union of Vehicle Builders (NUVB) and the Amalgamated Union of Engineering and Foundry Workers (AEF); the unions support for the strike made it official. As the stock of car seats began to run out, Ford production in Britain was increasingly brought to a standstill. 9,000 workers were laid off. Some of the male colleagues offered support, despite the layoffs; others offered abuse, suggesting women only worked for 'pin money' and that they should get back to work. With the company losing a million pounds a day (the equivalent of more than twenty million pounds in modern money), the dispute gained huge attention, and strong pressure was exerted on the women to reach some sort of an agreement. Panic grew, and the government was asked to intervene, but no-one wanted to focus on the issue of grading and skill; this was seen as opening a whole can of worms. The unions had after all been involved in negotiating the new grading agreement with Ford. The notion of equal pay was seen as a more palatable rallying cry, which as Chapter 4 suggested, politicians and industrialists had supported for years in principle, just not in practice.

Eight of the women travelled to Whitehall to meet Barbara Castle, Secretary of State for Employment, creating an uproar when one of their banners, which stated, 'We want Sex Equality' was not properly unfurled, and instead read, 'We want Sex'. Taxi drivers were prompted to lean out the windows of their vehicles, and let the women know they would be available that evening.[9] At the meeting, a deal was agreed to end the three-week strike; the women were awarded a 7% pay increase (giving them 92% of the rate paid to unskilled male workers), with the promise equal pay legislation would be introduced and a court of inquiry would be appointed to investigate the dispute independently. Shop Steward, Lil O' Callaghan, reflected years later, 'We mucked it up. We should have left it open to fight another battle on another day.'[10] Likewise, shop steward, Rose Boland, noted, 'we did get more money, we did not gain the point, we won a battle but lost the war.[11] Whilst Vera Sime also remarked that although they got their money, still they were not classed as skilled: 'That's what we fought for wasn't it, But it all got turned around which was to everybody's convenience wasn't it?'[12] Sir Jack Stamp, an industrial conciliator and chairman of the Motor Industries Joint Labour Council, chaired the Court of Inquiry which reported on 14 August. He noted that the strike was about re-grading and recommended that the machinists' job profile be reviewed.[13] However, the machinists did not receive equal pay or a re-grading until after the 1983 Equal

Pay (Amendment) Regulations were introduced, when their case was looked at by the Advisory, Conciliation and Arbitration Service (ACAS).[14]

The Equal Pay Act was introduced in 1970, with employers given 5 years to implement its requirement for equal pay to be paid for equal work. By then, the 1975 Sex Discrimination Act had also made it illegal to discriminate against women in work, education and training, whilst the Employment Protection Act in the same year, introduced statutory maternity provision and made it illegal to sack a woman because she was pregnant. The Equal Opportunities Commission came into being in 1976, to oversee the operation of these acts, and to campaign on gender related issues. However, the implementation of the new laws was often resisted by employers, claiming that women did not do equal work to men and therefore were not entitled to equal pay. In the years between 1972 and 1979, roughly 43 per cent of women-led industrial disputes were around equal pay.[15] Many women found there were loopholes in the Equal Pay Act, which did not live up to its promise, and when they took their cases to Industrial Tribunals, the rulings seemed bizarre. Furthermore, women sometimes faced hostility around equal pay from male co-workers. Frances Galt has pointed out, 'during the six-week equal pay strike at GEC Spon Street Works, Coventry, in 1973, AUEW convenor Albert Beardmore refused to bring his section out on strike, encouraged delivery drivers to cross the picket lines and swore at pickets, justifying his behaviour by stating that he 'couldn't possibly bring his breadwinner men out in support of mere girls.'[16]

Marion Blanche Jones who worked in the Hoover Factory, which employed about 7,000 at Merthyr Tydfil, Wales in the 1970s, recalled how for the quarter of the workforce who were women, 'it was alright in the beginning when we had our segregated jobs you know – women and men separate. But once the Equality (Act) came in you could feel the bitterness coming in with the men, you know. They didn't want us to have equal pay... not by no means.'[17] When the management agreed to the women's request for equal pay, not all in the unions were so convinced. They argued that, 'the women weren't doing the work the same as the men', because women were doing sub-assembly, small jobs, while the men undertook the final assembly of the machines. The pay differentials were significant, and even though women appreciated the cheap or free domestic appliances they received as perks for working at the factory, they also wanted equal pay. Despite going on strike for two days, the men eventually had to accept management's decision to give women equal pay.[18] This led to animosity: 'you know you're having equal pay so you should do equal jobs...it wasn't a very pleasant time at all... not at all'[19] – animosity which resurfaced when the women took strike action to oppose 'women out first' redundancy plans at the factory in 1980.

As the economic crisis deepened, women in Merthyr Tydfil in South Wales were called upon to support male trade unionists in the many long months of the 1984–85 Miners' Strike. The proposed closures of mines announced by the National Coal Board on 6 March, 1984, involved an initial 20,000 redundancies, the decimation of communities, and the beginning of the end for the mining industry. Legislation passed in 1842, prevented women in Britain from working down mines but miner's wives, sisters and daughters supported the miner's strike and formed the Women Against Pit Closure Group (WAPC), which gained associate membership of the National Union of Mineworkers in December 1984. The women not only joined men on the picket lines, but also ran soup kitchens, created leaflets and badges to promote their cause, raised funds, held sit-ins in mine shafts, chained themselves to colliery gates, addressed rallies across Britain and Europe and sent miner's pit lamps across the country to inspire support.[20] Despite their efforts, the bitter dispute ended when miners returned to work in 1985, having won no concessions. Julie Hayward's fight against Cammell Laird for equal pay for equal value, began the same year as the Miner's Strike, but, with the support of her male colleagues at the shipyard in Birkenhead, Liverpool, it had a more successful outcome.

In the late 1970s and 80s, jobs were hard to come by in the Liverpool area; as the hard realities of recession and Margaret Thatcher's economic policies hit home, unemployment was rife. When Julie Heywood heard that there were apprenticeships going at the Cammell Laird shipyard, she applied, hopeful of getting a secure job. She was virtually the only girl who sat the qualifying tests in a large hall with approximately fifty others, and welcomed the subsequent news that she had been awarded an apprenticeship. She would earn a regular wage, go to college part-time and gain City and Guilds qualifications and skills. Her uniform and tools would be paid for by her employer. Her apprenticeship, she was informed, would be in catering, whilst the other male apprentices the company took on, were learning to be fitters, joiners or laggers in the shipyard. Julie was staggered to discover that she alone did not receive an increase in pay when, like all the others, she had completed her apprenticeship, passed her assessments and had qualified as a cook. At this point, she discovered that her work was not as valued, or considered as skilled, as men's work. They were categorised as craftsmen; she was apparently only a labourer, and therefore her wages were lower.

Neither Julie Haywood, the GMB Union, to which she belonged, nor the Equal Opportunities Commission considered this fair. Importantly, in 1975, the European Community had issued an Equal Pay Directive clarifying that equal pay was required when work of equal value was performed. The British

Government took no action to modify the Equal Pay Act until ordered to do so by European Court of Justice in 1982, after which time they introduced the Equal Pay (Amendment) Regulations in 1983. What was now needed, was for the law to be tested by cases taken to industrial tribunals; so the GMB Union and the Equal Opportunities Commission funded the legal team needed to give Julie Haywood the best chance of forcing Cammell Laird to reconsider their assessment of her work. Her legal team argued that the skill, danger and physical demands of Julie's work were on a par with joiners, fitters and laggers. As David Pannick, the lead barrister on the case, explained, 'We all had a sense that this was historic, in a sense it was the first case, but we were all very much proceeding in the dark. No one really had any clear idea as to how tribunals, far less the courts would deal with the matter. The new legislation was very ambiguous, very unclear.'[21]

When Julie's case came before a local industrial tribunal in April 1984, she attended with the support of three of her male co-workers, who had been apprentices with her, but now received higher pay. Photographs of Julie Haywood carrying huge trays of meat pies and loading them into hot oven, and video clips of her at work, were presented to the court, to demonstrate the physical demands of her job. The tribunal agreed that the case should be looked at by an independent expert, who would visit the factory and follow Julie around, observing the skill, danger and physical demands of her work, and the work of others at the shipyard. Although the independent expert and the initial industrial tribunal went in Julie's favour, she did not get her pay rise. Instead, her employers put her under pressure by, for example, demanding that she worked night shifts. Once again, backed by the GMB Union and the Equal Opportunities Commission, Julie had to go to a regional tribunal, where Cammell Laird appealed against the initial decision. By then, as Julie Haywood was aware, 'it was much bigger than just my small job in Cammell Laird. It became escalated to do with this big massive thing that was going to happen.'[22]

As the significance of the test case became clearer, the Confederation of British Industry (CBI) and teams of lawyers and consultants became involved. Cammell Laird argued that Julie Haywood received other benefits that made her contract more valuable – for example, the ability to have a free lunch from any leftovers. Slowly but steadily, over many months and years, the case trundled its way through three industrial tribunals, into more intimidating and alien parts of the judicial system. However, even when the Court of Appeal favoured the employers, as The *Liverpool Echo* in March 1987 noted, Julie remained defiant, prepared for the case to go all the way to the House of Lords.[23] She received widespread support from other workers, who were familiar to her both from the workplace and from their shared enthusiasm for football, but her employers continued to make her working life more difficult. It was reported; 'Her local chip shop – run by the Chinese community – produced newspapers from China with her name on the front pages.'[24] But Julie did not relish the publicity the case gave her, as some campaigners do: press photographers pursued her, and she was briefly compelled to move home.

The case finally did indeed reach the House of Lords in 1988. Julie's recollection was of two days of legal arguments, which were often hard to follow. By this time, she was receiving £130 a week and claiming an extra £27 to bring her wages in line with joiners, fitters and laggers.[25] It was then several months before the Law Lords made their unanimous ruling in Julie's favour. Cammell Laird remained truculent, and lawyers had to return to the House of Lords to ensure that she was paid the money she was owed, approximately £2,000 (£6,399 in contemporary currency).[26] Julie Haywood continued to find herself in the spotlight, and there was even an offer of money and a chauffeured car to take her to appear on the Terry Wogan television show. But she turned it down: the achievement had been for her, a political campaign about a principle. When it was over, she left the shipyard and trained as a youth worker, moving from Liverpool to Bromley, where she set up a drop-in centre for young people and where she was able to live in anonymity.[27]

A flurry of other cases around equal pay for equal value took place alongside and following the ruling of *Haywood versus Cammell Laird*; individuals and also groups of workers sought the backing of the trade unions to get legal recognition of their status as skilled workers. In what became the longest running case in legal history, NHS speech therapist, Pam Enderby, began her action for equal pay for equal value in 1986. She argued that she and her colleagues, mostly women, were of equal value to clinical psychologists who were at the time mostly men. She later recalled, she was 'heading quite a large department that was doing quite a lot of research, a lot of personal clinical responsibility and my psychologist friend, great chap but had much limited, much less of a portfolio.'[28] Pam Enderby was head of the speech therapy department at Frenchay Hospital in Bristol, earning approximately £11,000 a year, and her male psychologist colleague earned £17–18,000. The speech therapist's union was small and the legal costs were high, and this created huge stress for Pam Enderby, whose husband feared that they would lose their house over the case.

However, once again, the case was supported and part-funded by the Equal Opportunities Commission, who, as Sheila Wild later explained, felt that Pam Enderby offered a:

> lead applicant who was the most articulate spokesperson for her profession which was a way of disarming the opposition. You know when you support an equal pay case you get the official opposition which is the respondent defending the claim, but you can also get quite a lot of opposition from the media... if they think, you know, it's completely out of order. The scare stories around equal value when equal value came in, was that you would get the cleaner in the bank claiming equal pay with the chief executive you know.[29]

The media could see that Pam Enderby was highly professional, doing a very important job, and finally, after endless court appearances, in 1993, the European Court of Justice ruled in her favour. In the aftermath of the decision, the health service had to review its pay grades across the board; as the organisation employed so many women this was an important fight to have been won.

Local authorities also began to undertake job evaluation schemes, with various jobs allocated places on their pay scale, although comparisons were hard to make. As Ray Gray – Regional Officer National Union of Public Employees (NUPE), in the 1980s – has pointed out, this was hard to explain:

> you can't compare a refuse person with a home help person, using this scheme was quite difficult for people to grasp because their logic was well I'm out in all weathers lifting the bin and the home helps in somebody's warm comfortable house just looking after granny and trying to say it's not like that. It's not as easy as that. You know, you know your job well, they know their job well.[30]

However, after all these careful assessments – completed in 1987 – compulsory competitive tendering was introduced. Local authorities had to put a range of services, from cleaning to school dinners, out to competitive tender. Much of this work relied upon women workers, and as employers sought to keep their prices down, they reduced wages and cut conditions of work; women were no longer being given equal pay for equal value. Dorothy Ratcliffe a Dinner lady for twenty-five years, remembered how:

> They actually just came in one day and said your terms and conditions are changing. You're going to be 3 pounds an hour and that will be it, everything was taken away. The holiday pay and the laundry allowance, the bank holidays and all that was taken away and I think we were given 14 days holiday a year and that was it, so, you know, we had lost everything

cos we got paid through the holidays, we got £3.40 an hour at the time and we got 30 pence cleaning money and we also got all the you know – we got three weeks holiday then, so it changed drastically.[31]

Although the women lost their benefits, because it seemed that the company existed in name only, Susan Crosby, a dinner lady for sixteen years, recalled: 'nobody wanted to leave the job. I mean, we all liked the job anyway, particularly the schools we were working for. You know a lot of the ladies that worked with me had been there 30 years so it was part of their lives.'[32] Once again, their recourse was a lengthy legal action, supported by their union, and in 1995, the House of Lords found in their favour and a total of 2 million pounds of back pay was awarded to the women.

By the end of the twentieth century, the gender pay gap was reducing and the National Minimum Wage had been introduced on 1 April 1999, which made a significant difference to women's rates of pay. Many women, due to domestic and caring responsibilities, continued to find their promotion limited, or had to work part time; this is where the gender pay gap is highest.[33] Women working in the 1990s and beyond, continue to have to undertake long, stressful and expensive battles through the courts to get their skills and contribution to the workplace recognised, as the Dagenham machinists, Julie Haywood, Speech Therapists and the Yorkshire Dinner Ladies, had all done. Furthermore, as Hazel Conley, Frances Galt, Louise Jackson, and Tanya Rhodes have argued 'No Win No Fee lawyers, led to over 60,000 equal pay cases being taken to employment tribunals. Recent cases in supermarket chains have used the principles established in these public sector cases to extend the fight for equal pay for equal value to the private sector.'[34]

Chapter 15

Tell me what you want, what you really, really want' – Girl Power (1996)

The debut single of the all–girl group, the Spice Girls was released by Virgin records on July 7, 1996. The *Wannabe* song, as it became known, entered the British charts initially at number three, before taking the number one slot, where it remained for the next seven weeks. It was a hit in 37 countries, and the group produced both the best-selling debut album by an all-girl group and the all-time best-selling single by a girl group. The confident, feisty lyrics and the five young girls who sang them, became a global phenomenon. They personified Girl Power, giving a voice to a new politics, which used music, print, film, television and social media, to tell the world that independent young women wanted to call the shots; girls were not going to be pushed around by anyone. These were girls who challenged inequality, and who, like the lads, wanted it all and weren't afraid to say so. This was a political campaign which did not seek to change laws, welfare provision, media, government or employers' behaviour; it sought to change to the way young women felt about themselves.

From the opening lines of the *Wannabe* song, 'I'll tell you what I want, what I really, really want', the Spice Girl's lyrics made it clear that girls wanted to define their own priorities, needs and wants. There was also an up-beat physicality in their performance, as they jumped and danced and travelled across ground space in the *Wannabe* pop video, suggesting they were taking control of the street, public spaces and places. The *Wannabe* song also made it clear who in any relationship would be making compromises, stating 'If you wanna be my lover, you have got to give. Taking is too easy, but that's the way it is.' The song, the accompanying video and the public image the girls portrayed, placed a high premium on female friendship, as the girls sang 'If you wanna be my lover, you gotta get with my friends.' But this was sisterhood with a new twist: it was fun. The excitement and novelty of the women's movement of earlier decades looked jaded and passé to many young girls by the 1990s; the media, and most particularly the popular press, often ridiculed feminists as kill-joys and dungaree dykes. The Spice Girls made the idea of Girl Power ubiquitous; the *Wannabe* song was the anthem of young, apparently confident, optimistic generation of girls, seeking to be in control of their own bodies and their own sexuality.

Historically, girls have made up the least powerful group in society; their sexuality and their bodies have always been subject to control and constraint. Girls, as Carol Dyehouse has argued, were repeatedly seen as 'trouble', worrying, threatening or a cause for concern.[1] In the twentieth century, as girls progressed from a life lived primarily in the domestic space of the home, to take their place in the public spheres of work, leisure and politics, there have been multiple moral panics over their bodies, brains and behaviour. Any open admission or display by teenagers of their sexuality has been treated with apprehension by social reformers and the chattering classes, castigated in the popular press and media. At the beginning of the twentieth century young girls' admiration for military men, was labelled first as 'scarlet fever', and then in First World, as 'khaki fever', to reflect the colour of the men's uniform. The use of the term 'fever', suggested that girls' sexual desire was some sort of hysterical disease. Local newspapers spread alarm about girls' apparent vulnerability. In 1915, in Swansea, it was claimed that girls of the respectable class were being led astray by Norwegian sailors, whilst the National Union of Women Workers of Great Britain and Ireland (NUWW) suggested that wartime had thrown girls off balance, and they were consequently being led into grave moral danger.[2]

The mobility of young men and women who joined the services or the war industries in Second World War, was also greeted with waves of anxiety directed at young women's sexual behaviour. The Bishop of Norwich warned that nothing was 'more alarming than the decay of personal standards of sexual morality . . . nothing threatens more the future of our race.'[3] Anxiety about girls' increased freedom and independence put them under greater scrutiny. Sexual restraint was seen as a national responsibility in wartime, particularly when the American GI's appeared.[4] There is little evidence to support the assumption that girls were more promiscuous in the war, even when they encountered the charms of USA soldiers who were seen as 'over paid, over sexed and over here.' Young girls were, however, becoming more visible, going to dances and the cinema, and going out unchaperoned. In the post-war era, it was youth culture, music and dancing, which became the focus of concerns about young girls' behaviour.

From the 1950s, teenage girls' musical taste defined their sense of identity, what they wore, how they spent their leisure time and who they really were. Initially, in their enthusiasm for modern jazz, rhythm & blues, or rock and roll, the girls' tastes overlapped with those of many young lads, as they listened to music on transistor radios, in booths at record shops, on juke boxes in milk-bars, or even enjoyed television programmes such as *Top of Pops* (1964- 2006) and live gigs. At the tail end of 1966, the hugely popular American television show, *The Monkees*, was first broadcast in Britain. The action-packed sit-com featured the group of the same name and exuded a sense of irreverent, wacky fun. It struck a chord with many youngsters of the sixties, who were enjoying a new sense of freedom and independence. Rosemary Reedman recalled watching the programme with her sister and being impressed by how it felt very 'different from anything that the BBC produced for children.' Some of the dialogue seemed improvised, 'the pace and energy of each episode was infectious and it avoided excessive sentimentality and cynicism.'[5] The following year, in 1967, the Monkeys' hit, 'I'm a believer', reached the number one spot in the British charts, four weeks in a row. A fan, aged ten, who attended one of their concerts, recalled how she, 'danced and sang along with all our favourite songs. It was awesome! The glow of the stage, staying out way past my bedtime and knowing that my favourite singers were right there in person!'[6]

Whilst records, radio and television were consumed in the home, live events brought girls onto the streets, screeching their adulation and intense lust for male stars, and causing panic, scorn and alarm amongst others. There were hordes of noisy teenyboppers rampaging the streets, for whom, as Nicolette Rohr has pointed out, 'screaming was essential to the experience' to create 'chaos, exuberance and subtle rebellion.'[7] They were 'breaking down barriers between them and their idols and abandoning gender appropriate behaviour.'[8] For girls, the appeal of becoming a screaming fan arguably lay in having the chance to openly express sexual desire, in a safe space, directed at someone who could not be touched or, just as importantly, could not touch them.[9] Fandom of groups such the Beatles, the Monkees and Bay City Rollers in the 1960s and 70s, provided young girls – teenyboppers aged 8–14 – with their own space to join the sexual revolution.

The public display of physical attraction by young fans to the Monkees and the Beatles, clearly surprised, shocked, even frightened onlookers. A *Daily Mail* reporter described a Beatles fan as, 'Screaming like an animal and wearing almost as much leather as one', going on to note that 'the young girl writhed and shook in some sort of private ecstasy'.[10] The music of these bands was disparaged, whilst young girl fans, just like their predecessors who had shown an enthusiasm for the soldiers, were scathingly spoken about as immature, vulnerable, and hysterical. Fandom was given names such as Beatlemania and Rollermania, suggesting that it was a fever or an infectious disease. For the girls, their enthusiasm for boy bands provided an opportunity for them to explore their sexuality without any of the tricky consequences usually accompanying sexual awakening; no one gets pregnant screaming at a boy band. The girls also revelled in being part of a group of like-minded fans and avoided having to walk the perilous tightrope of being categorised as a slag or a drag.

Adult hatred of the girls' choice of music re-enforced their sense of 'us against the world.'[11] The public behaviour of fans in the 1970s, of the phenomenally successful Scottish group, the Bay City Rollers, was reviewed unsympathetically by newspapers. However, much of the joy of fandom was hidden from public view, manifesting itself, for example, on bedroom walls adorned with posters. When Sheryll Garratt was interviewed about her time as a Bay City Roller fan, she struggled to remember the gigs, songs or the physical attributes of the band members. She did, however, vividly recall how she enjoyed with her friends, 'running home from school together to get to someone's house in time to watch *Shang- a-Lang* on TV, dancing in lines at the school disco and sitting in each other's bedroom discussing our fantasies and compiling our scrapbooks.'[12]

The fans did not just passively consume music; they wanted to be musicians. Girls created their own girlie culture by making and listening to music. Maureen Nolan and Roma Singleton recalled how groups like the Beatles, the Merseybeats and Gerry and Pacemakers, changed the sound of popular music, and also encouraged teenagers to form groups with their mates, sign a hire purchase agreement to buy a guitar or drums, or imagine themselves as a lead singer of a group.[13] In the 1990s, the Spice Girls, as one of the first really popular all-girl groups, was, for many young girls, the realisation of this fantasy. It was not just the lyrics and the style of the Spice Girls which was revolutionary, but it was also how they as an all-girl group foregrounded themselves as creators of their own music.

The five Spice Girls – Victoria Beckham (*née* Adams), Melanie Brown, Emma Bunton, Geri Halliwell and Melanie Chisholm – who were respectively known as Posh Spice, Scary Spice, Baby Spice, Ginger Spice and Sporty Spice – got together in 1994. The group was formed following an auditioning process by their first managers, Bob and Chris Herbert, who were seeking an all-girl group to compete with the popular boy bands of the era. The managers placed the girls in a house-share, where they began practicing their choreography and singing, while also taking song writing lessons. The following year, they apparently ditched their managers and left the house in Geri's car, claiming that they were being artistically restricted and encouraged to adopt a childlike image. Within months, they were signed up by Simon Fuller's management company, and a record deal with Virgin followed. At the Spice Girls' insistence, the *Wannabe* song was their first release, hitting the shops on 7 July, 1996. The accompanying video, lyrics of *Wannabe,* and the widely circulated narrative of their formation, cultivated a sense of them as assertive proponents of Girl

Power. As Jane Middlemiss says, 'For a group of five young women to not only be having writing credits but to have an input into what they were singing [then] was absolutely huge. That was not done, even with boy bands.'[14]

The Spice Girls, however, borrowed rather than invited the term Girl Power, which was first used by a US punk group, called Bikini Kill in 1991. This group were part of the Riot grrrl movement, which is remembered as a rough-and-tumble music scene populated by teenagers in second-hand dresses and Hello Kitty hair clips. 'Riot grrrl was an exuberant underground movement of mouthy, anarchic women's bands, such as America's Bikini Kill and Brighton's Huggy Bear, which enjoyed a brief moment in the spotlight in the early 90s before melting away.'[15] It combined feminism, punk music, and politics, which carried its influence into a number of countries as it called for girl-style revolution and sought to confront inequality, abuse, rape and eating disorders.[16]

Bikini Kill was made up of Kathleen Hanna, Kathi Wilcox, Tobi Vail and Bill Karren, had been formed in 1990, and played music with feminist lyrics to a sexually abrasive, fiery stage performance. Their angry Girl Zine, which was published to coincide with their first tour in 1991, carried a message of female friendship, and, some 35 years before the MeToo movement, articulated an unwillingness to accept any form of sexual harassment or abuse. For example, the opening feature included lines such as 'I am in protest against the whole world. My body says it, slung into my clothes. I won't stop talking. I'm a girl who you have no control over. There is not a gag big enough to handle this mouth, I'm gonna tell everyone what you did to me.'[17] Their music, lyrics and performance articulated many of the messages for a new generation, that had been voiced by the women who disrupted the Miss World Competition, or were involved in the Off the Shelf and Women against Rape campaigns, twenty years previously.

Furthermore, whilst the fans of the Beatles, the Bay City Rollers, and even Take That, watched boy bands, as music journalist El Hunt has pointed out: 'Riot grrrl bands in general were very focused on making space for women at gigs. They understood the importance of giving women a platform and voice to speak out against abusers.'[18] Bikini Kill's first six-track EP was released in 1991, and their debut album, *Pussy Whipped,* came out in September 1993, and their last *Reject all American,* three years later. The Riot grrrl movement was discussed in the British music magazine, *Melody Maker,* but as the 1990s progressed, Girl Power became associated with the much more mainstream Spice Girls. It found its way into many areas of the British music, television and the films that young women consumed, as well as clothing styles and girls' magazines. *Company* Magazine explained,

> A new girl has arrived, who's gutsy, irrelevant and fun. A girl who's glad to be a girl and into all that baggage that goes with it. A girl who loves fashion, make-up and men (so long as they know their place) and has the balls to get exactly what she wants.... Ok its's a twist on feminism, but this time round it has a sense of humour – who wants to waste time burning a bra when you could be out having a laugh.[19]

Simon Fuller's astuteness in signing the Spice Girls group paid off for his management company: the band became a money-making machine, with tie-ins to soft drinks companies and TV Channels – such as the new Channel 5 – as well as a stream of merchandise, all of which offered commodity feminism to the younger generation. The fashion chain, Miss Selfridge, was quick to align itself to the Spice Girls, and the slogan, Girl Power, appeared on the band's stationery, T-Shirts, and other merchandise for many years to come. However, despite the popularity of the Spice Girls and schemes such as the Take Our Daughter to Work Day, which came in their wake, Rebecca Haines has argued that Girl Power and commodity feminism had its limitations; it was about marketing, serving corporate interests, and selling the idea of empowerment, rather than ensuring that individual young girls actually became more empowered.[20] Others have suggested the message of Girl Power had lost the hard edge and the overtly political tone of the punk group Bikini Kill and the Riot grrl movement.

The Spice Girls, however, pushed back against the attacks on both feminism and young girls' progression towards sexual freedom and equality in Britain, and they did so at a time when, as feminist Susan Faludi argued, a counterattack against feminism was in full swing.[21] Her book, which was published in the USA, where it won the National Book Critics Circle Award for non-fiction, identified a backlash against the progress women had made towards equality – something she saw as a historical trend. Women and particularly feminism were being blamed for any number of problems experienced by men, women and children. Single mothers were being criticised for being idle and living off the state and working mothers came in for abuse for abandoning their children.[22] The term post-feminism entered popular discourse, because, some suggested, women had apparently achieved equality, and even gone too far and got the upper hand. There was horror, in some quarters, at girls' repeated ability to gain better GCSE results than boys. Critiquing feminism, and even women and girls' behaviour, was a source of apparently tongue-in-cheek humour. Young lads openly pored over magazines such as *Loaded* (1994–2015), revelling in a world of liberty, sex, drink, football and scantily glad young women. In the 'lad mag' culture characterised by *FHM* and *Loaded*, as the journalist Rebecca Nicholson has suggested, 'Sexism was fine, as long as it was couched in irony.'[23]

The music industry was also harsh for women in the 1990s, as journalist and broadcaster, Miranda Sawyer has pointed out: 'female artists were "pitted against each other" and "shamed" by the publication of revealing photographs.'[24] The Spice Girls responded by promoting what has been described as 'diluted feminism', but it was at least a move in a positive direction.[25] As Sporty Spice, Mel C, explained: 'Feminism has become something of a misused and abused word, Girl Power is the 1990s version. If women band together and show a unified front, solidarity creates power.'[26] The Spice Girls seemed to acknowledge criticisms of feminism, but also took feminism's aims for granted. They wanted equality, the right to work and define their image. Geri Haliwell, Ginger Spice, acknowledged the problems and unpopularity of feminism in the 1990s: 'It's about labelling', she told *The Guardian*, 'For me feminism is bra-burning lesbianism. It's very unglamorous. I'd like to see it rebranded. We need to see a celebration of our femininity and softness.'[27] Youngsters should be able to have equality and all the girlie clothes and make-up, to be soft, feminine and not always have to fight hard battles for basic human rights.

The idea of Girl Power and women banding together, was further enhanced by the release of the film, *Spice World* (1997). The five Spice Girls played themselves in a fictionalised plot about the challenges of fame. In the film, they encountered a series of obstacles on their way to perform a concert at the Albert Hall, which was to be broadcast across the world. Like the narrative of the Spice Girls' rise to fame and the *Wannabe* song, the film portrays the girls as active agents of their own destiny. Interestingly, the young girl fans also feature prominently in the film. These consumers of popular music are not ridiculed or seen as threatening, but as a force to be reckoned with: they have Girl Power. Predictably perhaps, the film received negative reviews from the critics, but *Spice World* was a box office success in Britain and the United States. It was a fantasy for teenagers, and was enjoyed by them.

Most importantly, in *Spice World*, all five Spice Girls appear comfortable in their own bodies, wearing skimpy or tight, revealing clothing, lounging comfortably, or at times sitting with legs apart, not having to conform to gender stereotypes of appropriate female dress or body positioning. Girls are riotous in *Spice World*. There is no sign of the controlled decorum of the contestants in a Miss World contest in the 1970s and 80s, or of insecure women sitting cross-legged, trying to take up as little room as possible, who were often witnessed in films of the 1950s. Nor did Spice Girls talk of sexual abuse, as Bikini Kill did. The band's assertiveness seems to banish the very idea these girls could ever be sexually abused; victimhood, for them, seemed preposterous. This perspective is given further creditability by a video clip of them, which has been available online for years. It portrays a crew member on a shoot for a Polaroid advert asking them to reveal more cleavage. Mel C confronts him: 'Well, you can fuck off', as Geri and Victoria join the chorus of disapproval.[28]

The Spice Girls' version of Girl Power included young women comfortably owning their sexuality. This, and their very short shorts and skirts or skimpy tops, may not seem radical to a generation of women who have grown up listening and watching the music of Britney Spears and Beyoncé. However, in the 1990s, the idea of young women feeling confident about their own bodies and exploring their sexuality was under attack. Magazines aimed at older teenage girls, but predictably read by younger girls, with problem pages which took a straight-talking, frank approach to sexuality, were at the forefront of the mid-90s wave of anxiety about teenage girls' virtue. Publications such as *More*, a fortnightly magazine launched in 1988, and *Just Seventeen*, which found its way into the shops in 1983, encouraged an informed assertiveness amongst young women regarding sex. The magazines were greeted with enthusiasm by girls thirsty for a more unembarrassed approach to such topics than they were likely to encounter in any discussions with their teachers or parents. However, on February 6, 1996, the Conservative MP, Peter Luff, introduced the Periodicals (Protection of Children) Bill in the House of Commons. It sought to require magazines aimed at young girls to place a notice of age advisory restrictions on their front covers – on a par with film classifications. The bill was not successful, but it garnered considerable support across different political parties and in the press. Commentators, as Fan Carter argues, often saw girls 'as sexually passive and innocent, devoid of sexual desire' – a perspective which was in 'conflict with the more progressive and permissive construction of female sexuality articulated in the pages of teenage magazines of the period.'[29]

Despite the unease created by girls' sexuality and some aspects of Girl Power, its popularity grew. The Spice Girls created a very British version of the phenomenon, relishing the incorporation of the Union Jack into their outfits. In 1997, Geri Halliwell, Ginger Spice, wore a mini-dress featuring this flag on one side, and the Campaign for Nuclear Disarmament symbol on the back; the anti-nuclear message of the Greenham Common was also it seemed part of commodity feminism. The dress symbolised both Girl Power and Cool Britannia, and reclaimed the Union Jack from its use by far-right groups such as the National Front with which it had become associated in the 1970s and 80s. Nevertheless, the songs, film and music videos of the Spice Girls chime with a range of media texts in the era, which often originated in the USA. In films like the coming-of-age teen comedy, *Clueless* (1995), starring

Alicia Silverstone, girls were ironic, self-aware and used pastiche to celebrate multiple different, arguably contradictory ideas of girlhood. This was just one of a number of films which were popular with teenage girls and their younger siblings for their portrayal of sassy, confident young women with Girl Power.

This 1990s generation of young women also reveled in female action heroes, who, as Susan Hopkins has suggested, showed a strong correlation with many of the ideas of Girl Power.[30] *Buffy the Vampire Slayer* (1992), a young woman who battled evil forces, with endurance, intuition and agility, was the focus of this film, as well as, five years later, a supernatural television drama, novels, comics and tie-ins. On the other hand, *Sabrina the Teenage Witch* (1996), who apparently discovered her magical powers on her sixteenth birthday, entertained the millions of youngsters who regularly watched the sitcom. Such media texts offered one blond, white, thin, conventionally attractive middle-class, suburban version of being a young woman – albeit one who was strong, independent and in control of their own destiny. That said, one of the reasons the Spice Girls was so successful, was because they offered five different versions of femininity to emulate. Young girls could take their choice, fluidly shifting between or combining the range of ways of being a young woman at the close of the twentieth century. Perhaps most importantly, the Spice Girls seemed comfortable and confident with their sexuality and their bodies.

The effectiveness of this new media politics of the Spice Girls and Girl Power remains open to question. It may seem frivolous compared to the campaigns of the Glasgow Rent Strikers, Radclyffe Hall or the Wages for Housework Campaign. But encouraging young girls to believe in themselves, to be more confident and assertive, and to be comfortable in their own bodies and with their sexuality, is important. There remains much to celebrate in the potential of the Spice Girls and Girl Power to improve young girls' lives. As journalist, Meg Walters, has suggested, 'for millions of women who grew up in the Nineties, Girl Power taught us to use our voices as women, and singers like Adele, Lauren Mayberry, and even Beyonce have cited it as a source of inspiration.'[31] Likewise the growth of women's sport in Britain, and ultimately to the success of English Lionesses football team at the Euros the summer of 2022, owe much to Sporty Spice.

The Spice Girls were catalysts for change, but they stood on the shoulders of many previous political campaigns. The shifts in women's working lives, political representation and health, the greater availability of contraception and childcare, gave women new senses of freedom and possibility. Perhaps most of all, the Spice Girls phenomenon relied upon changing attitudes towards the representation of women and their sexuality, which occurred in the twentieth century.

Notes

Introduction
1. See for example: Bartley, Paula. *Women's Activism in Twentieth-Century Britain: Making a Difference Across the Political Spectrum.* Palgrave Macmillan, (2022). Thomlinson, Natalie. *Race, ethnicity and the women's movement in England, 1968–1993.* Basingstoke: Palgrave Macmillan, 2016. Purvis, June, and Sandra Stanley Holton, eds. *Votes for women.* Psychology Press, 2000. Purvis, June, and June Hannam, eds. *The British Women's Suffrage Campaign: National and International Perspectives.* Routledge, 2020.
2. Rowbotham, Sheila. *Women in Movement (Routledge Revivals): Feminism and Social Action.* Routledge, 2013. P. 245.

Chapter 1: Glasgow Rent Strikes (1915)
1. Hughes, Annmarie. *Gender and Political Identities in Scotland, 1919–1939.* Edinburgh University Press, 2010.
2. Mooney, Gerry. London House protests echo Glasgow Strikes of 100 years ago' *The Conversation*, September 29, 2015. https://theconversation.com/london-housing-protests-echo-glasgow-rent-strikes-of-100-years-ago-48274 Accessed 4/4/2022.
3. https://www.counterfire.org/women-on-the-left/16331-mary-barbour-and-the-glasgow-rent-strike Accessed 4/4/2022.
4. Hughes, Annmarie, *op cit*. P. 20.
5. Mooney, Gerry. *op cit.*
6. Dewey, P.E. *British Agriculture in the First World War.* Oxford: Routledge 1989, reprinted 2014.
7. *Worcester Herald* 8 August, 1914.
8. *Falkirk Herald* 17 April, 1915.
9. See for example Andrews, Maggie, Adrian Gregson and John Peters. *Worcestershire's War: Voices of the First World War.* Amberley Publishing Limited, 2014.
10. https://www.parliament.uk/about/living-heritage/transformingsociety/parliament-and-the-first-world-war/legislation-and-acts-of-war/kdjgh/#:~:text=The%20Munitions%20of%20War%20Act,of%20certificates%20and%20of%20tribunals. Accessed 4/4/2022.
11. https://www.counterfire.org/women-on-the-left/16331-mary-barbour-and-the-glasgow-rent-strike Accessed 4/4/2022.
12. Memoirs of Helen Crawfurd, kept in the Marx Memorial Library, London. Quoted in https://remembermarybarbour.wordpress.com/mary-barbour-rent-strike-1915/ Accessed 4/4/2022.
13. Hughes, Annmarie, *op cit*. P. 20.
14. Currie, Pam. "'A Wondrous Spectacle': Protest, Class and Femininity in the 1915 Rent Strikes." *Rent and Its Discontents. A Century of Housing Struggle* (2018): 3–16. P. 6.
15. Orr, Lesley. https://www.heraldscotland.com/opinion/15240274.importance-dangerous-lesley-orr-pays-tribute-unsung-scotswomen-fought-peace-justice-wwi/ Accessed 4/4/2022.

16. Currie, Pam. *op cit*. P. 13.
17. See Burgess, Catriona. *Mary Barbour*. remembermarybarbour.com and Taudevin, A. J. *Mrs Barbour's Daughters*. Bloomsbury Publishing, 2015
18. https://dangerouswomenproject.org/2017/03/02/mary-barbour-dangerous-woman/ Accessed 4/4/2022.
19. Currie, Pam. *op cit* . P. 6.
20. *Ibid*. P6.
21. Memoirs of Helen Crawfurd, *op cit*.
22. *The Courier* October 13, 1915.
23. Banner at the Great March in St Enoch's Square, Glasgw 7th October 1915, quoted in Castells, Manuel. *The city and the grassroots: a cross-cultural theory of urban social movements*. No. 7. Univ of California Press, 1983. P32.
24. *The Evening Telegraph and Post* October 29, 1915.
25. *The Evening Telegraph and Post* October 29, 1915.
26. Gray, Neil, ed. *Rent and its discontents: a century of housing struggle*. Rowman & Littlefield, 2018.
27. *The Scotsman* 2 December 1915.
28. Hughes, Annmarie, *op cit*.
29. Pankhurst, Estelle Sylvia. *The home front: a mirror to life in England during the World War*. Hutchinson, London 1932.
30. Iris Barry, 'We Enjoyed the War' *Scribners Magazine*, 1934, pp 279–283.
31. https://www.bbc.co.uk/programmes/p02b2jng Accessed 4/4/2022.
32. Mr Ewart, SOHCA /O19/031/ Glasgow quoted in Hughes, Annmarie, and Valerie Wright. "What did the rent strikers do next? Women and housing struggles in interwar Scotland." (2018): 17–32. P. 19.
33. https://www.bbc.co.uk/programmes/p02b0m0s Accessed 4/4/2022 and Beddoe, Deirdre. *Out of the shadows: A history of women in twentieth-century Wales*. University of Wales Press, 2000. P. 50.
34. Hunt, Karen. "A Heroine at Home: the housewife on the First World War home front." In *The Home Front in Britain*, pp. 73–91. Palgrave Macmillan, London, 2014.
35. Moorhouse, Bert, Mary Wilson, and Chris Chamberlain. "Rent strikes-direct action and the working class." *Socialist Register* 9 (1972).
36. https://www.counterfire.org/women-on-the-left/16331-mary-barbour-and-the-glasgow-rent-strike Accessed 4/4/2022.
37. Andrews, Maggie. *The Acceptable Face of Feminism: The Women's Institute as a Social Movement*. New and revised edition. London: Lawrence and Wishart. 2015).
38. Rowan, Caroline. "Women in the Labour Party, 1906–1920." *Feminist Review* 12, no. 1 (1982): 74–91.
39. *Forward* May 3, 1919.
40. https://dangerouswomenproject.org/2017/03/02/mary-barbour-dangerous-woman/ Accessed 4/4/2022.
41. Moorhouse, Bert, Mary Wilson, and Chris Chamberlain. "Rent strikes-direct action and the working class." *Socialist Register* 9 (1972).
42. *The Yorkshire Post,* November 19, 1924.
43. Swenarton, Mark. *Homes fit for heroes: The politics and architecture of early state housing in Britain*. Routledge, 2018.
44. http://hansard.millbanksystems.com/commons/1923/may/02/housing-etc-no-2-money Accessed 4/4/2022.

45. *Home and Country,* July 1940. P. 121.
46. *Keeping Ourselves Informed,* London: NFWI publication, 1981. P. 132.
47. Bullock, Nicholas. "Re-assessing the Post-War Housing Achievement: the Impact of War-damage Repairs on the New Housing Programme in London." *Twentieth Century British History* 16, no. 3 (2005): 256–282.
48. Bryan, Beverley, Stella Dadzie, and Suzanne Scafe. *The heart of the race: Black women's lives in Britain.* Verso Books, 2018. Kindle edition 58%.
49. *Ibid.*
50. Reeve, Kesia. "Squatting since 1945." In *Housing and Social Policy,* pp. 205–224. Routledge, 2005.
51. Report on Housing and Demolition Survey, 1975, GLC Policy Studies Unit, Table C13, P. 41. Quoted in Wall, Christine. "Sisterhood and squatting in the 1970s: Feminism, housing and urban change in Hackney." In *History Workshop Journal,* vol. 83, no. 1, pp. 79–97. Oxford University Press, 2017.
52. Franklin, A. S. *Squatting in England 1969–79: a case study of social conflict in advanced industrial capitalism.* University of Bristol, School for Advanced Urban Studies, 1984.
53. Quote taken from Wall, Christine. "Sisterhood and squatting in the 1970s: Feminism, housing and urban change in Hackney." In *History Workshop Journal,* vol. 83, no. 1, pp. 79–97. Oxford University Press, 2017. P. 85.
54. *Ibid.* P 86.
55. Wall, Christine. "Sisterhood and squatting in the 1970s: Feminism, housing and urban change in Hackney." In *History Workshop Journal,* vol. 83, no. 1, pp. 79–97. Oxford University Press, 2017.
56. https://remembermarybarbour.wordpress.com/about-mary-barbour/ Accessed 4/4/2022.
57. https://www.dailyrecord.co.uk/incoming/castlemilk-housing-activist-takes-top-8740658 Accessed 4/4/2022.
58. Reproduced in Penny Kitchen *For Home and Country: War, Peace and Rural Life as Seen through the pages of the WI Magazine 1919–59.* Edbury Press.1990 p 45.

Chapter 2: *Voters Awake* **(1920s)**
1. The *Leeds Mercury,* 14 December 1918.
2. The *Leeds Mercury,* 14 December 1918.
3. *Citizens,* 21 October, 1926.
4. *Worcester Herald,* 28 September 1918.
5. Letter of Ida Chamberlain 8 December 1918 Diary letters 100.
6. *Birmingham Mail,* 14 December 1918.
7. *Birmingham Mail,* 14 December 1918.
8. Reproduced in *The Guardian* 16 December 2018 https://www.theguardian.com/politics/from-the-archive-blog/2018/dec/14/women-vote-uk-general-election-first-time-1918 Accessed 5/5/2022.
9. *Sunday Pictorial,* 15 December 1918.
10. Reproduced in *The Guardian,* 16 December 2018. https://www.theguardian.com/politics/from-the-archive-blog/2018/dec/14/women-vote-uk-general-election-first-time-1918 Accessed 5/5/2022.
11. Muggeridge, Anna. "The Missing Two Million: The Exclusion of Working-Class Women from the 1918 Representation of the People Act." *Revue Française de Civilisation Britannique. French Journal of British Studies* 23, no. XXIII-1 (2018).

12. *Leamington Spa Courier and Warwickshire Standard* 1 March, 1918.
13. Jarvis, David. "Mrs Maggs and Betty: The Conservative Appeal to Women Voters in the 1920s." *Twentieth Century British History* 5.2 (1994): 129–152. P 138.
14. Stanley Baldwin "Why the Sugar Duty was not reduced" *Home and Politics* August 1923 quoted in Thackeray, David. "Home and politics: women and Conservative activism in early twentieth-century Britain." *Journal of British Studies* 49.4 (2010) pp. 826–848.
15. Lawrence, Jon. "The Culture of Elections in Modern Britain." *History* 96.324 (2011): 459–476.
16. *Birmingham Gazette*, 14 December 1918.
17. Lawrence, Jon. (2011): 'The Culture of Elections in Modern Britain'. *History* 96.324, pp 459–476. P 466.
18. Braithewaite, Brian, et al. *Good Housekeeping* 1923 reproduced in *Ragtime to Wartime the Best of Good Housekeeping 1922–1939*, Edbury Press, 1986. P 56.
19. *The Pall Mall Gazette* 22 September 1921.
20. *Good Housekeeping* March, 1923.
21. Logan, Anne. "In Search of Equal Citizenship: the campaign for women magistrates in England and Wales, 1910–1939." *Women's History Review* 16, no. 4 (2007): 501–518.
22. Beaumont, Caitriona. *Housewives and citizens: Domesticity and the women's movement in England, 1928–64*. Manchester University Press, 2016.
23. Braithewaite, Brian, et al. *Good Housekeeping* 1923 reproduced in *Ragtime to Wartime the Best of Good Housekeeping1922–1939*, Edbury Press, 1986. P. 21.
24. *Woman's Journal* March 1934. P. 22.
25. For a history of the formation of the Women's Institute Movement – see Andrews, Maggie *op cit*.
26. *Keeping Ourselves Informed*, London: NFWI publications, 1981, P. 82.
27. Colpus, Eve. "Women, service and self-actualization in inter-war Britain." *Past and present* 238, no. 1 (2018): 197–232.
28. *Daily Herald*, 7 December 1922.
29. Lady Olivier, *Jubilee Book*, London: NFWI Publications, 1965.
30. H. McCarthy, 'Parties, voluntary associations and democratic politics in inter-war Britain' *The Historical Journal*, 2007, 50, pp. 891–912, P. 910.
31. 1931 NFWI Annual Report, P. 73.
32. 1926 NFWI Annual Report, P. 46.
33. Hughes, Annmarie, and Valerie Wright. "What did the rent strikers do next? Women and housing struggles in interwar Scotland." (2018): 17–32. P 17.
34. *Home and Country*, July 1923, P. 17.
35. Forward 7 November, 1922 quoted in Hughes, Annmarie, and Valerie Wright. "What did the rent strikers do next? Women and housing struggles in interwar Scotland." (2018): 17–32.
36. Neville, Julia. "Challenge, Conformity and Casework in Interwar England: the first women councillors in Devon." *Women's History Review* 22, no. 6 (2013): 971–994
37. https://womenssuffragescotland.wordpress.com/main-sections/women-as-active-citizens-politics-and-feminism-in-interwar-scotland/ Accessed 5/5/2022.
38. Frankish, Carol. 'Ada Croft Baker'in Andrews, Maggie, and Janis Lomas. *Hidden Heroines: The Forgotten Suffragettes*. The Crowood Press, 2018.
39. For more about Emma Spronson see https://nicolagauld.wordpress.com/2015/03/09/emma-sproson-wolverhamptons-first-female-councillor/ Accessed 5/5/2022.

40. Mitchell, Hannah. *The Hard Way Up. The Autobiography of Hannah Mitchell, Suffragette and Rebel.* Faber & Faber, 1968.
41. Barnes, Annie in conversation with Kate Harding and Caroline Gibbs. *Tough Annie.* Stepney Book Publications 1980.
42. 'Do "Workington Man" and "Worcester Women" decide elections"*The Spectator.* 9 November 2019.
43. Electoral Commission report on Gender and Political Participation, published in April 2004 https://www.electoralcommission.org.uk/sites/default/files/electoral_commission_pdf_file/Final_report_270404_12488-9470__E__N__S__W__.pdf Accessed 5/5/2022.

Chapter 3: The Suppression of *The Well of Loneliness* (1928)

1. Souhami, Diana. *The Trials of Radclyffe Hall.* Open Road Media, 2014.
2. *ibid.*
3. Quoted in Love, Heather. "Hard Times and Heartaches: Radclyffe Hall's *The Well of Loneliness.*" *Journal of Lesbian Studies* 4, no. 2 (2000): 115–128, P. 121.
4. *ibid.* P. 117.
5. https://www.themarginalian.org/2016/11/09/well-of-loneliness-trial-of-radclyffe-hall-virginia-woolf/ Accessed 2/2/2022.
6. Radclyffe, Hall, M. *The Well of Loneliness.* General Press (1928) reprinted 2021. P11.
7. Madden, Ed. "*The Well of Loneliness*, or The Gospel According to Radclyffe Hall." *Journal of homosexuality* 33, no. 3–4 (1997): 163–186.
8. *Ibid.* PP. 163–4.
9. *Ibid.* PP. 163–4.
10. *Ibid.* P. 163–4.
11. William Acton, *The Functions and Disorders of the Reproductive Organs in Childhood, Youth, Adult Age and Advanced Life Considered in Their Physiological, Social and Moral Relations* (London: John Churchill and Sons, 1862), P. 212.
12. https://hansard.parliament.uk/Lords/1921-08-15/debates/79d32ffb-c9ba-46f7-a46f-0020f1269fd5/CommonsAmendment Accessed 2/2/2022.
13. https://hansard.parliament.uk/Lords/1921-08-15/debates/79d32ffb-c9ba-46f7-a46f-0020f1269fd5/CommonsAmendment Accessed 2/2/2022.
14. https://hansard.parliament.uk/Lords/1921-08-15/debates/79d32ffb-c9ba-46f7-a46f-0020f1269fd5/CommonsAmendment. Accessed 2/2/2022.
15. https://hansard.parliament.uk/Lords/1921-08-15/debates/79d32ffb-c9ba-46f7-a46f-0020f1269fd5/CommonsAmendment. Accessed 2/2/2022.
16. Love, Heather. *op cit.* P. 123.
17. National Archives (Catalogue ref: DPP 1/88) https://www.nationalarchives.gov.uk/education/resources/twenties-britain-part-two/well-of-loneliness/ Accessed 2/2/2022.
18. https://www.nationalarchives.gov.uk/education/resources/twenties-britain-part-two/well-of-loneliness/ Accessed 2/2/2022.
19. *The Scotsman*, 24 August, 1928.
20. *The Evening Telegraph*, 9 November 1928.
21. Vargo, Marc E. *Scandal. Infamous Gay Controversies of the Twentieth Century.* Routledge, 2013. PP. 72–3.
22. *Hull Daily Mail* 16 November 1928.
23. https://blog.britishnewspaperarchive.co.uk/2020/06/15/the-well-of-loneliness/ Accessed 2/2/2022.

24. https://www.theguardian.com/books/2019/jan/10/it-has-made-me-want-to-live-public-support-for-lesbian-novelist-radclyffe-hall-over-banned-book-revealed Accessed 2/2/2022.
25. Marshik, Celia. "History's" abrupt revenges": censoring war's perversions in The Well of Loneliness and Sleeveless Errand." *Journal of Modern Literature* 26, no. 2 (2003): 145–159, at P. 145.
26. Taylor, Leslie A. ""I Made up My Mind to Get It": The American Trial of "The Well of Loneliness" New York City, 1928–1929." *Journal of the History of Sexuality* 10, no. 2 (2001): 250–286. P. 20.
27. *Yorkshire Post*, 30 August, 1929.
28. *Leeds Mercury* March 13, 1931.
29. Souhami, Diana. *op cit.* PP. 22–25.
30. Cook, Blanche Wiesen (1979). "'Women Alone Stir My Imagination': Lesbianism and the Cultural Tradition". *Signs*. 4 (4): 718–739, at P. 719.
31. *Dunn, Sara; Warland, Betsy; Munt, Sally (1994). "Inversions: Writings by Dykes, Queers and Lesbians by Betsy Warland; New Lesbian Criticism: Literary and Cultural Readings by Sally Munt". Feminist Review* (46): 106–108. Souhami, Diana. "The case for the well of loneliness." *The Gay & Lesbian Review Worldwide* 21, no. 6 (2014): 22–2
32. https://publishingtriangle.org/best-lesbian-gay-novels/ Accessed 2/2/2022.
33. Love, Heather. *op cit.* P. 116.
34. *ibid.* P. 117.
35. *Souhami, Diana op cit.*
36. https://www.bl.uk/sisterhood/articles/sexual-pleasure-sexual-rights Accessed 2/2/2022.
37. https://www.bl.uk/sisterhood/articles/sexual-pleasure-sexual-rights Accessed 2/2/2022.
38. Bindel, Julie (). 'My sexual Revolution' *The Guardian* 30 January, 2009.

Chapter 4: 'Every mother should be entitled to anaesthetic' (1930)
1. Vincent De Brouwere (2007) 'The Comparative Study of Maternal Mortality over Time: the role of the professionalisation of childbirth', *Social History of Medicine*, 20(3), pp. 541–562.
2. Tilghman, Carolyn. "Autobiography as dissidence: subjectivity, sexuality, and the Women's Co-operative Guild." *Biography* (2003): 583–606, at P. 585.
3. *Maternity: Letters* from Working *Women*. G Bell. 1915. P69.
4. *ibid.* P39.
5. Stanley, Heather Michelle. "Vested interests: the 1902 Midwives Act as a case study in professional identity." PhD diss., 2006.
6. Bourke, Joanna. "Childbirth in the UK: suffering and citizenship before the 1950s." *The Lancet* 383, no. 9925 (2014): 1288–1289.
7. *Maternity: Letters. op cit.* PP. 79–80.
8. *ibid.* P. 77.
9. Quoted in Winter, Jay. *The great war and the British people*. Springer, 2003. p 193.
10. De Groot, Gerard J. *Blighty: British Society in the era of the Great War*. Addison-Wesley Longman, 1996. P. 218.
11. *Stirling Saturday Observer* 25 November 1916.
12. *British Medical Journal*, 'Infant Mortality and Stillbirth' published 31 August 1912. *British Medical Journal*

13. https://register-of-charities.charitycommission.gov.uk/charity-search/-/charity-details/4045112 Accessed 20/2/2022.
14. https://register-of-charities.charitycommission.gov.uk/charity-search/-/charity-details/4045112 Accessed 20/2/2022.
15. https://www.lookandlearn.com/history-images/YW031851L/National-Birthday-Trust-Fund-flags-for-hel?t=1&q=national+birthday+trust Accessed 20/2/2022.
16. *Western Mail and South Wales News,* December 20, 1928.
17. Jones, Helen. *op cit.* P. 75.
18. Williams, A. Susan. "Relief and research: The nutrition work of the National Birthday Trust Fund, 1935–9." *Nutrition in Britain: Science, scientists and politics in the twentieth century* (1997): 99–122.
19. Report of Maternal Mortality Committee Conference 1932. https://cdm21047.contentdm.oclc.org/digital/collection/health/id/2100. Acessed 10 January 2022.
20. *British Medical Journal,* 'Infant Mortality and Stillbirth' published 31 August 1912.
21. Rijks, Miranda. *The Eccentric Entrepreneur: Sir Julien Cahn Businessman, Philanthropist, Magician and Cricket-Lover.* The History Press, 2011. P. 69.
22. Baker, Penelope A. "Illustrations from the Wellcome Institute Library: The National Birthday Trust Fund records in the contemporary Medical Archives Centre." *Medical History* 33, no. 4 (1989): 489–494.
23. *British Medical Journal* 1: 220. doi:10.1136/bmj.1.3604.220. PMC 2312642. Accessed 20/2/2022.
24. *ibid.*
25. *The Fife Free Press* July 29, 1939.
26. Baker, Penelope A. "Illustrations from the Wellcome Institute Library: The National Birthday Trust Fund records in the contemporary Medical Archives Centre." *Medical History* 33, no. 4 (1989): 489 – 494.
27. Williams, A. Susan. "Relief and research: The nutrition work of the National Birthday Trust Fund, 1935–9." *Nutrition in Britain: Science, scientists and politics in the twentieth century* (1997): 99–122.
28. Towler, Jean, and Joan Bramall. *Midwives in history and society.* Taylor & Francis, 1986.
29. Bourke, Joanna. *op cit.* 1288–1289.
30. Bourke, Joanna. *op cit.* 1288–1289.
31. "Lucy Baldwin Apparatus For Obstetric Analgesia" (PDF). *British Journal of Anaesthesia.* XXXIV (3). March 1962.
32. Thorn, Gill ' 'Eighteenth Century Obstetric Forceps' Andrews, Maggie, and Janis Lomas. *A History of Women in 100 Objects.* The History Press, 2018. P 10.
33. https://memoriesofnursing.uk/articles/midwifery-in-britain-in-the-twentieth-century Accessed 20/2/2022.
34. Thorn, Gill. *op cit.* P. 109.
35. https://www.bbc.co.uk/news/magazine-36194677 Accessed 20/2/2022.
36. https://www.google.com/search?q=aims+of+the+national+childbirth+trust&rlz=1C5CHFA_enGB916GB916&oq=aims+of+the+national+childbirth+trust&aqs=chrome..69i57j33i22i29i30l9.14841j0j9&sourceid=chrome&ie=UTF-8 Accessed 20/2/2022.

Chapter 5: Equal Pay in the Aeronautical Industry (1943)
1. https://ukvote100.org/2020/08/31/women-mps-1931-1945/ Accessed 14/4/2022.
2. *Daily Mail,* 7 July, 1915.
3. *Labour Gazette,* March, 1915.

4. Spurgeon, Anne. "Mortality or Morality? Keeping Workers Safe in the First World War." In *The Home Front in Britain*, pp. 57–72. Palgrave Macmillan, London, 2014. P. 58.
5. Holloway, Gerry. *Women and Work in Britain since 1840*. Routledge, 2007.
6. Bartley, Paula. *Women's Activism in Twentieth-Century Britain: Making a Difference Across the Political Spectrum*. Palgrave Macmillan, London. 2022. P. 42.
7. *ibid*. P. 42.
8. Hunt, Cathy. *'The Weather Was Hot, The Way was Long"*: the 1918 strike for equal pay online blog https://cathyhunthistorian.com/2018/07/24/the-weather-was-hot-the-way-was-long-the-1918-strike-for-equal-pay/ Accessed 14/4/2022.
9. *Ibid*.
10. *Ibid*.
11. http://www.ampltd.co.uk/collections_az/Sex+Gender04/editorial-introduction.aspx Accessed 14/4/2022.
12. Holloway, Gerry. *op cit*.
13. Smith, Harold L. "British Feminism and the Equal Pay issue in the 1930s." *Women's History Review* 5, no. 1 (1996): 97–110. P. 98.
14. Bourke, Joanna, *Working Class Cultures in Britain, 1890–1960: Gender, Class and Ethnicity*, Routledge 2008. P. 86.
15. Kean, Hilda, and Alison Oram. "'Men Must be Educated and Women Must Do If: the National Federation (later Union) of Women Teachers and contemporary feminism 1910-30." *Gender and Education* 2, no. 2 (1990): 147–167. P. 147.
16. West, Rebecca. 'Equal Pay for Men and Women Teachers' *Time and Tide* 6 February, 1923.
17. Kean, Hilda. *op cit*. P. 154.
18. https://hansard.parliament.uk/Commons/1920-03-18/debates/e35c8c5b-033d-42d2-8e56-a26f2c0a2664/CivilServants(EqualPayForMenAndWomen); https://hansard.parliament.uk/Commons/1928-03-26/debates/f11dd2ea-4dd1-4e5e-b998-f143bf084b6f/EqualPay Accessed 14/4/2022.
19. Pugh, Martin. *Women and the Women's Movement in Britain since 1914*. Bloomsbury Publishing, 2015. P. 97.
20. *Time and Tide* November 30, 1923.
21. Smith, Harold L. *op cit*. P. 101.
22. *Ibid*.
23. *ibid*. P. 102.
24. *ibid*. P. 104.
25. https://hansard.parliament.uk/Commons/1935-07-09/debates/b0a719e4-e193-4bc2-b334-5f6ac0e68dae/CivilService(EqualPay) Accessed 14/4/2022.
26. Hansard 3 March, 1936.
27. *Women's Leader*, 7 November, 1924.
28. Hansard 1 April, 1936.
29. Glew, Helen. "The slow road to victory: The equal pay campaigns from 1939 to 1954." In *Gender, rhetoric and regulation*, pp. 146–177. Manchester University Press, 2016.
30. Smith, Harold L. "The womanpower problem in Britain during the Second World War." *The Historical Journal* 27, no. 4 (1984): 925–945, at P. 931.
31. https://api.parliament.uk/historic-hansard/commons/1939/oct/24/personal-injuries-emergency-provisions Accessed 14/4/2022.

32. Smith, Harold. "The Problem of" Equal Pay for Equal Work" in Great Britain during World War II." *The Journal of Modern History* 53, no. 4 (1981): 652–672.
33. *Ibid* P. 661.
34. *Ibid* P. 661.
35. *Ibid*. P. 658.
36. See Holloway, Gerry *op cit*. Andrews, Maggie, and Janis Lomas. "Home fronts, gender, war and conflict." *Women's History Review* 26, no. 4 (2017): 523–527.
37. Smith, Harold. *op cit*.
38. Little, Stephen E. and Grieco, Margaret (2011). Shadow factories, shallow skills? An analysis of work organisation in the aircraft industry in the Second World War. Labor History, 52(2) pp. 193–216.
39. Calder, Angus. *The People's war: Britain 1939–1945*. Random House, 2012. P. 466
40. Little, Stephen E. and Grieco, Margaret (2011). Shadow factories, shallow skills? An analysis of work organisation in the aircraft industry in the Second World War. Labor History, 52(2) pp. 193–216. https://oro.open.ac.uk/31226/1/little-grieco-shadowfactory.pdf Accessed 14/4/2022.
41. Smith, Harold. *op cit*. P. 667.
42. Smith, Harold. *op cit*. P. 668.
43. https://hansard.parliament.uk/commons/2015-07-01/debates/15070135000001/EqualPayAndTheGenderPayGap Accessed 14/4/2022.
44. Fox, Jo. https://blog.history.ac.uk/2018/10/equal-pay-for-equal-work-jill-craigies-to-be-a-woman/ Accessed 14/4/2022.
45. Smith, Harold L. "The Politics of Conservative Reform: the equal pay for equal work issue, 1945–1955." *The Historical Journal* 35, no. 2 (1992): 401–415.

Chapter 6: Gowns and Mortarboards (1940s and 1950s)
1. Strachey, Ray. *A Short History of the Women's Movement in Great Britain*. G Bell and Sons 1928.
2. https://researchbriefings.files.parliament.uk/documents/SN04252/SN04252.pdf Table 8 Students obtaining university degrees. Accessed 8/5/2021.
3. https://www.bl.uk/collection-items/the-daughters-of-england-by-sarah-stickney-ellis Accessed 8/5/2021.
4. Stickeny Ellis, Sarah, *The Daughters of England*. 1845.
5. https://recipes.hypotheses.org/18239 Accessed 8/5/2021.
6. Maudsley, Henry 'Sex in Mind and Education'. *Popular Science Monthly Volume*, 5 June, 1874.
7. https://www.varsity.co.uk/science/17020 Accessed 8/5/2021.
8. https://www.britain-magazine.com/features/history-of-women-at-cambridge-university/
9. Evans, J. L. Prelude and Fugue: and autobiography, 1947. P 21 quoted in Dyhouse, Carol. *No distinction of sex?: Women in British universities, 1870–1939*. Routledge, 2016. P. 192.
10. https://www.ox.ac.uk/about/oxford-people/women-at-oxford/centenary#:~:text=The%20first%20women's%20colleges%20%2D%20Somerville,expense%20of%20the%20other%20foundations. Accessed 8/5/2021.
11. Dyhouse, Carol. *No distinction of sex?: Women in British universities, 1870–1939*. Routledge, 2016. P. 194.
12. https://www.varsity.co.uk/science/17020 Accessed 8/5/2021.

13. Richmond, Marsha L. "" A Lab of One's Own": The Balfour Biological Laboratory for Women at Cambridge University, 1884–1914." *Isis* 88, no. 3 (1997): 422–455, at P. 422.
14. https://www.girton.cam.ac.uk/pioneering-history/student-experience Accessed 8/5/2021.
15. Dyhouse, Carol. *op cit.* P. 189.
16. *Aberdeen Press and Journal*, 11 November, 1908.
17. *The Scotsman*, 11 January, 1909.
18. See Dyhouse, Carol. *op cit.* PP. 189–216.
19. Brittain, Vera. *Testament of Youth*, Victor Gollancz (1933) reprinted Kindle. At P. 84 and P. 44.
20. *Ibid.* P. 84.
21. https://www.varsity.co.uk/science/17020 Accessed 8/5/2021.
22. https://www.sciencefocus.com/science/10-amazing-women-in-science-history-you-really-should-know-about/ Accessed 8/5/2021.
23. October 1920: the first degrees https://www.ox.ac.uk/about/oxford-people/women-at-oxford Accessed 8/5/2021.
24. https://www.britain-magazine.com/features/history-of-women-at-cambridge-university/
25. *Time and Tide*, 3 December 1920 as quoted in Spender, Dale. "Time and tide wait for no man." (1984). P. 240.
26. *Ibid.*
27. https://www.britain-magazine.com/features/history-of-women-at-cambridge-university/ Accessed 8/5/2021.
28. *Time and Tide. op cit.* P. 253.
29. https://blackcantabs.herokuapp.com/earliest-african-women/ Accessed 8/5/2021.
30. https://www.telegraph.co.uk/only-in-britain/oxford-university-allows-women-to-graduate/ Accessed 8/5/2021.
31. https://www.varsity.co.uk/features/17317
32. Watts, Ruth. 'Review of Spencer, Stephanie. Gender, Work and Education in Britain in the 1950s'. https://reviews.history.ac.uk/review/689 Accessed 8/5/2021.
33. Nicholson, Virginia. *Perfect wives in ideal homes: The story of women in the 1950s.* Penguin UK, 2015.
34. https://www.cambridgenetwork.co.uk/news/cambridge-science-festival-celebrates-pioneering-women-science Accessed 8/5/2021.
35. Maitland, Sara, ed. *Very heaven: looking back at the 1960's.* Virago Press, 1988. P. 9.
36. Coote, Anna, and Beatrix Campbell. *Sweet Freedom the Struggle for Women's Liberation.* Virago, 1982. P. 17.
37. Kennedy, Mary, and Brec'hed Piette. *From the margins to the mainstream: issues around women's studies on adult education and access courses.* na, 1991.
38. https://www.bl.uk/sisterhood/articles/womens-studies-and-womens-history Accessed 8/5/2021.
39. https://socialhistory.org.uk/shs_exchange/women-adult-education-1970s/ Accessed 8/5/2021.
40. https://socialhistory.org.uk/shs_exchange/women-adult-education-1970s/ Accessed 8/5/2021.

Chapter 7: 'We got a little hall and took our children there with their toys' (1961)
1. https://www.independent.co.uk/news/education/schools/here-s-to-the-early-years-the-preschool-learning-alliance-s-playgroups-are-facing-an-uncertain-future-2161653.html Accessed 3/3/2021.
2. Mamoojee, Farhanah 'The Hidden History of the Ayahs of Britain' *Women's History: The Journal of the Women's History Magazine.* Vol 2 Issue 17. (2021) : 4–8.
3. Arnot, Margaret L. "Infant death, child care and the state: the baby-farming scandal and the first infant life protection legislation of 1872." *Continuity and Change* 9.2 (1994): 271–311.
4. *Worcester Herald*, September 1914.
5. https://www.early-education.org.uk/about-froebel Accessed 3/3/2021.
6. https://www.early-education.org.uk/about-froebel Accessed 3/3/2021.
7. Darling, Elizabeth. "Womanliness in the Slums: A Free Kindergarten in Early Twentieth-Century Edinburgh." *Gender & History* 29, no. 2 (2017): 359–386.
8. Heren, Louise. 'British Nannies and the First World War' (http://ww1centenary.oucs.ox.ac.uk/?p=3680) Accessed 3/3/2021.
9. Connelly, Katherine. "Sylvia Pankhurst, the First World War and the struggle for democracy." *Revue Française de Civilisation Britannique. French Journal of British Studies* 20, no. XX-1 (2015).
10. Liebovich, Betty. "Margaret McMillan's Contributions to Cultures of Childhood." *Genealogy* 3.3 (2019): P. 43.
11. Quoted in Steedman, Carolyn. *Childhood, Culture* and *Class* in *Britain: Margaret McMillan, 1860–1931.* New Brunswick: Rutgers, 1990. P. 186.
12. https://eastendwomensmuseum.org/blog/2018/8/7/women-babies-and-bombs-how-day-nurseries-contributed-to-working-womens-lives-during-wwii Accessed 3/3/2021.
13. https://eastendwomensmuseum.org/blog/2018/8/7/women-babies-and-bombs-how-day-nurseries-contributed-to-working-womens-lives-during-wwii Accessed 3/3/2021.
14. Day, Ann. 'The forgotten Matey's: women workers in Portsmouth Dockyard England 1939–45' *Women's History Review* 1998, Issue 3. pp 361–382.
15. https://www.independent.co.uk/news/education/schools/here-s-to-the-early-years-the-preschool-learning-alliance-s-playgroups-are-facing-an-uncertain-future-2161653.html Accessed 3/3/2021.
16. https://www.independent.co.uk/news/education/schools/here-s-to-the-early-years-the-preschool-learning-alliance-s-playgroups-are-facing-an-uncertain-future-2161653.html Accessed 3/3/2021.
17. https://www.independent.co.uk/news/education/schools/here-s-to-the-early-years-the-preschool-learning-alliance-s-playgroups-are-facing-an-uncertain-future-2161653.html Accessed 3/3/2021.
18. https://www.independent.co.uk/news/education/schools/here-s-to-the-early-years-the-preschool-learning-alliance-s-playgroups-are-facing-an-uncertain-future-2161653.html Accessed 3/3/2021.
19. *The Guardian Obituary*, 18 September, 2002.
20. https://www.stjohnswoodmemories.org.uk/content/amenities/schools-and-playgrounds/st_johns_wood_terrace_-_a_1960s_childhood Accessed 3/3/2021.
21. https://www.independent.co.uk/news/education/schools/here-s-to-the-early-years-the-preschool-learning-alliance-s-playgroups-are-facing-an-uncertain-future-2161653.html

22. *The Guardian* 25 February, 2019. https://www.theguardian.com/politics/2019/feb/25/inspired-by-belle-tutaev-1961-letter-on-pre-school-playgroups Accessed 3/3/2021.
23. *Spare Rib* 41, November 1975.
24. *Ibid.*
25. Crowe, Brenda. *The playgroup movement*. Routledge, 2013, first published in 1973.
26. *Ibid.* P. 14.
27. https://www.bl.uk/sisterhood/articles/families-and-parenting Accessed 3/3/2021.
28. https://www.bl.uk/sisterhood/articles/families-and-parenting Accessed 3/3/2021.
29. https://www.bl.uk/sisterhood/articles/families-and-parenting Accessed 3/3/2021.
30. https://www.bl.uk/sisterhood/articles/families-and-parenting Accessed 3/3/2021.
31. https://www.bl.uk/sisterhood/articles/families-and-parenting Accessed 3/3/2021.
32. https://www.bl.uk/sisterhood/articles/families-and-parenting Accessed 3/3/2021.
33. https://holdingthebaby.org/podcasts/2019/12/18/bonus-track-doing-it-ourselves Accessed 3/3/2021.
34. https://holdingthebaby.org/podcasts/2019/12/18/bonus-track-doing-it-ourselves Accessed 3/3/2021.
35. *Spare Rib,* November, 1977.
36. *Spare Rib* 70, May, 1978.
37. *Spare Rib* 88 November, 1979.
38. https://www.familyandchildcaretrust.org/?utm_source=domain%20redirect&utm_content=daycaretrustorguk/mod.php?mod=userpage&menu=901&page_id=3 Accessed 3/3/2021.
39. http://www.educationengland.org.uk/documents/rumbold/rumbold1990.html Accessed 3/3/2021.
40. House of Lords Select Committee on Affordable Childcare Report of the Session 2014-15. https://publications.parliament.uk/pa/ld201415/ldselect/ldaffchild/117/117.pdf Accessed 3/3/2021.
41. Littler, J. & Winch, A., (2016) "Feminism and Childcare: A Roundtable with Sara de Benedictis, Gideon Burrows, Tracey Jensen, Jill Rutter and Victoria Showunmi", *Studies in the Maternal* 8 (1), p.2. doi: https://doi.org/10.16995/sim.212 Accessed 3/3/2021.

Chapter 8: Avoiding Unwanted Pregnancy for the Young (1964)
1. *Spare Rib,* May 1980.
2. Chamberlain, Mary. *Fenwomen*. Virago, 1975 P. 77.
3. https://www.open.edu/openlearn/body-mind/health/health-studies/brief-history-sex-education Accessed 8/8/2021.
4. Thane, Pat. *Happy Families History and Family Policy* A Report prepared for the British Academy 2010 revised 2011. https://www.thebritishacademy.ac.uk/publications/happy-families-history-family-policy/ Accessed 8/8/2021.
5. Lampe, David. *Pyke, the Unknown Genius,* Evans Brothers, 1959, pp. 35–36, 51–53.
6. https://collection.sciencemuseumgroup.org.uk/objects/co96297/rubber-vault-cap-london-england-1915-1925-vault-cap Accessed 8/8/2021.
7. https://www.history.com/topics/germany/eugenics Accessed 8/8/2021.
8. Hubback, Eva. (27 February 1931). 'Correspondence' 'Eugenic Sterilisation'. The *Woman's Leader* XXIII.4: 31 quoted in Makepeace, Clare (2009). 'To What Extent was the Relationship Between Feminists and the Eugenics Movement a 'Marriage of Convenience' in the Interwar Years?. *Journal of International Women's Studies,* 11(3), 66–80.

Notes 179

9. *The Daily Mirror,* November 9, 1935.
10. https://archives.lse.ac.uk/Record.aspx?src=CalmView.Catalog&id=8SUF%2fB%2f149 Accessed 8/8/2021.
11. *The Guardian,* 20 December, 1935.
12. https://archives.lse.ac.uk/Record.aspx?src=CalmView.Catalog&id=8SUF%2fB%2f177 Accessed 8/8/2021.
13. https://feministlibrary.co.uk/reviewed-lesley-a-hall-the-life-and-times-of-stella-browne-feminist-and-free-spirit/ Accessed 8/8/2021.
14. https://publications.parliament.uk/pa/cm200607/cmselect/cmsctech/1045/1045we14.htm Accessed 8/8/2021. Hall, Lesley A. *The Life and Times of Stella Browne, Feminist and Free Spirit.* IB Tauris, 2011.
15. Women's Co-operative Guild. *Maternity; letters from working-women.* G. Bell and Sons, Limited, 1916.
16. https://publications.parliament.uk/pa/cm200607/cmselect/cmsctech/1045/1045we14.htm Accessed 8/8/2021.
17. Wilson, Dr Libby. *Sex on the Rates: Memoirs of a Family Planning Doctor.* Argyll, 2004. P. 78.
18. *Ibid.* P. 79.
19. *The Guardian,* 6 June, 2010.
20. Durant, Alan. "Kenneth Thompson ed., Media and Cultural Regulation; Bob Mullan, Consuming Television: Television and its Audience." (1998): 313–318.
21. Gorer, Geoffrey. *Sex & Marriage in England Today: Study of the Views and Experience of the Under-45s.* London: Nelson, 1971.
22. Thane, Pat. *Happy Families History and Family Policy* A Report prepared for the British Academy 2010 revised 2011. https://www.thebritishacademy.ac.uk/publications/happy-families-history-family-policy/ Accessed 8/8/2021.
23. Maitland, Sara, ed. *Very heaven: looking back at the 1960's.* Virago Press, 1988. P. 151.
24. HUMANAE VITAE http://www.vatican.va/holy_father/paul_vi/encyclicals/documents/hf_p-vi_enc_25071968_humanae-vitae_lt.html Accessed 8/8/2021.
25. *The Guardian,* 6 June, 2010.
26. Thane, Pat. *op cit.*
27. *Independent* 9 October, 1997.
28. Brook Advisory Centre. 1964. Aims and Principles, July 1964.
29. https://legacy.brook.org.uk/about-brook/helen-brooks-obituary Accessed 8/8/2021.
30. Brook, H. 1967. SA/BRO/J1/7. London: Wellcome Library.
31. Rusterholz C. Med Humanit Epub ahead of print: doi:10.1136/ medhum-2021-012206
32. Dyhouse, Carol. *op cit.*
33. Wilson, Dr Libby. *op cit.* P. 84.
34. *Ibid.* P. 85.
35. *Ibid.* P. 86.
36. Sex Teaching in Schools: Statement by the Executive of the National Union of Teachers. London: National Union of Teachers, 1944.
37. https://www.open.edu/openlearn/body-mind/health/health-studies/brief-history-sex-education Accessed 8/8/2021.
38. Maitland, Sara, *op cit.* P. 144.
39. *Ibid.*
40. Cousins, Jane. *Make it happy: what sex is all about.* Penguin, 1978.
41. https://legacy.brook.org.uk/about-brook/quotes-about-brook Accessed 8/8/2021.
42. BBC 27 July, 1989.

Chapter 9: The Miss World Protest (1970)
1. https://www.historyextra.com/period/20th-century/miss-world-1970-what-happened-feminist-civil-rights-protest-documentary/ Accessed 11/11/2021.
2. Rockliff-Steiin, Consuelo Marie. "Pre-Raphaelite Ideals and Artistic Dress." *CM Rockliff-Steiin.[электронный ресурс]*. URL: https://web. archive. org/web/20110930101322/http://www. glily. com/preraphs. htm (дата обращения 12. 02. 2019) (2010).
3. Hoggart, Richard. *The uses of literacy*. 1957 reprinted Routledge, 2017.
4. Hobsbawn, Eric. *Industry and empire: the birth of the industrial revolution*. Penguin Group, 1999.
5. Cavendish, Richard, 'The First Miss World Contest'. *History Today* Vol 52 April 4, 2001
6. 'What was Miss World and why did feminists disagree with it?' https://www.bl.uk/collection-items/jo-robinson-miss-world-contest Accessed 11/11/2021.
7. https://www.dailymail.co.uk/femail/article-6356311/Full-story-1970-Miss-World-final-protestors-triggered-feminist-revolution.html Accessed 11/11/2021.
8. Political Voices Sally Alexandra interviewed by Andrew Whitehead https://www.andrewwhitehead.net/political-voices-sally-alexander.html Accessed 11/11/2021.
9. Political Voices Sally Alexandra interviewed by Andrew Whitehead https://www.andrewwhitehead.net/political-voices-sally-alexander.html Accessed 11/11/2021.
10. Political Voices Sally Alexandra interviewed by Andrew Whitehead https://www.andrewwhitehead.net/political-voices-sally-alexander.html Accessed 11/11/2021.
11. https://www.mirror.co.uk/film/miss-world-protest-brought-cause-21642388 Accessed 11/11/2021.
12. Jo Robisnon 'Miss World 1970: Our aim was to stop the Spectacle.' *Socialist Review* 4 May, 2020. https://socialistworker.co.uk/socialist-review-archive/miss-world-1970-our-aim-was-stop-spectacle/ Accessed 11/11/2021.
13. https://www.royalalberthall.com/about-the-hall/news/2020/october/unstoppable-voices-how-the-1970-miss-world-contest-sparked-a-revolution/ Accessed 11/11/2021.
14. *Waltham Forest Echo* 26 December, 2020 https://walthamforestecho.co.uk/how-we-took-on-the-patriarchy/ Accessed 11/11/2021.
15. https://www.refinery29.com/en-us/2020/09/10047819/misbehaviour-true-story-real-jennifer-hosten Accessed 11/11/2021.
16. https://www.dailymail.co.uk/femail/article-6356311/Full-story-1970-Miss-World-final-protestors-triggered-feminist-revolution.html Accessed 11/11/2021.
17. *New York Times* 8 November 8, 1984.
18. https://womenslibrary.org.uk/2021/08/26/spray-it-loud-feminist-culture-jamming-in-the-1980s/ Accessed 11/11/2021.
19. https://womenslibrary.org.uk/2021/08/26/spray-it-loud-feminist-culture-jamming-in-the-1980s/ Accessed 11/11/2021.
20. *Guardian* I February, 2018 https://www.theguardian.com/lifeandstyle/2018/feb/01/joan-bakewell-1970s-might-woman-one-day-read-the-news-absolutely-not Accessed 11/11/2021.
21. https://archiveshub.jisc.ac.uk/search/archives/1f6315e9-2fa1-3c15-913c-e197a514329b Accessed 11/11/2021.
22. *The Daily Telegraph* 19 September, 2002.

23. https://womenshistorynetwork.org/womens-history-month-spare-rib/ Accessed 11/11/2021.
24. https://www.bl.uk/collection-items/shrew-magazine-1976 Accessed 11/11/2021.
25. https://www.theguardian.com/culture/2018/jun/11/how-we-made-spare-rib-magazine Accessed 11/11/2021.
26. Nye, Louise Kimpton. https://www.bl.uk/sparerib/articles?authors_sorted=Louise%2AKimpton%20Nye Accessed 11/06/2022.
27. Bryan, Beverley, Stella Dadzie, and Suzanne Scafe. *The heart of the race: Black women's lives in Britain*. Verso Books, 2018.
28. See for example: MacKinnon, Catharine A., Andrea Dworkin, and N. D. Andrea Dworkin, eds. *In harm's way: The pornography civil rights hearings*. Harvard University Press, 1997. Morgan, Robin. *Going too far: The personal chronicle of a feminist*. 1977 reprinted Open Road Media, 2014.
29. https://www.birminghammail.co.uk/news/midlands-news/page-3-row-clare-short-8513283 Accessed 11/11/2021.
30. *Ibid.*
31. https://www.independent.co.uk/news/uk/politics/clare-short-my-day-in-the-sun-and-other-page-3-stories-535382.html Accessed 11/11/2021.
32. Short, Clare. *Dear Clare-this is what women feel about Page 3*. Vintage, 1991. P. 82.
33. *Ibid*. P. xxi.
34. *Ibid*. P. xvi.
35. *Ibid*. P. xvii.
36. https://www.bishopsgate.org.uk/collections/campaign-against-pornography
37. Short, Clare. *Dear Clare-this is what women feel about Page 3*. Vintage, 1991. P. 12.
38. Short, Clare. *Dear Clare-this is what women feel about Page 3*. Vintage, 1991. P. 13.
39. Short, Clare. *Dear Clare-this is what women feel about Page 3*. Vintage, 1991. P. 13.

Chapter 10: 'We appreciate the cards and flowers but they are not enough' (1972)
1. *Spare Rib* 58, May 1977.
2. https://globalwomenstrike.net/the-independent-i-founded-the-wages-for-housework-campaign-in-1972-and-women-are-still-working-for-free/ Accessed 20/12/2021.
3. Perkins Gilman, Charlotte. *Women and Economics: A Study of the Economic Relation Between Men and Women as a Factor in Social Evolution in 1898*. Small, Maynard & Company, et al 1898. P. 7. Digital.library.unpenn.edu/women/gilman/economics/economics.html Accessed 20/12/2021.
4. *Ibid*. P. 317.
5. Barash, Carol. 'Dora Marsden's Feminism, the "Freewoman", and the Gender Politics of Early Modernism'. *The Princeton University Library Chronicle*, Vol. 49, No. 1 (Autumn 1987), pp. 31–56.
6. Andrews, Maggie.*op cit*. Beaumont, Caitriona. *Housewives and citizens*. Manchester University Press, 2016.
7. Andrews, Maggie. *op cit* and. Scott, Gillian. *Feminism, Femininity and the Politics of Working Women: The Women's Co-Operative Guild, 1880s to the Second World War*. Routledge, 2005.
8. Rowbotham, Sheila. *Women in Movement (Routledge Revivals): Feminism and Social Action*. Routledge, 2013. P. 245.

9. John, Angela V. *Turning the Tide: the life of Lady Rhondda.* Parthian Books, 2014. Kindle edition P. 231.
10. Pedersen, Susan. *Eleanor Rathbone and the politics of conscience.* Yale University Press, 2004.
11. Rathbone, Eleanor Florence. *The disinherited family: A plea for the endowment of the family.* London, Arnold, 1924.
12. *Ibid.*
13. *The Scotsman.* October 13, 1924.
14. *The Scotsman.* October 13, 1924.
15. *The Scotsman.* October 13, 1924.
16. Pedersen, Susan. *op cit.*
17. Andrews, Maggie. *Women and Evacuation in the Second World War: Femininity, Domesticity and Motherhood.* Bloomsbury Publishing, 2019.
18. Padley, Richard, and Margaret Cole, eds. *Evacuation survey: a report to the Fabian Society.* Routledge & Sons, 1940. p 3.
19. *Home and Country* June 1942. p.114.
20. *Keeping Ourselves Informed,* London: NFWI publication, 1981, P. 148.
21. *Home and Country,* July 1945, P. 109.
22. Thane, Pat. *op cit.*
23. BBC Written Archive. R51/642, Eileen Molony, 5 February, 1948.
24. Dyhouse, Carol. *Love Lives: From Cinderella to Frozen.* Oxford University Press, 2021. P. 77.
25. *Ibid.* P. 75.
26. Titmuss, Richard M. "The position of women: some vital statistics." In *Essays on The Welfare State*, Policy Press, 2018. PP. 54–64.
27. Dyhouse, Carol. *op cit.* P 79.
28. *Ibid.* P. 81.
29. https://genius.com/The-rolling-stones-mothers-little-helper-lyrics Accessed 20/10/2022.
30. Harpwood, Diane. *Tea and Tranquilizers.* Virago 1981.
31. *Spare Rib* 1970.
32. *Independent* 8 March 2000, https://www.independent.co.uk/voices/international-womens-day-wages-housework-care-selma-james-a9385351.html?r=33999 Accessed 20/12/2021.
33. https://www.plutobooks.com/blog/wages-housework-campaign-history/ Accessed 20/12/2021.
34. https://www.plutobooks.com/blog/wages-housework-campaign-history/ Accessed 20/12/2021.
35. https://www.plutobooks.com/blog/wages-housework-campaign-history/ Accessed 20/12/2021.
36. *The Guardian* 1976 quoted in https://www.theguardian.com/books/2012/jun/08/life-in-writing-selma-james Accessed 20/12/2021.
37. *The Guardian* 1976 quoted in https://www.theguardian.com/books/2012/jun/08/life-in-writing-selma-james Accessed 20/12/2021.
38. *The Guardian* 1976 quoted in https://www.theguardian.com/books/2012/jun/08/life-in-writing-selma-james Accessed 20/12/2021.
39. *Spare Rib* 45, April 1976.
40. Oakley, Ann. *The sociology of housework.* 1974 reprinted Policy Press, 2018.
41. *Ibid.* P. 183.

42. *Ibid.*. P. 154.
43. https://globalwomenstrike.net/the-independent-i-founded-the-wages-for-housework-campaign-in-1972-and-women-are-still-working-for-free/ Accessed 20/12/2021.
44. House of Commons Debate, 13 May 1975, c 330.
45. *Belfast Telegraph* 21 March 1977.
46. Jennifer Simon writing in *The Aberdeen Evening Express* 23 March, 1979.
47. Jennifer Simon writing in *The Aberdeen Evening Express* 23 March, 1979.
48. *Sunday Life* April 15, 1989.
49. https://www.carersuk.org/about-us/who-we-are/our-history Accessed 20/12/2021.
50. https://www.carersuk.org/for-professionals/policy/policy-library/carers-uk-wbg-commission-2019 Accessed 20/12/2021.
51. https://www.independent.co.uk/voices/international-womens-day-wages-housework-care-selma-james-a9385351.html?r=33999 Accessed 20/12/2021.
52. https://www.theguardian.com/world/2000/mar/07/gender Accessed 20/12/2021.

Chapter 11: Airport Protest against Virginity Tests (1979)
1. See some further details via https://www.facebook.com/watch/?v=651008679282921
2. Evan Smith and Marinella Marmo, 'Uncovering the "Virginity Testing" Controversy in the National Archives: The Intersectionality of Discrimination in British Immigration History' *Gender & History*, Vol.23 No.1 April 2011, pp. 147–165. P. 148.
3. Parmar, Pratibha. "Gender, race and class: Asian women in resistance." In *Empire Strikes Back*, pp. 235–274. Routledge, 2004. P. 245.
4. https://raveetawrites.com/2018/07/29/virginity-testing-immigration-and-the-brown-female-body-in-1970s-britain/ Accessed 20/1/2022.
5. *The Guardian* 8 May, 2011. *For more, see* Smith, Evan, and Marinella Marmo. "Uncovering the 'Virginity Testing' controversy in the national archives: The intersectionality of discrimination in British immigration history." *Gender & History* 23, no. 1 (2011): 147–165.
6. For more details on the Ayahs see for example Robinson, Olivia. "Travelling Ayahs of the Nineteenth and Twentieth Centuries: Global Networks and Mobilization of Agency." In *History Workshop Journal*, vol. 86, pp. 44–66. Oxford Academic, 2018. Chakraborty, Satyasikha. "" Nurses of Our Ocean Highways": The Precarious Metropolitan Lives of Colonial South Asian Ayahs." *Journal of Women's History* 32, no. 2 (2020): 37–64.
7. *Daily Mail,* 30 December, 1913.
8. Bryan, Beverley, Stella Dadzie, and Suzanne Scafe. *The Heart of the Race: Black women's lives in Britain.* Verso Books, 2018. Kindle edition – 2427.
9. *Ibid.*
10. Goulbourne, Harry. *Race Relations in Britain since 1945.* Bloomsbury 1998.
11. https://pastinthepresent.net/2018/06/28/remembering-the-windrush-generation-in-gentrified-notting-hill/ Accessed 20/1/2022.
12. Bryan, Beverley, *op cit.*
13. https://artsandculture.google.com/exhibit/a-history-of-notting-hill-carnival-black-cultural-archives/eALiDoHj8Po6Kg?hl=en Accessed 20/1/2022.
14. https://www.findmypast.co.uk/blog/history/notting-hill-carnival?ds_kid=397000523 27871087&gclid=EAIaIQobChMIts3fmLOG8QIVj77tCh036Qs6EAMYASAAE gLFSfD_BwE&gclsrc=aw.ds Accessed 20/1/2022.

15. https://archive.voice-online.co.uk/article/rhaune-laslett-true-founder-notting-hill-carnival Accessed 20/1/2022.
16. https://archive.voice-online.co.uk/article/rhaune-laslett-true-founder-notting-hill-carnival Accessed 20/1/2022.
17. *Kensington Post*, 23 September, 1966.
18. https://www.theguardian.com/tv-and-radio/2021/may/19/black-kids-were-written-off-the-scandal-of-the-children-sent-to-dustbin-schools Accessed 20/1/2022.
19. https://www.theguardian.com/tv-and-radio/2021/may/19/black-kids-were-written-off-the-scandal-of-the-children-sent-to-dustbin-schools Accessed 20/1/2022.
20. https://djmag.com/content/children-windrush-generation-pioneering-djs-who-paved-way-uk-dance-music Accessed 20/1/2022.
21. https://www.theguardian.com/tv-and-radio/2021/may/19/black-kids-were-written-off-the-scandal-of-the-children-sent-to-dustbin-schools Accessed 20/1/2022.
22. https://www.bbc.co.uk/news/uk-57099654 Accessed 20/1/2022.
23. https://www.bl.uk/collection-items/mia-morris-owaads-campaigns Accessed 20/1/2022.
24. https://www.barca-leeds.org/news/gertrudemarettapaul Accessed 20/1/2022.
25. https://www.leedsbeckett.ac.uk/blogs/carnegie-education/2022/03/celebrating-the-life-and-legacy-of-gertrude-paul/ Accessed 20/1/2022.
26. https://www.blackhistorymonth.org.uk/article/section/the-windrush-generation/louise-da-cocodia-and-the-discrimination-faced-by-black-nurses-in-the-infant-days-of-the-nhs/ Accessed 20/1/2022.
27. https://www.bl.uk/womens-rights/articles/remembering-the-grunwick-dispute Accessed 20/1/2022.
28. https://web.archive.org/web/20070904100203/http://www.irr.org.uk/faces/desai.html Accessed 20/1/2022.
29. https://www.bl.uk/womens-rights/articles/remembering-the-grunwick-dispute Accessed 20/1/2022.
30. https://web.archive.org/web/20070904100203/http://www.irr.org.uk/faces/desai.html Accessed 20/1/2022.
31. Lambert, Caitlin. "'The objectionable injectable': recovering the lost history of the WLM through the Campaign Against Depo-Provera." *Women's History Review* 29, no. 3 (2020): 520–539. P. 6.
32. Douglas, Jenny. "Black women's activism and organisation in public health-struggles and strategies for better health and wellbeing." *Caribbean Review of Gender Studies* 13 (2019): 51–68. P. 57.
33. Campling, Jo. *Woman, nation, state*. Edited by Nira Yuval-Davis, and Floya Anthias. London: Macmillan, 1989. P. 20.
34. Douglas, Jenny. *op cit*. P. 58.
35. Bryan, Beverley, *op cit.*.
36. Brent Community Health Council, Brent Community Health Council. 1981. *Black People and the Health Service*. London: Brent Community Health Council. 1981. p.24.
37. *Speak Out*, Numbers 1 and 3.
38. https://www.bl.uk/collection-items/mia-morris-owaads-campaigns Accessed 20/1/2022.
39. Douglas, Jenny. *op cit*. P. 57.
40. https://www.bl.uk/collection-items/rowena-arshad-contraception-and-controlling-poor-womens-bodies Accessed 20/1/2022.

41. Lambert, Caitlin. "'The objectionable injectable': recovering the lost history of the WLM through the Campaign Against Depo-Provera." *Women's History Review* 29, no. 3 (2020): 520–539. P. 7.
42. *Ibid.* P. 7.
43. *Ibid..* P. 14.
44. https://gal-dem.com/collective-past-amrit-wilson-reflects-anti-racist-feminist-work/ Accessed 20/1/2022.
45. https://www.bl.uk/collection-items/stella-dadzie-owaad Accessed 20/1/2022. Bryan, B., Dadzie, S., & Scafe, S. (2018). *The heart of the race: Black women's lives in Britain.* Verso Books.
46. Akala, *Natives: Race and Class in the Ruins of Empire* (London: Two Roads, 2018), p.8.
47. https://irr.org.uk/article/reclaiming-our-collective-past-meeting-amrit-wilson/ Accessed 20/1/2022.
48. https://irr.org.uk/article/reclaiming-our-collective-past-meeting-amrit-wilson/ Accessed 20/1/2022.
49. Gupta, Rahila, ed. *From homebreakers to jailbreakers: Southall black sisters.* Zed books, 2003. P. 1.
50. *Ibid.* P. 245.
51. *Ibid.* P. 241.
52. *Ibid.* P. 241.
53. Douglas, Jenny. *op cit.* P 51.
54. https://www.bl.uk/collection-items/stella-dadzie-owaad Accessed 20/1/2022.

Chapter 12: Prostitutes Sit-in at Holy Cross Church (1982)

1. *Southall Gazette* 7 June, 1974.
2. *The Guardian* 28 April, 2014.
3. *The Guardian* 28 April, 2014.
4. https://www.bbc.co.uk/news/uk-england-london-59064064 Accessed 10/12/2021.
5. https://www.bbc.co.uk/news/uk-england-london-59064064 Accessed 10/12/2021.
6. *Harrow Observer*, 8 November, 1974.
7. *Acton Gazette* 25 April, 1974.
8. James, Dickie. Women's Aid Slogan in Andrews, Maggie, and Janis Lomas. *A History of Women in 100 Objects.* The History Press, 2018.
9. James, Dickie. Women's Aid Slogan in Andrews, Maggie, and Janis Lomas. *A History of Women in 100 Objects.* The History Press, 2018.
10. See https://www.bbc.co.uk/news/uk-england-london-59064064 and Pizzey, Erin, and Jeff Shapiro. *Prone to violence.* London: Hamlyn, 1982.
11. https://womenslegallandmarks.com/2017/08/08/first-rape-crisis-centre-opens-1976/
12. Walby, Sylvia, Alex Hay, and Keith Soothill. "The social construction of rape." *Theory, Culture & Society* 2, no.1 (1983): 86–98.
13. https://womenslegallandmarks.com/2017/08/08/first-rape-crisis-centre-opens-1976/ Accessed 10/12/2021.
14. https://womenslegallandmarks.com/2017/08/08/first-rape-crisis-centre-opens-1976/ Accessed 10/12/2021.
15. https://bradfordrapecrisis.org.uk/our-story.php Accessed 10/12/2021.
16. Jones, Helen, and Kate Cook. *Rape crisis: Responding to sexual violence.* Russell House Publishing, 2008.
17. https://www.ercc.scot/ Accessed 10/12/2021.
18. https://www.ercc.scot/about-us/timeline/ Accessed 10/12/2021.

19. https://womenslegallandmarks.com/2017/08/08/first-rape-crisis-centre-opens-1976/ Accessed 10/12/2021.
20. https://devonrapecrisis.org.uk/about-us/myths-facts-and-statistics/ Accessed 10/12/2021.
21. https://www.theweek.co.uk/98330/when-did-marital-rape-become-a-crime 6 December 2018 Accessed 10/12/2021.
22. https://againstrape.net/wp-content/uploads/2018/05/1977-When-rape-like-charity-begins-at-home.jpg Accessed 10/12/2021.
23. https://assets.publishing.service.gov.uk/government/uploads/system/uploads/attachment_data/file/228746/0167.pdf Accessed 10/12/2021.
24. https://www.womens.cusu.cam.ac.uk/reclaim-the-night/history/
25. *Liverpool Weekend Echo* April 7/8, 1979.
26. *Liverpool Weekend Echo* April 7/8, 1979.
27. *Spare Rib*, June 1981 https://www.bl.uk/collection-items/spare-rib-magazine-issue-107 Accessed 10/12/2021.
28. *Ibid*.
29. https://www.closebrothers.com/pride-month-2021/maureen-colquhoun-pioneering-mp
30. *Spare Rib*, June 1981 https://www.bl.uk/collection-items/spare-rib-magazine-issue-107 Accessed 10/12/2021.
31. *Spare Rib*, June 1981 https://www.bl.uk/collection-items/spare-rib-magazine-issue-107 Accessed 10/12/2021.
32. https://www.bl.uk/collection-items/newsbeat-report-from-holy-cross-occupation Accessed 10/12/2021.
33. https://www.bl.uk/collection-items/newsbeat-report-from-holy-cross-occupation Accessed 10/12/2021.
34. https://www.bl.uk/collection-items/newsbeat-report-from-holy-cross-occupation Accessed 10/12/2021.
35. https://www.bl.uk/collection-items/newsbeat-report-from-holy-cross-occupation Accessed 10/12/2021.
36. https://www.bl.uk/collection-items/newsbeat-report-from-holy-cross-occupation Accessed 10/12/2021.
37. https://www.bl.uk/collection-items/newsbeat-report-from-holy-cross-occupation Accessed 10/12/2021.
38. See footage of the news coverage – https://www.facebook.com/watch/?v=2219384014985191 Accessed 10/12/2021.
39. See footage of the news coverage – https://www.facebook.com/watch/?v=2219384014985191 Accessed 10/12/2021.
40. https://prostitutescollective.net/church-occupation-1982/ors Accessed 10/12/2021.
41. For further discussion see – Andrews, Maggie. "Calendar ladies: Popular culture, sexuality and the middle-class, middle-aged domestic woman." *Sexualities* 6, no. 3–4 (2003): 385–403. Andrews, Maggie, and Sallie McNamara, eds. *Women and the Media: Feminism and Femininity in Britain, 1900 to the Present*. Routledge, 2014.
42. https://www.theguardian.com/society/2021/may/23/fewer-than-one-in-60-cases-lead-to-charge-in-england-and-wales Accessed 10/12/2021.

Chapter 13: 'How dare the government presume the right to kill others in our name?' (1982)

1. https://www.walesonline.co.uk/news/news-opinion/remembering-women-men-children-who-20124575 Accessed 10/9/2021.

2. https://www.walesonline.co.uk/news/news-opinion/remembering-women-men-children-who-20124575 Accessed 10/9/2021.
3. https://www.walesonline.co.uk/news/news-opinion/remembering-women-men-children-who-20124575 Accessed 10/9/2021.
4. Schreiner, Olive. *An Olive Schreiner Reader: Writings on women and South Africa.* Pandora Press. 1987. pp. 206–7.
5. Oldfield, Sybil. *Women Humanitarians: A Biographical Dictionary of British Women Active Between 1900 and 1950:'doers of the Word'*. Continuum International Publishing Group, 2001.
6. https://blog.history.ac.uk/2019/05/women-and-peace-helen-crawfurd/ Accessed 10/9/2021.
7. *Birmingham Gazette*, 4 October, 1933.
8. https://www.walesonline.co.uk/news/news-opinion/remembering-women-men-children-who-20124575 Accessed 10/9/2021.
9. https://artsandculture.google.com/story/women-s-international-league-for-peace-and-freedom-lse-library/MAWxop-EIuSvKA?hl=en Accessed 10/9/2021.
10. https://heritage.humanists.uk/dora-russell/ https://digitalcollections.mcmaster.ca/pw20c/case-study/only-learning-love-one-another-can-our-world-be-saved-dora-black-russells-work Accessed 10/9/2021.
11. https://www.theguardian.com/newsroom/story/0,,1865423,00.html Accessed 10/9/2021.
12. Notes taken from 'The Greenham Factor', courtesy of Rebecca Johnson https://www.theguardian.com/newsroom/story/0,,1865509,00.html Accessed 10/9/2021.
13. http://feministarchivesouth.org.uk/collections/dora-russells-peace-caravan/ Accessed 10/9/2021.
14. Pettitt, Anne. *Walking to Greenham: how the peace-camp began and the Cold War ended* Honno. 2006.
15. https://www.theguardian.com/newsroom/story/0,,1865509,00.html Accessed 10/9/2021.
16. Statement to Newbury Magistrates Court, April 14 1982. https://www.theguardian.com/newsroom/story/0,,1865509,00.html Accessed 10/9/2021.
17. https://www.opendemocracy.net/en/opendemocracyuk/greenham-common-womens-peace-camp-changed-the-world-and-my-life Accessed 10/9/2021.
18. https://www.opendemocracy.net/en/opendemocracyuk/greenham-common-womens-peace-camp-changed-the-world-and-my-life/ Accessed 10/9/2021.
19. https://www.opendemocracy.net/en/opendemocracyuk/greenham-common-womens-peace-camp-changed-the-world-and-my-life/ Accessed 10/9/2021.
20. http://news.bbc.co.uk/1/hi/special_report/1999/11/99/greenham_common/514324.stm Accessed 10/9/2021.
21. Pettitt, Anne. *Walking to Greenham: how the peace-camp began and the Cold War ended* Honno. 2006.
22. *Reading Evening Post*, 5 June, 1991.
23. *Suffolk and Essex Free Press*, 29 March 1984. *Aberdeen Press and Journal*, 31 August, 1983.
24. Harford, Barbara, and Sarah Hopkins. *Greenham Common: Women at the wire*. Women's Press (UK), 1984.
25. *Reading Evening Post*, 15 August 1983.
26. *Belfast Telegraph*, 24 December 1983.
27. https://biblio.co.uk/book/embrace-base-greenham-common-womens-peace/d/1243694373 Accessed 10/9/2021.

28. https://ttin.uk/memories-of-greenham Accessed 10/9/2021.
29. https://www.walesonline.co.uk/news/news-opinion/remembering-women-men-children-who-20124575 Accessed 10/9/2021.
30. *The Guardian* 29 August 2021. https://www.theguardian.com/uk-news/2021/aug/29/greenham-common-at-40-we-came-to-fight-war-and-stayed-for-the-feminism Accessed 10/9/2021.
31. *The Guardian*, July 30 1983 https://www.theguardian.com/newsroom/story/0,,1865509,00.html Accessed 10/9/2021.
32. Lynne Jones quoted in https://www.theguardian.com/newsroom/story/0,,1865509,00.html
33. https://blog.history.ac.uk/2019/05/women-and-peace-pat-arrowsmith-and-greenham-common/
34. *The Guardian*, 29 August 2021 https://www.theguardian.com/uk-news/2021/aug/29/greenham-common-at-40-we-came-to-fight-war-and-stayed-for-the-feminism Accessed 10/9/2021.
35. https://www.theguardian.com/newsroom/story/0,,1865509,00.html Accessed 10/9/2021.
36. https://www.opendemocracy.net/en/opendemocracyuk/greenham-common-womens-peace-camp-changed-the-world-and-my-life/ Accessed 10/9/2021.
37. http://www.fredsakademiet.dk/abase/sange/greenham/song4.htm Accessed 10/9/2021.
38. https://www.riseupandsing.org/songs/cant-kill-spirit https://joanszymko.com/works/ind/mountain Accessed 10/9/2021.

Chapter 14: Equal Pay for Equal Value (1988)
1. https://www.bl.uk/sisterhood/articles/equal-pay-and-equality-legislation Accessed 28/8/2021.
2. Hazel Conley, Frances Galt, Louise Jackson and Tanya Rhodes 'Campaigning for equal pay – 50 years on' https://www.genderequalitiesat50.ed.ac.uk/2022/11/20/equalpayday/ Accessed 28/8/2021.
3. TUC History online. 'Just Desserts' https://www.tuc.org.uk/about-the-tuc/our-history Accessed 28/8/2021.
4. Conley, Hazel., Frances Galt, Louise Jackson and Tanya Rhodes 'Campaigning for equal pay – 50 years on' https://www.genderequalitiesat50.ed.ac.uk/2022/11/20/equalpayday/ Accessed 28/8/2021.
5. Moss, Jonathan. "'We didn't realise how brave we were at the time': the 1968 Ford sewing machinists' strike in public and personal memory." *Oral History* (2015): 40–51.
6. *The Guardian*, 6 June, 2013.
7. Moss, Jonathan *op cit*. 40–51.
8. *Ibid*.
9. *The Guardian* 6 June, 2013. https://www.theguardian.com/politics/2013/jun/06/dagenham-sewing-machinists-strike Accessed 28/8/2021.
10. Moss, Jonathan. *op cit*.
11. *Ibid*.
12. *Ibid*.
13. https://www.parliament.uk/about/living-heritage/transformingsociety/tradeindustry/industrycommunity/collections/equal-pay/ford-strike/ Accessed 28/8/2021.
14. Conley, Hazel. 'Revisiting the 1968 Ford Dagenham Dispute (again)' https://www.genderequalitiesat50.ed.ac.uk/2022/03/08/iwd2022-revising-the-1968-ford-dagenham-dispute-again/ Accessed 28/8/2021.

15. Stevenson, George. *The Women's Liberation Movement and the Politics of Class in Britain.* Bloomsbury Publishing, 2019.
16. Galt, Frances. 'The Equal Pay Act 1970 and Women-led Industrial Disputes, 1964–86' https://www.genderequalitiesat50.ed.ac.uk/2021/11/15/the-equal-pay-act-1970-and-women-led-industrial-disputes-1964-86/ Accessed 28/8/2021.
17. Jones, Marion Blanche Hoover, Merthyr. VSE028, http://www.factorywomensvoices.wales/search.php?func=search&searchfor=Hoover&in_facname=on Accessed 28/8/2021.
18. *Ibid.*
19. *Ibid.*
20. For more about women and the Miners' Strike see for example Rowbotham, Sheila, and Jean McCrindle. "More than just a memory: Some political implications of women's involvement in the miners' strike, 1984–85." *Feminist Review* 23, no. 1 (1986): 109–124. Kelliher, Diarmaid. "The 1984–5 miners' strike and the spirit of solidarity." *Soundings* 60, no. 60 (2015): 118–129.
21. TUC History online. 'Cooking Up a Storm' https://www.tuc.org.uk/about-the-tuc/our-history Accessed 28/8/2021.
22. *Ibid.*
23. *Liverpool Echo* March 6, 1987.
24. BBC Website 'One Woman's fight to Equal Pay' http://news.bbc.co.uk/1/hi/business/8032750.stm Accessed 28/8/2021.
25. *Liverpool Echo* March 6, 1987.
26. TUC History online. 'Cooking Up a Storm' https://www.tuc.org.uk/about-the-tuc/our-history Accessed 28/8/2021.
27. BBC Website 'One Woman's fight to Equal Pay' http://news.bbc.co.uk/1/hi/business/8032750.stm Accessed 28/8/2021.
28. TUC History online. 'Speaking Out for Change'. https://www.tuc.org.uk/about-the-tuc/our-history Accessed 28/8/2021.
29. http://www.unionhistory.info/britainatwork/emuweb/objects/common/webmedia.php?irn=1060 Accessed 28/8/2021.
30. TUC History online. 'Just Desserts'. https://www.tuc.org.uk/about-the-tuc/our-history Accessed 28/8/2021.
31. *Ibid.*
32. *Ibid.*
33. https://www.bl.uk/sisterhood/articles/equal-pay-and-equality-legislation Accessed 28/8/2021.
34. Hazel Conley, Frances Galt, Louise Jackson and Tanya Rhodes 'Campaigning for equal pay – 50 years on' https://www.genderequalitiesat50.ed.ac.uk/2022/11/20/equalpayday/ Accessed 28/8/2021.

Chapter 15: Tell me what you want, what you really, really want' – Girl Power (1996)

1. Dyhouse, Carol. *Girl trouble: Panic and progress in the history of young women.* Bloomsbury Publishing, 2014.
2. Levine, Philippa. "" Walking the Streets in a Way No Decent Woman Should": Women Police in World War I." *The Journal of Modern History* 66, no. 1 (1994): 34–78.
3. Rose, Sonya O. *Which People's War?: national identity and citizenship in wartime Britain 1939–1945.* Oxford University Press on Demand, 2003. 78–79.
4. Rose, Sonya O. "Sex, citizenship, and the nation in World War II Britain." *The American Historical Review* 103, no. 4 (1998): 1147–1176.

5. https://www.monkeeslivealmanac.com/blog/a-british-fans-perspective-on-the-monkees-by-rosemary-reedman Accessed 7/7/2022.
6. http://mandyischaos.blogspot.com/2017/02/concert-memories-monkees-and-weird-al.html Accessed 7/7/2022.
7. Rohr, Nicolette. "Yeah yeah yeah: The sixties screamscape of Beatlemania." *Journal of Popular Music Studies* 29.2 (2017): e12213.
8. *Ibid.*
9. Ehrenreich, Barbara, Elizabeth Hess, and Gloria Jacobs. "Beatlemania: Girls just want to have fun." *The adoring audience: Fan culture and popular media* (1992): 84–106.
10. *Daily Mail* 2 October, 1963.
11. Frith, Simon, Andrew Goodwin, and Lawrence Grossberg, eds. *Sound and vision: The music video reader*. Routledge, 2005.
12. *Ibid.*
13. Maitland, Sara.*op cit.*
14. https://www.independent.co.uk/arts-entertainment/music/spice-girls-channel-4-documentary-b1920183.html Accessed 7/7/2022.
15. https://www.theguardian.com/world/2001/feb/13/gender.uk2 Accessed 7/7/2022.
16. https://www.theguardian.com/world/2001/feb/13/gender.uk2 Accessed 7/7/2022.
17. http://www.artzines.info/wp-content/uploads/2017/06/Bikini-Kill.pdf Accessed 7/7/2022.
18. https://www.bbc.co.uk/news/entertainment-arts-48381340 Accessed 7/7/2022.
19. *Company,* November 1996 P. 5.
20. Hains, Rebecca C. *Growing up with girl power: Girlhood on screen and in everyday life.* New York: Peter Lang, 2012.
21. Faludi, Susan. *Backlash: The undeclared war against American women.* Crown, 1991 reprinted 2009.
22. Woodward, Kath. "Representations of motherhood." In *Gender, identity & reproduction*, pp. 18–32. Palgrave Macmillan, London, 2003.
23. https://www.theguardian.com/tv-and-radio/2021/sep/14/spice-girls-how-girl-power-changed-britain-review-fabulous-and-intimate Accessed 7/7/2022.
24. https://www.independent.co.uk/arts-entertainment/music/spice-girls-channel-4-documentary-b1920183.html Accessed 7/7/2022.
25. https://www.theguardian.com/tv-and-radio/2021/sep/14/spice-girls-how-girl-power-changed-britain-review-fabulous-and-intimate Accessed 7/7/2022.
26. Spice Girls. *Official Spice Girl Power.* London Zone Chamberlain Books 1997. P. 34.
27. https://inews.co.uk/culture/spice-girls-tory-fans-girl-power-geri-horner-nadine-dorries-selfie-1773991 Accessed 7/7/2022.
28. https://www.theguardian.com/tv-and-radio/2021/sep/14/spice-girls-how-girl-power-changed-britain-review-fabulous-and-intimate Accessed 7/7/2022.
29. Carter, Fan. "What's Luff Got to Do with It? Teenage Magazines, Sexuality and Regulation in the 1990s (Too much, too young? Teenage Magazines, Sexuality and Regulation)." In *Women and the Media*, pp. 245–257. Routledge, 2014.
30. Hopkins, Susan. *Girl heroes: The new force in popular culture.* Pluto Press, 2002.
31. https://inews.co.uk/culture/spice-girls-tory-fans-girl-power-geri-horner-nadine-dorries-selfie-1773991 Accessed 7/7/2022.